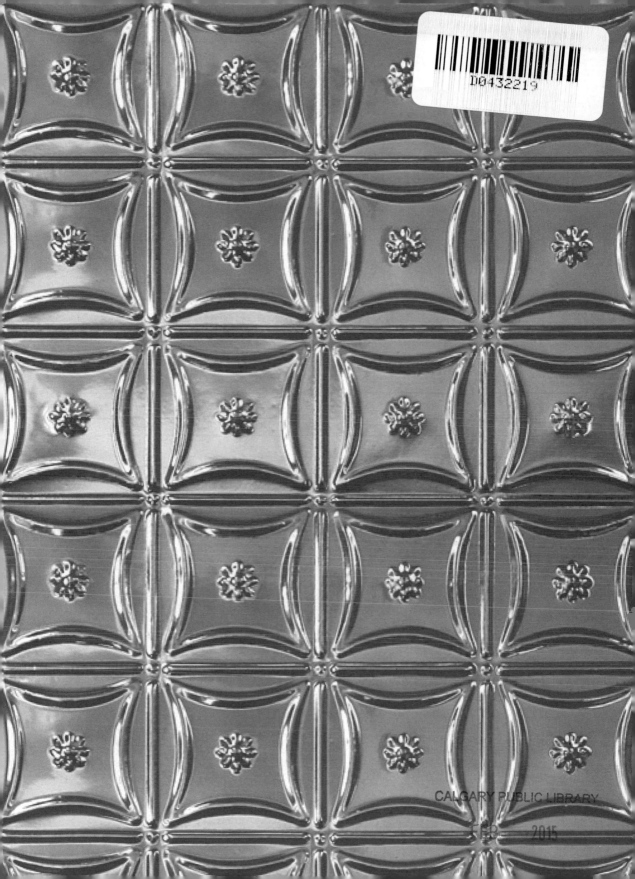

DI PALO'S GUIDE TO THE ESSENTIAL FOODS OF ITALY

ONALI
IIA

DI

R

200

SINCE
1910

100 YEARS OF WISDOM AND STORIES
FROM BEHIND THE COUNTER

DI PALO'S
GUIDE TO THE
ESSENTIAL FOODS
OF ITALY

LOU DI PALO
with RACHEL WHARTON

FOREWORD BY
MARTIN SCORSESE

BALLANTINE BOOKS
NEW YORK

Published in the United States by Ballantine Books,
an imprint of Random House, a division of Random House LLC,
a Penguin Random House Company, New York.

BALLANTINE and the HOUSE colophon are
registered trademarks of Random House LLC.

Photo insert, frontispiece, and chapter opener photography copyright © Evan Sung

See page 211 for further photo credit details.

LIBRARY OF CONGRESS CATALOGING-IN-PUBLICATION DATA

Di Palo, Lou, author.
Di Palo's guide to the essential foods of Italy : 100 years of wisdom
and stories from behind the counter / Lou Di Palo with Rachel Wharton;
foreword by Martin Scorsese. —First edition.
pages cm
Includes index.
ISBN 978-0-345-54580-0 (hardback) — ISBN 978-0-345-54581-7 (ebook)
1. Food—Italy. 2. Italy—Social life and customs. 3. Italians—Ethnic identity.
4. Italian Americans—New York (State)—New York.
5. Cooking, Italian. I. Wharton, Rachel, author. II. Title. III.
Title: Di Palo's guide to the essential foods of Italy.
TX360.I8D53 2014
641.5945—dc23   2014018032

Printed in the United States of America on acid-free paper

www.ballantinebooks.com

2 4 6 8 9 7 5 3 1

FIRST EDITION

Book design by Barbara M. Bachman

THIS BOOK IS DEDICATED TO MY WIFE,

CONNIE, WHO SUPPORTED ME ALL THESE YEARS

AND GAVE MORE OF HERSELF THAN

I COULD EVER HAVE HOPED. WITHOUT HER,

THIS BOOK WOULD HAVE NEVER COME TO BE.

..

DI PALO'S

CONTENTS

..

MARTIN SCORSESE

..

Back in the late 1930s, my uncle Mike got a 16-mm camera and shot home movies of our family. When I finally saw those images sixty years later, there was the fruit and vegetable stand in our neighborhood that my grandparents had briefly owned. They had it for only a few years before I was born. I had often heard about it and tried to picture it, and there it was—a small storefront, piled with tomatoes and celery and onions, among many other stands and carts on a street bustling with shoppers. It's a brief glimpse, but for me a precious one. That was the way it was in the old neighborhoods, before the supermarkets. The people from the old country and their children made traditional meals at home, and they'd buy the ingredients at the vegetable stands and the latterias—they made and ate the food that they knew and that had always nourished them. It wasn't just sustenance; it was as much a part of what made them who they were as their language and their faith and their memories of home.

My family has been going to Di Palo's for generations. My mother shopped at the store back when it was a latteria, and I've gone myself since I was a kid. Now, when I take my daughter to Di Palo's, I feel like I'm home. Here's Marie behind the counter in 1996, just like today.

Of course, many things had changed by the time I was a teenager, but you'd still buy fresh fruits and vegetables in outdoor markets and get your cheeses at the latteria. My mother used to go to a shop called Di Palo's, which had started as a latteria. And she remained a loyal customer through the years as they expanded and started importing and selling more and more products.

In 2001, right after the terrorist attacks on 9/11, we made a little film about the old neighborhood for The Concert for New York City. I immediately thought to myself: We have to go to Di Palo's. At the time, the store was just down the street—Grand Street, to be specific—from where it is now. Both of my parents were gone by then, and everything in the old neighborhood was changing. My life had changed in many ways too since I'd left, but when I walked into the store and saw Lou behind the counter, I was home. We bought delicious cheeses and meats and oils and balsamic vinegars; we talked with Lou and his wife and his brother and sister, just like they talk to everyone who comes into the store: It was as if the camera had disappeared. My daughter Francesca was with me, and she was just two years old at the time. I'll never forget Lou cutting her a little piece of Parmesan—"It's just like candy for children," he said. She loved it. On that day, Di Palo's didn't feel like home only because it was back in my old neighborhood. It went deeper than that. The food, the familiarity, the time everyone took to talk to one another, the way Lou and his family offered a taste of this cheese or that olive oil to everyone in the store—it was the heart of the world I came from at its most generous.

And that world, that culture—it was alive at Di Palo's, and it still is. If you walk through the neighborhood today, the dramatic changes that were happening in 2001 are now complete. There are historic tours that take you to this shop and that church, and Little Italy is mostly a memory. But not at Di Palo's. And that's because Lou and his family adapted to the changes as they came. Back in 2001, Lou said that someone walked in one day and asked him what made him open an Italian store in the middle of a Chinese neighborhood. Over the years, Chinatown kept expanding, and new immigrants continued to come from Southeast Asia. But Lou and his family understood that this was simply the way things were. Di Palo's is now next door to a Vietnamese sandwich shop, but they haven't just kept their family business going but have deepened the practice of their own traditions and culture, which is based in generosity. They're not just selling food, they're sharing their knowledge of where it came from, how it was grown and cultivated and pre-pared over the centuries in different regions of Italy, where different climates and land-scapes and traditions yield variations in the taste and texture of different olive oils and cheeses and meats. My friend visited the store recently and heard Lou's brother, Sal, tell a customer, "I've never worked a day in my life." For him, and for Lou as well, as you'll see, the making and importing and selling and sharing of food, and the honoring of its origins, is life.

INTRODUCTION

..

When people ask me how many years I've worked in New York City's Little Italy, where my family has owned an Italian food shop for 104 years, I usually ask them to guess. "I'm going to give you one clue," I say to them, "I am sixty-one years old." The real answer, I eventually tell them, is sixty-two. I've been behind the counter since before I was born. My mother worked at Di Palo's until the day she went to the hospital to give birth to me.

For as long as I can remember, I've sold Italian food, made mozzarella, and cut sixty-pound wheels of Pecorino Romano from behind the counters at Di Palo's just as my father, grandfather, and great-grandfather did. I don't work seven days a week from dawn to dusk for the money, nor does my brother, Sal, or my sister Marie. We could have worked half as hard in many other careers, but we wouldn't be as happy. This is the life we chose, the business we love.

This book is not only about my six decades behind the counter, or the story of my family's store. It is also about the history *behind* the foods of Italy, and the traditions we love.

I first went to Italy in 1973. I was twenty-two and on my honeymoon. Connie and I traveled from Sicily to Lombardia, stopping along the way in the rural region of Basilicata, where my paternal family came from. I would wake Connie up early to visit the places where our products were made, and the shops like ours that sold them. This trip changed everything for me: it opened my eyes to what I didn't know. Since then I have gone to Italy often to meet the people who make what we sell, to learn about the products firsthand and bring new ones back to our store in Little Italy.

I wasn't interested in visiting only the factories that made the cheese or the pasta, or a *frantoia*, where the olives are pressed into oil, though those visits are essential to understanding these products and explaining them to our customers. I wanted to take it a step further: I wanted to meet the cowherds marching the cows up the mountains, the wheat growers in the plains, the olive growers in the hot southern hills; I wanted to witness the traditions of all the foods that Di Palo's sells. My mission was to discover the world my great-grandfather Savino Di Palo left behind in Basilicata in 1903, when he came to the United States and eventually opened the first Di Palo's.

Though my family is all from Southern Italy—the regions of Basilicata and Sicily—I made it a point to visit all twenty regions of Italy and every province within them. I went to Italy to meet the small farmers and learn how the products were made hundreds of years ago, as well as how the process is automated today. And then, and only then, could I come home and say that I know what I'm talking about.

I learned about products we sell by going to the source, and literally breaking bread with those who made these foods for generations. These people are more than my business associates: I spend days with them, share their meals, and meet their parents and grandparents. They tell me the old stories about how things came to be. Are they all true? Maybe not, but they are worth hearing, and it helps me understand the traditions. I am still learning, every trip I make.

In this book, I hope to give you a sense of what it's like to travel through Italy, though this is not a culinary travel guide. I hope to show you how to identify a good piece of *Parmigiano-Reggiano* or *prosciutto crudo*—but this book is not an encyclopedia with every little fact about every cheese or cured meat. Instead I have tried to capture the stories behind what you'll find at Di Palo's, just as if you came into the store in Little Italy. I want to tell you about the *affinatore* who wraps his cheese in sweet Alpine hay before he ages it. I want to describe the *contessa* with the magical olive groves in Sicily, the seventeenth generation of vinegar makers with a petrified chunk of 300-year-old vinegar in Modena, the old Parmigiano-Reggiano cheesemaker in Reggio-Emilia who likes to dangle his elbow in the warm leftover whey, as a cure-all for his arthritis. I want to tell you about the aroma of prosciutto and how to savor that long-lasting flavor. (Don't cut off the fat! It's one of God's gifts.) Hold a full slice up to your face and smell the country breezes of the hills of Langhirano, just as I have.

I don't just sell the food in my store—I live it. This book is about living it.

—LOU DI PALO

DI PALO'S GUIDE
TO THE
ESSENTIAL FOODS
OF ITALY

The street scene in Little Italy in the early 1900s, when horse-drawn buggies and automobiles shared cobblestoned streets with Italian pushcart vendors.

A CENTURY IN
LITTLE ITALY

..

Before I tell you about the food at Di Palo's, let me begin with a little Italian-American history, and the mass migration of Italians to America between 1880 and 1920. My paternal great-grandfather, Savino Di Palo, was among them, and like so many others, New York City's Little Italy was where he landed. By the time he arrived in 1903, the neighborhood was essentially one large open-air market, the cobblestoned streets crowded with pushcarts and lined with shops run by Italian immigrants. You heard no English—only Italian, and mostly dialect Italian. Little Italy was as segmented as Italy itself: Sicilians on Elizabeth Street, Italians from Naples and Campania on Mulberry Street, and on Mott Street, where my great-grandfather lived and eventually opened his store, a blend of immigrants from the regions of Puglia, Calabria, and Basilicata.

Basilicata, where my great-grandfather came from, was then part of a larger territory in Southern Italy that the ancient Romans called Lucania, or "the land of the wolves." Savino grew up in a small mountain farming town called Montemilone, where his family kept dairy cows and made fresh cheese. Life was hard in Basilicata, where the terrain was very difficult to farm. It has some of the tallest mountain ranges in Southern Italy, and in the nineteenth century most people spent their entire life on their particular mountain. Some still do. Even though the towns are geographically close together, they tend to be on the mountaintops, so it takes a long time to travel between them. It took Great-grandfather Savino a day just to get down the mountain to the main road.

On a recent trip to the region, I went to meet a farmer outside the town of Stigliano who still lived in the mountains much as my great-grandfather had. His name is Mario Vaccaro—*vaccaro* is Italian for cowboy—and his melodious, singsong Basilicata accent sounds exactly like my great-aunt Nancy's. Mario is a shepherd and a cowherd who keeps sheep, goats, and podolica cows, which are found only in Basilicata and give rich, buttery milk. He cures his own sausages, bakes his own bread, grows some vegetables, and produces a little mozzarella, *caciocavallo,* and ricotta—just as my great-grandfather did before he moved to Little Italy. Mario still heats his milk in a big cauldron over a wood fire; he still cleans his wooden tools with whey, and hangs his cheeses to age in the old curve of an ancient cave under his house where he lives with his wife and three children. He makes cheese by hand, often hunched over the pot of curds and whey on a little stool that must be twice as old as I am.

Today this craftsmanship is rare, even in Italy. But Basilicata is still the most rural, dispersed region in the country, home to just 450,000 people and some of Italy's biggest mountain forests, some of which recently became pristine state parks. Imagine the culture shock for Savino to leave his mountain town and go to the most crowded part of one of the world's biggest cities, leaving his family behind—a wife and six children. He wouldn't see them again until they journeyed to Little Italy eleven years later, in 1914.

Opportunity, however, was not really what brought my great-grandfather to New York. Like many other immigrants, he'd been told that there was "gold in the streets of New York City." But the real gold was the ability to make money, to find work, which was then scarce in Italy. In my great-grandfather's case, he was in a feud with the noble landowners in his region. He was a poor subsistence farmer, a *contadino,* and from the nobles' point of view, if a farmer grew three oranges, two of them belonged to the noble. My great-grandfather couldn't stomach this: he was a difficult man with a very short temper. But since the nobles held the power, Savino decided to join the migration to America.

(Today my oldest daughter, Allegra, who married into a noble Italian family a hundred years after my great-grandfather left Italy, is now a contessa, and my two grandsons are counts. My great-grandfather is either laughing, or spinning in his grave.)

An updated photo of Savino Di Palo, my great-grandfather,
in his small latteria on Mott Street with two customers.
He opened the shop in 1910.

It was probably a good thing that Savino was a tough man, because New York's Lower East Side, of which Little Italy is a part, was a tough place to be at the turn of the twentieth century. By 1910 he was living on Mott Street and had saved enough money working for a relative to rent a very small storefront half a block down in the heart of the overcrowded neighborhood. At this point, Italians were still one of the most discriminated-against groups in the country. It was hard for them to find jobs, so they created their own opportunities. Savino decided to do what he knew best, making and selling cheese. He opened a small *latteria*—a dairy—in between Grand and Hester streets.

Milk was delivered daily in old-fashioned metal milk pails from the dairy farms that operated in upper Manhattan. Customers would come in with their own pitchers, and my great-grandfather would pull down the pail from the shelf and ladle out the milk. With the leftovers, he made ricotta, as he had done in Basilicata. He would also make mozzarella from fresh cow's milk and rounds of *caciotta,* a soft fresh cheese aged just a few days, the same way we do in our store today.

In 1914, Savino had saved enough money to bring his family to New York. He had an ulterior motive, the family joke goes: he needed the free labor. My grandmother Concetta, then fourteen, was immediately put to work alongside her father in the store with her brothers and sisters. By age twenty Concetta was married; she knew her husband—my grandfather Luigi Santomauro, my namesake—before she got here. Luigi was from the city of Potenza, and they arrived on the same ship in 1914. Luigi first worked as a barber, but once he married Concetta, an already skilled cheese-maker, he decided he was going to open up a latteria on East Eighty-Sixth Street in Yorkville in upper Manhattan, where there was no competition. The store was large and rent was cheap, but Luigi's shop lasted all of five months. Yorkville was a German enclave, and not many Germans wanted fresh mozzarella. So now my grandfather was out of work, and had a child—my uncle Michael, who was almost two. My grandmother Concetta was pregnant with my father.

There happened to be an empty store on the corner of Mott and Grand Street a half-block north of Savino's latteria. At first, Luigi didn't want to take the space fearing that he might hurt not just his father-in-law, Savino, but his sister Anna, who ran a latteria called Santomauro Dairy with her husband a block away on Mulberry Street. But my great-grandfather generously said, "Look, you have to live too." The neighborhood was still teeming with Italians then: the Falangas sold cheese, the Fretta brothers sold meats, the Carusos sold fruits and vegetables, the Parisi family sold bread. It was a thriving marketplace, and it wasn't uncommon for different members of a family to have stores within two or three blocks of each other, much like Chinatown today. These families weren't really competing—there was a tremendous immigrant market, and shoppers were often loyal to shopkeepers from their own region or from their own block of Little Italy.

So in 1925 my grandparents, Concetta and Luigi Santomauro, took the shop at 206 Grand Street at the northeast corner of Mott, a prime location in Little Italy right in the heart of the main shopping district. The shop was barely four hundred square feet with one icebox and one small counter, and they called it C. Di Palo, after Concetta and out of respect for my great-grandfather, who had encouraged them to open up at that location—and because my grandfather's sister Anna already ran Santomauro Dairy around the corner. My real last name is of course Santomauro too, but in the store I use Di Palo, as I am proud of its history.

In those days, my grandmother Concetta and grandfather Luigi had room only for a very small inventory. Like my great-grandfather Savino, they made fresh mozzarella, ricotta, and caciotta every day, kept a few tins of Italian tomatoes, olive oil, or bags of pasta on the shelves behind the counter, and sold fresh raw milk at two cents a ladle. I love to tell the story my father told me about Grandfather Luigi and his milk. In the basement of the store, there was a social club, where the men would meet over home-made wine sold for five cents a glass during Prohibition. One of my grandfather's drink-ing buddies sent his son to the store with a pitcher to buy milk. One night in the wine bar, the boy's father yelled at my grandfather. "You cheated me!" he said. "You didn't give me enough milk for my two cents." Luckily Luigi did not have the same temper as Savino. "Don't worry," he said, "send your son back to me and I'll give him some more milk." So the little boy came back with the pitcher, and my grandfather gave him a ladle and a half. But the father came back with a half-empty pitcher, and this time he was even angrier. "Are you fooling me?" said my grandfather. "If anything I gave your son too much milk!" So the next time the boy came in, my grandfather followed him home and he saw him sneak behind the stairwell and drink right out of the pitcher. My grandfa-ther dragged him upstairs to his father with the proof. My grandfather felt so bad when the boy got a beating that from then on, he gave him some milk to drink in the shop *and* a full pitcher to take home.

My own father—his name was Savino too, though everybody called him Sam—also grew up in that store. He was born while Concetta and Luigi were setting it up, and I like to joke that my grandmother breast-fed him between making the batches of mozzarella. My father would tell me that when he was eleven years old he worked all day, then immediately went to the candy stand run by two Jewish brothers, Izzie and Louie, who were still there in the 1960s when I was growing up. My father would hand over the three cents he'd just earned for an ice cream. Sam worked alongside his mother, father, and his brother Michael until the early 1940s. Mussolini had come to power in Italy, and was no friend to Americans. Although they had been born in Italy,

My grandmother Concetta Di Palo selling milk, ricotta,
and caciotta in the store she opened in 1925 on the northeast
corner of Mott and Grand streets, just a few blocks
away from her father's store.

many Italians in America had already begun to integrate, and willingly sent their children to fight for the United States in World War II. My father was seventeen when he joined the U.S. Army Air Corps, the precursor to the air force, and my uncle joined the infantry.

My father happened to be stationed in Puglia, at an airfield very close to Basilicata. One day he visited his cousins, who were so happy to see him. He vowed to return, but shortly after his visit, his plane was shot down over what was then Yugoslavia. He was taken captive by local factions who were fighting each other. Since the Americans paid in gold for the return of their flyboys, my father was kept safe in enemy territory as a valuable commodity. He was an *Americano*! He kept getting tossed around from group to group until finally somebody took him to the American front line to collect the reward.

My uncle, meanwhile, was in the Battle of the Bulge—and the only member of his platoon to survive. Both Sam and Michael came home from the war unscathed. Our family attributed their survival to Concetta's prayers. She prayed every day while her sons were missing, and never doubted that they would come home. Concetta was one of those true neighborhood matriarchs: she respected not only the people she served at the store, but her greater community. During the Depression, before there was much in the way of public assistance, my grandmother and her latteria fed many families in need. An old man once came into our shop to tell me that when he was young, he lived above our store. "My mother had ten children," he told me, "and my father died. She had no money, and it was your grandmother who fed us every day. Every day there was milk, every day there was cheese, every day there was bread. We never went hungry." Over the years, I learned that my grandmother fed many families. She believed you took care of your community, and you had a duty to share what you could.

When Sam and Michael returned from the war, they went back to work with my grandparents. My grandfather took ill soon after, and passed away in 1947. Before the war, my dad had gone to trade school for photography, but now the store needed him, so my father felt it was his duty to stand by his mother, and so did Uncle Michael.

By then my father had met my mother, Violanda Cali, and they married just after my grandfather died. In the family tradition, she went to work in the store by my father's side. My mother's parents, Salvatore and Mary, had emigrated from Mount Etna, the active volcano on the eastern coast of Sicily. Their land was eventually destroyed in an eruption. My mother had grown up on Eldridge Street in Little Italy, across the street from my father. Amazingly she had never met my father until she started flirting with him from her window. He was "the soldier boy," as she puts it, home on leave—he called her down to the sidewalk to talk, and that was it.

Michael had gotten married too, so now instead of one family, the shop was supporting three, and it needed to grow. At the same time, a new wave of Italian immigrants was settling in Little Italy at the end of World War II. So Sam, Michael, and their wives expanded the inventory to include foods that could easily travel from Italy, like salamis and hard, aged cheeses like Pecorino Romano and provolone.

In the 1950s and early 1960s our family continued to add products to the store, sell-

Concetta and Luigi Santomauro and their son Savino,
my father, whom everybody called Sam.

ing more cheeses, then cured meats they sliced to order. They expanded the store twice, first in 1948 and again in 1961, eventually doubling its four hundred to eight hundred square feet. (They bought out a small egg store next door, then the candy store from Izzie and Louie, who were retiring.)

Business remained strong through all these years: When you first come to a new land, what's the first thing that you do? You try to blend in. You change the way you dress, you start changing your language. But the very last thing you change—even four or five generations later—is the food you eat. Americans with Italian heritage associate themselves with being Italian primarily because they eat *lasagne,* or because their mother makes *pasta e fagio-*

My paternal uncle Michael cutting a provolone to order, the same way we do today. Like his brother—my father, Sam—he came back to work in the store after serving in World War II.

lie, or because they buy fresh mozzarella or olive oil. Di Palo's was where they bought it.

My uncle passed away very young, at forty-six, and after he died his wife decided to leave Di Palo's. My parents now had to run the business by themselves, so the next generation—my brother, Sal; my sisters, Marie, Concetta, and Yolanda; and I—were called to work every holiday and every weekend, sacrificing all of our free time. But the business needed us, and our parents needed us. The spirit of my grandparents needed us. I worked so much that eventually my father sent me to a private boarding school in the Bronx, because he thought I wasn't applying myself academically. But I would still take the subway down to Little Italy every Friday to close the store. I'd spend Saturdays at home in Brooklyn, where we lived in the house my grandmother bought after World War II, and then work again on Sunday before I went back to school.

My father outside my grandmother's shop on Grand Street. We expanded this store twice before moving across the street in 2002, once in 1948 and again in 1961, when we changed the name to just Di Palo's.

I did that from the sixth grade to the eighth grade—and then in the ninth grade I came back to Brooklyn to attend a Catholic school. So now I could work Saturdays too! I did that all through high school, and when I was in college, just a few subway stops from the store, I used to schedule my courses around the business. I took an eight o'clock class in the morning, worked in the store from noon to three, then went back to school from four to eight. Not because I had to, but because I wanted to: I thought it was important. Sal did the same thing. My sisters worked on weekends until they graduated from college; while Concetta and Yolanda started new careers in education and finance, respectively, Marie came to work in the store full-time.

When I graduated from college in 1973, I had a marketing degree with a specialization in real estate. Until then I'd worked in the store practically my whole life, so I decided to try working at a real estate firm uptown on Madison Avenue. Every morning I would help my father open up our store, then I'd put on my suit and tie, take the train to Forty-Second Street, and go to work. At four o'clock I'd come back to the store, put my apron back on, and finish the day with my father. One day at the office I got a call for a big real estate sale worth a thirty-thousand-dollar commission. As I was talking to the client, the other line buzzed. It was my father calling: "Lou, I have a chance to buy this cheese—we can save four cents a pound." I went back to the client, and I told him, "Listen, I can't talk to you right now, I have an important call on the other line." Click! "Dad," I told my father, "you better buy fifty cases, we'll save fifty dollars on all of that cheese!"

After I got off the phone, it struck me that I was working on a huge deal, but I hung up on the guy to save a few bucks on some cheese. I got up, left the office, and took the subway downtown to the store. "What are you doing here?" my father said.

"I'm not going back uptown," I told him. "I don't belong there. *This* is where I belong."

I never looked back, and neither did my sister or my brother. They have as much passion and devotion to our business as I do—I just talk more. We worked together and grew the business with my father, and even though we argued, the final decision was always his. (Most of the time, he was right.) The three of us worked side by side with him until 1990, when he had a heart attack. We took him to the hospital, where the doctors wanted him to have a quadruple bypass right away, but it was a week before Christmas, our busiest time of the year. My father told the doctor, "I'm not gonna have surgery until after the New Year. It's my busy season."

"Dad," I told him, "if you don't have this operation now, you're gonna drop dead, and there's not going to be any busy season." My father was released from the hospital on Christmas Eve, and at Christmas dinner, he came to the table and dangled the keys to the shop in his hand. "Do you want them?" he asked the three of us. "If you don't, we'll close the place. The business is now for you, if you want to maintain it."

By then, our Little Italy neighborhood had been changing dramatically. By 1963, immigration quotas had changed: immigrants were coming from Latin America, Asia, and Eastern Europe, not Italy. By the 1990s all our Italian neighbors on Mott Street had left for Brooklyn, Long Island, New Jersey, or Connecticut, and most of the shops selling cheese or meat had left too. Di Palo's was now one of the last true Italian stores on Mott Street. There were a few Italian restaurants on Mulberry Street, which has continued to grow into a tourist attraction, rather than a place where Italian-Americans would come to shop or eat, but everywhere else it was Chinese because Chinatown, once a few blocks south, had expanded into Little Italy.

It was inevitable that the neighborhood would grow and then fade away. As my grandmother said, nothing lasts forever, not even the stars in heaven: from the death of a star comes new life. And our neighborhood, the Little Italy neighborhood, is just like that. Today it is changing yet again, as the chic neighborhood of SoHo moves south and east and Chinatown shrinks. Today new immigrants can't afford to live or work here and are leaving just as the Italians did.

It doesn't upset me because I believe the *spirit* of the Italian immigrant is still here in our neighborhood. I feel we are even more in focus: we stand out. That is why, when my father was sick and offered the store to us, I said to Sal and Marie, "Our store is either going to be an eyesore in a changing neighborhood or a shining jewel. Let's make it a shining jewel. So let's not look forward, let's look backward." And by that I meant, let's do everything the way our father, our grandparents, and our great-grandparents would have done it, not the way a modern supermarket would do it. It's not how *many* people we serve, but rather *how* we serve them.

Sharing, not selling, is our business philosophy. Following my grandmother Concetta's lead, our business has always been to share—food and knowledge, certainly, but we also try to share our good karma, our good spirits, and we feel we get a blessing back. People often come in and ask, "Who owns this place?" We'll point to the wall, where

Wooden pushcart vendors worked the streets of Little Italy up until the 1960s and 1970s. In the background you can see the old store.

pictures of my grandmother, grandfather, and father hang, and say: "We're just caretakers. The owners are up there."

That's the feeling we try to maintain in our store by keeping the old cash registers, where we still have to punch in the sale. That's what our marble counters are meant to portray. Italian dining room tabletops are often made of marble, and our counters are meant to represent sitting at our table and sharing our food. Our store is very small and not that easy to browse, we don't put up a lot of product information, and you will have

A picture of me in my early teens, when I had just started making mozzarella.

to take a number and wait—you might even wait forty minutes or more on a busy weekend. But when your turn comes, you are the only customer in the world. You can ask as many questions as you want, sample as many things as you like. We take our time, we talk to you, we try to explain what it is you are seeing and tasting. You'll get the same treatment from me, Sal, and Marie and every one of our employees.

It might be more efficient to post product information or have a point-of-sale system or a dedicated checkout person. But that's the whole point—we want you to talk to us, just as customers did in my grandmother's day. We want you to go home with a little bit of what Italy is all about, what doing business in this store a hundred years ago was like. We're not the most efficient shop: there's a right way to do business, and there's a wrong way, and then there's my grandmother Concetta's way. We do things my grandmother's way.

I was the first of the Di Palos raised in the United States to visit Italy repeatedly, not just to reclaim our heritage, but to learn about what we were selling. By the 1990s, when we took over the store, I'd already spent nearly twenty years visiting Italy several times a year, meeting producers and farmers and artisans and bringing back new products.

Marie and Sal also traveled to Italy many times to learn more about the country, just as I did. Marie tells a story from her travels that I love. We buy figs from a wonderful farm called Artibel in southern Calabria, where the steep mountain slopes go straight

From right to left, my mother, Viola; my father, Sam; me; and my maternal aunt Anna Nicosia around the 1970s. My father was famous for the provolone animals you see on the counter, which he would shape and form by hand.

down into the sea on either side of the narrow peninsula. It's the perfect terrain for fruit, and their wood-fired, dried figs are amazing. They dip them in chocolate, and they are one of the best things I have ever tasted; they slow-bake them wrapped in fig leaves, and that is almost better. Their fig jam, or *confettura,* spread on bread with ricotta is out of this world. Marie has always loved figs—the trees are really important to Italians, and my mother has a huge one in our Brooklyn backyard—so when the time came to visit a producer on the rugged southern slopes of Calabria, she was the one who went.

As she was driving up the coast to the farm and factory, Marie saw a yard with cacti covered with fat pink fingers. They were *fichi d'India*—sweet prickly pears, or what Italians call "Indian figs." They are all over Southern Italy, and our Sicilian maternal grandfather always brought a box of them at Christmas and cleaned them for us grandchildren, because to eat them you have to carefully remove the prickly spines on the outside of the fruit. Marie loves them as much as she loves figs, and she'd never seen them growing before. So she knocked on the door of the farmhouse: it was an elderly couple, peasant shepherds who lived off their land. The husband started to open a prickly pear for Marie,

just as our grandfather had always done. When she got up to leave, the old man refused Marie's money. Instead he took Marie's hand. "We were so happy to host you and to share our food with you," he told her. "Thank *you* for coming to see us."

With rich experiences like these, our store grew from an immigrant store to an Italian-American store devoted to authentic foods of Italy, embracing the feel of the country itself. The business

This photo was taken of me; my brother, Sal; and my sister Marie in 2009, just after we expanded our store and opened the wine shop next door, which you can see through the windows behind us.

grew, because reporters who wanted to know why we were still selling Italian food in what was now Chinatown were coming in and interviewing us and telling people what they found.

I like to tell the story of my mother and the lentils to illustrate how much our focus changed since my parents ran the store. In 1995, when my father could no longer walk, my mother took a three-year break from the store to take care of him full-time until he passed away. When she came back to work, a young man tried to buy some lentils and she asked me how much they cost. The lentils were very special, grown in Castelluccio di Norcia in Umbria. which is known for legumes. Thanks to the clay soils in this area these small, copper lentils have a wonderful, almost crunchy texture. They are also expensive. I called across the shop: "They're $7.99 a bag!"

Now, my mother grew up in the Depression. Her regular customers haggled with her over pennies, forget $8 lentils. So she said in a very loud, excited voice in the middle of the crowded shop: "Oh nooo! Toooo expensive! Don't buy these lentils! Go to the supermarket where they are $1.40 a pound!" He bought them anyway. Later, one night as we were cleaning up the store we found we had a broken bag of lentils—I couldn't sell them, so my mother took them home for dinner. The next night she called and said, "Louie, are there any more broken bags of those lentils? They're so good." (For my mother's lentil soup recipe, see page 161.)

By 2002 we had so many products like our lentils that we could barely fit them in the store. Our place was so cramped I had to use Ferrara's pastry shop across the street as my office. (I still do: in fact it's where I worked on a lot of this book; it's a great place, ten years older than our store.) So we decided to move across Mott Street to the northwestern corner of Grand Street, where we could increase our size to twelve hundred square feet. As we grew we stocked more products—we now sell more than three hundred cheeses alone. We also have cured meats, beans and grains and flours, preserves and honeys, condiments, fresh pasta, frozen pasta, gelato and sweets and on and on from every region of Italy. In 2006 we added two hundred more square feet to the store and a large kitchen downstairs where we now cook our family's sauces and minestrone, bake eggplant parmigiana, and stuff strombolis. We fry five-cheese rice balls called *arancini,* and make our *caponata* and lasagne and ricotta and pecorino meatballs. Each day we cook something a little different based on what we have or the season or who is coming to visit from Italy, something we couldn't do before.

We've started to get more and more press over the years for the products we stock, in addition to our history. We now see people from many different ethnic backgrounds who want to taste the roast Umbrian *porchetta* my brother makes, or the many olive oils we import from every region of Italy, or the dried red chilies we bring in from our friend we call Pasquale Pepperoni in Basilicata, or the real sea salt from a nature preserve on the western tip of Sicily. People say, "You're still here!" To which I reply, "As long as you keep coming, I'll be here." Today we're a tourist attraction, though we're not a tourist store: people make a pilgrimage for our food.

Each year we, too, make a pilgrimage. We go to Italy, and every time we go, we make the store better. We're still learning, finding, tasting. Every member of my family now has dual citizenship, proud to be both Italian and Italian-American. Sal, Marie, and I encourage our children to go back to Italy, to learn and reclaim their Italian heritage. My daughter Allegra—the contessa—lived in Rome for a year. My youngest daughter, Caitlin, studied in Florence. My niece Jessica spent a year in Bologna studying business and food. And when my second child, my son, Sam, wanted to go to Piemonte to live for four years at Slow Food's new University of Gastronomic Sciences in Bra, starting the very first year it opened, I gave him my blessing. After his studies, Sam stayed in Italy to work: He made ricotta. He worked in a winery. He spent time with our relatives who still live in Basilicata—he went full circle. And when he finally came back to Little Italy, we decided to expand the business yet another time, by letting Sam add his contribution, a true *enoteca* focusing on the best wines and spirits of the twenty regions of Italy, right next door to our shop. Caitlin, my niece Cali Ann, and my nephew Michael now help him run it.

And when you read this book, I hope that you too will want to go to Italy. I want you to be inspired to buy a bottle of Sagrantino from Umbria, to cook with our excellent tomato *passata,* or to taste a wedge of pecorino made the same way for a thousand years. Over the past decades I've helped people learn about Italian food, about Little Italy, and the real Italy. And I've helped a lot of authors, journalists, and chefs write books about these things too. Now it's time to write my own.

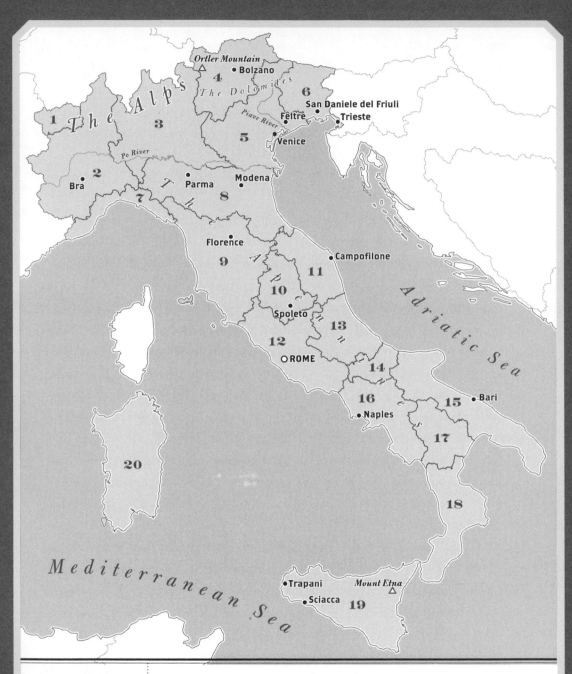

Ortler Mountain △ ● Bolzano

4

The Dolomites

6

San Daniele del Friuli ●

1 *The* *Alps* **3**

Piave River

Feltre ●

Trieste

5

Po River

Venice ●

2

Bra ●

Parma ●

Modena ●

7

The **8**

Florence ●

9

A *l* *p* *e* **11**

Campofilone ●

10

Spoleto ●

13

n *n*

12

○ ROME

14

16

15

Bari ●

Naples ●

17

Adriatic Sea

20

18

Mediterranean Sea

Trapani ●

Mount Etna △

Sciacca ●

19

ITALY
~AND ITS~
REGIONS

1 VALLE D'AOSTA	6 FRIULI-VENEZIA GIULIA
2 PIEMONTE	7 LIGURIA
3 LOMBARDIA	8 EMILIA-ROMAGNA
4 TRENTINO–ALTO ADIGE	9 TUSCANY
5 VENETO	10 UMBRIA

11 MARCHE	16 CAMPANIA
12 LAZIO	17 BASILICATA
13 ABRUZZO	18 CALABRIA
14 MOLISE	19 SICILY
15 PUGLIA	20 SARDINIA

THE
REGIONS OF ITALY

I refer to Italy as twenty countries in one because there are twenty regions, each with a distinct personality. Each region is divided into provinces, and they too have their own culture. At one time, these were hundreds of city-states functioning autonomously, and it wasn't until Garibaldi unified the country in the mid-nineteenth century that the city-states really became "Italy." For that reason, where a product is made or produced is an important consideration. The climate, terrain, crops, traditions, and even the languages can vary dramatically from region to region. My grandparents and their families moved to the United States before unification of the language arrived with the dictatorship of Mussolini, so my father couldn't understand his mother-in-law's Sicilian Italian. People thought my father's Lucanian language, on the other hand, was Chinese: Lucanian was a mountain dialect, mixed with a little bit of Greek and Albanian. And if you go up north, there are influences from Slovenia, Croatia, Austria, and France. It is the same with Italian food. That's why when you are in Italy, you drink the wine of the region and eat its food.

The other important thing to remember about regionalism is that the European Union has a system of noting when certain food products are special and traditional to a place. They are given a seal that says *Denominazione d'Origine Protetta,* or Protected Designation of Origin—which is shortened to DOP in Italian or PDO in English. This means that everything in that product is from a specific area of Italy, or that the product is made or processed following the local traditions. A DOP designation is governed by a consortium, which certifies the product and makes sure it is locally made and up to standards. There is also the label IGP, which stands for *Indicazione Geografica Protetta.* That means the product follows the consortium's guidelines for making the traditional product of the region, but they contain some ingredients that are from another area or are not generally considered traditional. For example, some cured meat headed to the United States is IGP because the pork is actually from USDA-approved slaughterhouses that operate in Denmark or Holland, while some balsamic vinegar is IGP because it is made with wine vinegar, instead of only fermented grape must, which is the pulp and skins of crushed grapes. When you see these two designations—which I refer to frequently in this book—it means that the product, whether it is olive oil, cheese, or preserves, has been recognized as both traditional and representative of that area's food traditions.

MOZZARELLA

By the early 1900s, New York City's Little Italy was rapidly expanding, and Italians had begun to move into narrow tenements on streets that had previously been Jewish. Along Orchard and Eldridge Streets in the Lower East Side, you now had Italians from Southern Italy and Sicily living next door to Eastern-European Sephardic and Ashkenazi Jews. Here you heard no English, only Italian and Yiddish. It's where my grandparents, Concetta and Luigi, moved, and it's where my parents grew up. When my mother was young, she was a *shabbos goy* for a rabbi—she turned off his lights on the Sabbath and did other small jobs—and my uncle Michael spent so much time playing with his Jewish friends that he mastered Yiddish as a kid.

My great-uncle Mauro, who had controversially married a Jewish girl from the neighborhood, was the only person who had the patience to show me how to make mozzarella. When Mauro and Doris met, their families weren't happy—for a while my great-grandfather refused to speak to his own son. But the couple got married anyway, and in a concession to both families, Mauro changed his name to Morris, and his wife, Doris, became Dora. Later, when they opened up their latteria on the corner of Union and Hicks Streets in Brooklyn near what is now the Brooklyn-

Queens Expressway, they called it Babitch Dairy after Dora's maiden name. When I was around fourteen, I asked my father to teach me how to make mozzarella, and he sent me to Great-Uncle Morris. During the summer of my sophomore year of high school, I would stay at Babitch Dairy for hours, slowly learning how to make caciotta, which is a simple Italian farmer–style cheese, and also ricotta and then mozzarella. "Work slowly, gently," Great-Uncle Morris would say when it came time to show me how to form the rounds of mozzarella. "Imagine yourself caressing a woman—imagine the tenderness with which you'd touch your girlfriend. You wouldn't be rough and squeeze her." As a teenager, that turned me red with embarrassment. But now, years later, I understand exactly what he was talking about.

Making mozzarella is not hard to do, but it is hard to do well. Great-Uncle Morris had learned how to make these cheeses in Basilicata, long before he came to work as a teenager in his father Savino's shop on Mott Street. When you grow up on a poor Italian farm like my great-uncle did, you learn to do everything. To sew. To cook. To cut hair. To slaughter pigs and cure meats and milk cows and make cheese. You can't buy, you have to do. Morris had been making these cheeses his whole life, and he learned to do it in Italy. I realized the importance of that part when I asked my father why he didn't teach me to make mozzarella. He said, "Who do you think taught me?"

The very first time I went to Italy—in 1973, when I was twenty-two and on my honeymoon—I insisted that Connie and I stop at a small latteria run by a Pugliese family in the province of Bari, a shop that made fresh cheeses like ours. I wanted to see how they made mozzarella in Italy, and was surprised to find these two old men in the shop doing it exactly the same way my family did: the only difference was the wooden tubs and paddles. With what little Italian I knew at the time, I asked if I could help them. You can imagine their surprise to see this young American guy from New York City making perfect rounds of their cheese. (Connie learned her lesson: she won't go to Italy with me anymore unless one of our children is getting married there.)

There are more than a thousand years of history behind the mozzarella we make. When I explain how we make cheese, I start with how milk is three components: a little bit of fat, a little bit of protein, and the rest is water, usually about 90 percent for cow's milk. Making cheese is separating the milk into fat and protein and getting rid of the extra water. We're really just mimicking nature: Mammals secrete a complex of enzymes called rennet. When babies drink their mother's milk, enzymes kick in to separate the milk into fat, protein, and water. The fat and protein are nourishment, and the water is voided out.

According to legend, making cheese began by accident some five thousand years ago in the Middle East, when a nomad tending his sheep and goats in the heat of the desert stored their milk in a makeshift canteen made from a lamb's stomach. To his surprise, so the story goes, when he tried to drink the milk, it had separated into curds, or in Italian, *cagliata,* and a pale green liquid called whey, or *siero.* The curd was the cheese, which satisfied his hunger, and the whey satisfied his thirst.

Today, cheese is made the same way, adding rennet to hot milk, then separating the curd from the whey. Rennet can come from the stomach of sheep, goats, or cows, or from vegetable or even microbial sources. The sap of some plants, such as figs, capers, thistles, and nettles, have long been used to make cheese across the Mediterranean. What type of rennet you add to the milk before it becomes curd—vegetable rennet, goat rennet, rennet from the dried stomach of a calf or lamb—gives you a different-tasting curd, and a different style of cheese. Today most rennet is processed; it's far more consistent and much more economical than slaughtering an animal. (I've seen small farmers make cheese with commercially available rennet, but some artisan cheesemakers still use the dried animal stomach.) You can also alter the flavor and style of cheese by heating the temperature of the milk to various degrees when you add the rennet, then cutting the curd into large or small pieces or adding in other flavors such as peppercorns, saffron, or truffles. How large the forms are and the amount of aging and the environment where the cheese is made and aged also affect how a cheese tastes. The more you tinker, the more complex cheese becomes.

Mozzarella itself was originally created by monks a thousand years ago, as a way to preserve milk from their water buffalo. These monks dedicated their lives to prayer. But they also focused on ways to store food. They made wines and beers and liquors, they pickled vegetables, and turned gallons of milk from their animals into cheese. In the hot, swampy region of Southern Italy called Campania—Naples is its major city—monks found the water buffalo to be the best animal for field work, as Campania was too hot and wet for cows. But water buffalo milk wasn't good for making cheese, except for the family of cheeses we now call *pasta filata.*

To Italians, "pasta" means more than just noodles. Pasta is any unfinished paste or dough that needs to be reworked to become the final product. And *filata* means "to spin" or "to stretch." Like the pasta dough we make into *fettuccine* or *pappardelle,* pasta filata cheese curds (including mozzarella) must be stretched into their final form. With pasta filata cheeses, traditionally made in Southern Italy, you make curds, let them rest, then reheat them in hot water, stretching them and forming them into rounds or other shapes that have a distinctive flavor and texture. Beside mozzarella, other common pasta filata cheeses are *scamorza, provolone, caciocavallo,* and *manteca,* all aged to some degree. Each is also typically made from a specific type of curd created with a specific type of rennet. These all used to be Southern Italian cheeses, made in Calabria, Campania, Basilicata, Puglia, Molise, and Abruzzo, but today large-scale production has moved north to Lombardia and Veneto where huge companies now make most of the country's cows' milk cheeses.

Scamorza, which is an aged mozzarella, is a yellow ball with a little knob on top. The curd is less acidic than the one used for mozzarella, and as a result the cheese is much drier and yellows as it ages. Provolone, on the other hand, was created when Italians found that if they added rennet from a goat, the cheese became sharper: *piccante,* but if they used rennet from a calf, it became milder and more delicate. So they make two kinds of provolone: some people like it young and mild, when it is almost the texture of mozzarella and good for a sandwich or for grilling; others when it "puts blisters on your tongue." Most Americans are used to the sandwich style, but in my opinion that's not experiencing a provolone at its fullest. Great provolone should have a strong aroma, a sharp bite at the beginning and a sweet finish. As provolone ages, it also develops tiny pinholes that grow into desirable cracks—what the Italian call *foglia,* or leaves.

Provolone is made by putting pasta filata into metal or plastic molds that range in size from a pound to a thousand pounds. After the cheeses are tightened up in a cold-water bath and then brined, the molds are hung to age for eight months to a year before being dipped in beeswax and delivered to stores. The three most common shapes are large tubes called salami, bells called *campanella,* or large rounds known as *mandarino,* because when they're tied up for hanging they look like slices of a mandarin orange. The latter is my favorite shape because as it ages the outside will get firm, but the interior stays creamy and moist.

Caciocavallo, which means "cheese horse," is similar to provolone—sharp and sweet at the same time. It takes its name because two rounds are tied together and hung to age—as they stretch and flatten, they look like saddlebags. First you make the pasta filata, then you shred it and recook it before you form the rounds. This makes the cheese denser and drier, so that it can be hung from a little knob. Caciocavallo was traditionally made in the summer, when the cheese becomes more compact.

Manteca, on the other hand, is more about what's inside the cheese. When you make lots of mozzarella (or any kind of pasta filata), eventually the butterfat rises to the top. Years ago my grandfather Luigi used to sell this *spuma*—he'd skim it off, put it in a milk can, and when that was full, he would sell it to a man in the neighborhood who made butter. Luigi made a lot of money for that can, because that spuma had the wonderful flavor of cultured milk fat, with a rich, cheesy taste. Sometimes we'd also put it on ice, and the next day it would be like a solid block of butter. We'd form it into a ball, massage out any remaining water or whey, and then we'd make the scamorza (aged mozzarella). We'd take that ball of butterfat and surround it with that cheese, creating an airtight environment. That's the way Italians preserved butter years ago: it never goes bad inside the cheese, even when the cheese dries or rots. That product was either called *burrino,* because "butter" in Italian is *burro,* or manteca, which comes from the Spanish word for "butter" or "lard." We still make it every once in a while, using fresh butter instead of spuma.

The season and what the animals are eating also affects how pasta filata tastes. We make mozzarella all year round, but winter milk is better for provolone because it is lighter in color and texture. Traditionally provolone was made in the winter and caciocavallo in summer, though today factories make them all year round. But when I went to visit Mario Vaccaro in Basilicata, the small farmer who still made cheese the way my great-grandfather once did, it was June: caciocavallo is what I watched him make, along with the drier braided forms of mozzarella.

Technically, to Italians, the mozzarella we make today in Little Italy is called *fior de latte,* because it is made with cow's milk. *Fior de latte* means "the top of the milk," or "the flower of the milk"—in other words, the very best part. True mozzarella—*mozzarella di bufala*—is still made from the milk of the water buffalo, and buffalo milk mozzarella made in Campania has been given DOP status by the European Union. We fly the real mozzarella di bufala Campana DOP into the States weekly. It is thinner-skinned, more delicate, and a little more tangy than fior di latte, thanks to the properties of the milk. In Italy, where fior di latte is sometimes still made from raw, unpasteurized cow's milk, which starts to ferment before it is made into cheese, you can often taste a little more tanginess than ours in the States.

Today, however, "mozzarella" meaning cow's milk cheese is accepted in most parts of Italy, and unless it specifically says *di bufala,* most Italian mozzarella is now from cow's milk too—and most of it is machine-made in massive latterias as most mozzarella is in America. (The stuff in your supermarket is likely a "low-moisture" or commercially made product that will last for several weeks, whereas ours only lasts for a few days.)

Whether handmade or machine-made, all mozzarella starts out the same way, with the curd, or milk solids. Milk is heated to about 100 degrees Fahrenheit, the cow's body temperature, to which you add *caglio,* or rennet. Fat and protein form curd, and the whey is discarded. (In Italy, the whey used to be used to make ricotta, see page 57.) Like most small shops that still make mozzarella by hand, we buy our curd from dairies. We've been doing that since the very beginning of our store, because my great-grandfather's and grandfather's shops had only a counter and an icebox. It takes four quarts of milk to make every pound of mozzarella, and even a small shop can sell hundreds of pounds of mozzarella each day. There wasn't room for storing that many gallons of fresh milk, or even that much curd. Though we now have five times the space my grandfather did, we still buy several types of curd from dairies in Wisconsin, Connecticut, and New York State. To make our mozzarella each week from scratch, we'd need a truckload of milk every day.

The important part of mozzarella is what happens after the curd is made. When we say we make fresh mozzarella, we mean *fresh.* Cow's milk mozzarella should be consumed within hours for best texture and milkiest flavor. That's why we make it all day long, seven days a week, by hand, the way our great-grandparents would have made it in Italy. First we soften a big rectangle of curd—it looks like a giant square of deli cheese—in a massive pot of water heated to about 180 degrees. Using my grandmother's old pasta cutter, we slice the curd into smaller pieces so that it heats through consistently—the outside doesn't get too soft, the inside doesn't stay too firm. Italians used to cut pasta with a tool called a *chitarra,* which means "guitar," a rectangular cutter made of stainless piano wire, strung between two pieces of metal that hold the wires together and keep them taut and uniformly spaced. You press the pasta across the wires, and it slices them uniformly. (You'll still see hand-cut pasta sold as *pasta alla chitarra.*

Depending on how far apart the strings are set, you will make spaghetti, fettucine, pappardelle, and so on.)

When my grandmother used our chitarra, the handles were wood, and so were the paddles we used to stir the curds in the hot water. I learned using a wooden paddle myself. But wood can splinter and get into the cheese, and it can hold bacteria. Eventually we switched to metal for everything.

Cold curd added to hot water gives off a little butterfat and lactic acid, and as it softens, the water temperature drops to about 105 degrees. So we add in a little more 180-degree water, to heat it back up. Experienced mozzarella makers know you keep some aside and recycle it, because the acidity in that water tenderizes the curd. Getting the balance right is important. If you keep too much water in the pot, the cheese will "overreact," and ferments too quickly, and won't stay fresh as long. But if you add too much new water and the water temperature of the pot is too high, the cheese will be tough and rubbery, because it releases too much butterfat too quickly. These are tiny details, but they must be mastered to make good mozzarella.

With your hands, you wait until you feel the butterfat leave the curd, and as soon as the curd is warmed through, you have to work it against your hands with the edge of the paddle. The longer you leave the curd in the water, the more butterfat it will release, and the more rubbery it will be. Ever felt 180-degree water? It's hot. But you become accustomed to it: my father's hands were permanently red, always puffy. Until we started wearing gloves for food safety reasons, we would eventually lose the outer layer of skin. You have to work very fast in that hot water, before the curd loses its stretch. The primary secret of good mozzarella is knowing when the texture is exactly right to form the cheese. Now that we wear gloves, we've learned to go not just by feel, but also by sight—when the stretch of the curd looks just right.

When the curd is ready to form into a round, there will be some resistance, but the curd will bend and move and stretch easily in your hands like taffy. That's when you have to work quickly. I fold a small piece into my hand and shape it into three layers, working out any lumps as I go, dipping the curd back in the water if I need to soften it—fold and dip, and fold and dip, and fold and dip. Then I cup the curd in my hand, pinch it tight at its base to form a smooth ball, then tear it away. In fact, that's where this cheese gets its name—*mozzare*, "to tear." The finished balls go straight into a cold water bath.

After a few minutes, the outer part of the cheese will be firm but the center will remain tender. You could serve it now as unsalted mozzarella, but we put it into a *sale moia,* or a saltwater bath. I prefer mozzarella made with a brine—which extends the life of the cheese and also tastes better. You can eat mozzarella before it goes into the salt water, when it is still very warm and has a bit of stretch—the milk will still seep out as you cut into it, and it tastes like cream. It's good, but a little rubbery, a little chewy. Great mozzarella needs to sit a bit, to settle. It's just like when you grill a steak: you need to let it rest, so that the milk, and in our case the salt from the brine, will be taken back up into the round of cheese. The final texture should be milky, juicy, and almost dissolve in your mouth.

It took me many, many years to learn all this. And though everyone at Di Palo's who makes mozzarella follows exactly the same procedure, we're each making it by hand. Everyone's mozzarella tastes a little different, maybe with a slightly unique texture or shape: I can pick out who made it—my brother, Sal, or our longtime employee Renee. My father made great mozzarella; customers would buy only the rounds he had formed. But he always insisted his mother's mozzarella was better—the best thing he'd ever tasted. This used to amaze me, because his was incredible. Now that he is gone, I understand what he meant.

BURRATA

BURRATA, A THIN ROUND OF MOZZARELLA USUALLY FILLED WITH CREAM AND shreds of more pasta filata called *stracciatella,* is the youngest cousin of mozzarella, and has become popular in America in recent years. I first saw it myself in the 1970s when I visited an Italian latteria that scooped up spuma, or butterfat, and shredded strands of curd and put it all in the center of another ball of mozzarella. They didn't call it burrata at that time, but stracciatella, the original name for those little butterfat-covered stretches that swim around the pot when you are making fior di latte. Thus the name burrata, which means "buttery," or "buttered." The story of this cheese was passed down to me by an old man in the Italian mozzarella industry, who said it was originally something that was made with the by-products of making mozzarella, to reuse things that would normally have been thrown away. Mozzarella makers would accumulate many shreds at the end of the day. The next day they would stuff them inside a mozzarella, and that would be the burrata. When it was cut open, the inside came pouring out.

Today, because there is demand for the product, it's fancier: the stretches aren't leftovers but fresh strips of reheated curd or shredded mozzarella. Many makers fill burrata with fresh cream. We make thin, soft stracciatella, then mix it with a little fresh cream and chill it down. The next day, we flatten out a disc of mozzarella, add a spoon-ful of the creamy mixture, then cup the disc and twist it closed. That's at Di Palo's—in Italy machines can now do the job.

Because the burrata is very thin-skinned, we sell it in a little plastic tub of water, so that it doesn't flatten out. Some producers wrap it in a paper leaf or wrap a real leaf around a plastic bag, because originally burrata was wrapped in a leaf of a plant that grew along the banks of the Adriatic that kept it moist and in shape and added a little flavor. Now we use paper. We do import burrata from Italy every once in a while, but it has such a short shelf life that by the time we get it we can sell it for only two days.

———

BUYING MOZZARELLA

LIKE ALL ITALIAN PRODUCTS, WITH FRESH MOZZARELLA YOU CAN HAVE *TIPO* AND *tipico*. *Tipo* means "type," which means it is made the same way, while *tipico* means "totally authentic," as in made in the same place the same way it has been for genera-tions with the same ingredients. We sell mozzarella both ways: tipico mozzarella di bufala DOP from Italy, and tipo fior di latte from Little Italy.

Unless you're cooking with it, fresh cow's milk mozzarella should be eaten the same day it's made. Ideally it should be consumed within hours, so that you can really enjoy its wonderful milky texture. Wherever you buy yours, it should be made that day, and if possible within a few hours. If the shop doesn't know when it was made—most will, even if they source it from another cheesemaker—think twice about buying it.

Note that while fior di latte, or cow's milk mozzarella, ages as you keep it in the refrigerator—it gets firmer as the days go on, and drier—buffalo milk mozzarella ripens, and is actually best after a few days. Ideally with buffalo mozzarella, the outside will still be firm but the inside will be tender. If it feels really soft in the package, which it often does, it's probably too ripe. (Pizza makers who use buffalo milk mozzarella, meanwhile, often prefer to buy it flash frozen; when it is defrosted it's drier than fresh and won't release as much moisture.)

Mozzarella comes in many sizes. We make half pounds called *ovolini,* or "little eggs," and tiny *bocconcini,* or "little bites," that are perfect for appetizers. We roll up long slabs with prosciutto into a pinwheel shape; we form some into a saltier, drier basket shape called *primo sale,* which means "first salt," and we tie some into stringy, twisted braids called *treccie,* which unravel into strings for a salad. We smoke it, and more recently, we fill very thin rounds of mozzarella with fresh cream and the thin shreds of mozzarella called stracciatella, to make burrata.

Even in Italy you'll see something called "pizza cheese," or mozzarella per pizza, which is a pasta filata closer to the low-fat, low-moisture highly processed versions of mozzarella you find in American supermarkets.

When you buy mozzarella, take note of its consistency. If you have to chew it, or it's soft in one spot and tough in another or uneven in texture, it's not made well. Good mozzarella should break down in your mouth, almost without chewing. It should be milky, juicy, and tender.

STORING MOZZARELLA

IF YOU AREN'T GOING TO EAT YOUR MOZZARELLA RIGHT AWAY, I RECOMMEND YOU buy it unsalted and put it in a bowl of water with a teaspoon of salt. (Salted mozzarella in water becomes mealy and mushy.) Cover the bowl to protect it from outside flavors, and refrigerate it—it will last several days. When you're ready to eat it, take it out and let it come up to room temperature in the water. It'll still be tender, but it won't be as juicy or as milky as when you bought it, because the butterfat is reabsorbed into the cheese and becomes a solid again. It will also lose some water, which means day-old mozzarella is better for cooking things that you don't want to get soggy, like pizza, eggplant parmigiano, or even a Caprese salad—I don't like salads to get milky from the cheese.

You can also freeze mozzarella for up to six weeks. We have customers from all over the world, including places where they can't find it fresh. They'll buy ten, twenty, forty balls, which we'll wrap in plastic, and they'll take it home to freeze it. If you freeze mozzarella when it's very fresh and wrapped tightly in plastic, it will be okay, just defrost it slowly in the refrigerator overnight. It will still be tender, but it won't be milky, and like day-old mozzarella, it will be best for cooking.

SERVING MOZZARELLA

REALLY FRESH ROUNDS OF MOZZARELLA NEED VERY LITTLE HELP. THEY SHOULD BE as fresh as possible, and taste best if they haven't been refrigerated. Then all you need to do is slice it about a half-inch thick onto a plate and—if you like—douse it with a little extra virgin olive oil, or salt and pepper. Don't cut it with a serrated knife, which leaves a ragged edge and ruins the texture.

If you're baking or cooking with mozzarella, you might want to buy it a day or two in advance, so it loses some moisture. Be sure to pay attention to whether you bought it salted or not. If your sauce is also salty, salted mozzarella can easily overpower a pizza or lasagne.

Different shapes of mozzarella serve different purposes. The drier treccia shape, the braid, is nice shredded into salads, and creamy burrata is excellent when topped with fresh tomatoes or preserved peppers. The little bites called bocconcini are perfect for appetizers: wrap them in prosciutto, marinate them in oil and herbs, or douse them with a good vinegar, then put out some toothpicks. Just be sure to let them come to room temperature before you serve them.

DI PALO'S SICILIAN EGGPLANT PARMIGIANA

SERVES 4

This is my maternal grandmother Mary's recipe for eggplant parmigiana, which like her, came from Mount Etna near the active volcano on the eastern side of Sicily. It is also an excellent example of a dish composed of traditional Sicilian ingredients: tomato, oil, eggplant, bread, and cheese combined very simply to make something incredibly good, and it is one of our bestsellers at the store. It's a really nice way to use day-old fresh mozzarella, and we traditionally make it on the stove instead of in the oven, which makes it easy in summer when eggplants and tomatoes are both at their peak. It also reheats well, is good at room temperature, and can be made in advance. Note that my grandmother would have used an aggressively flavored Sicilian cheese such as aged caciocavallo or *incanestrato* rather than Pecorino Romano, and you could try those too.

1/2 pound fresh, good quality whole milk ricotta

1/4 pound Pecorino Romano, grated

Freshly ground black pepper

1 quart marinara sauce, divided use

1 large eggplant

2 large eggs, beaten

2 cups seasoned breadcrumbs

Extra virgin olive oil, preferably from Sicily

3/4 to 1 pound day-old mozzarella, diced

1/4 pound Parmigiano-Reggiano, grated

1. Combine the ricotta, Pecorino Romano, black pepper, and 1/4 cup of marinara sauce together in a bowl, stir until very creamy.

2. Line a baking sheet with paper towels. Slice the eggplant into rounds about 1/4-inch thick, discarding the smaller slices at the end or reserving for another use. Spread the slices over the baking sheet and sprinkle both sides with salt. Let sit 5 to 10 minutes.

3. Prepare the dredge: place the eggs in one large bowl and the breadcrumbs in another. Blot the eggplant dry with paper towels. Dip a slice of eggplant into beaten eggs, and then coat each slice on all sides with breadcrumbs. Set aside on an unlined baking sheet and repeat until all slices have been battered.

4. Line another baking sheet with paper towels. In a large skillet, heat an inch of the olive oil over medium heat until it begins to shimmer. Working in batches so you don't crowd the eggplant slices, and watching the heat to make sure the oil doesn't burn, fry the eggplant on both sides until golden brown, about 4 to 5 minutes per side. Remove the slices from the skillet with a slotted spoon and set aside on baking sheet to absorb the excess oil. If the breadcrumbs begin to burn in the oil on the bottom of the skillet as you prepare later batches, discard and start with fresh oil.

5. Cover the bottom of a large skillet or saute pan with a lid with 1/4 inch of marinara sauce. Arrange 1/2 of the eggplant slices in the sauce. Add a generous dollop of the cheese mixture in the center of each slice, and top with 4 to 5 cubes of fresh mozzarella. Top cheeses with another slice of eggplant. Pour a generous amount of marinara on and around each tower, and then sprinkle the tops generously with Parmigiano-Reggiano.

6. Cover the skillet or saute pan and turn the heat to low. Cook for at least 10 minutes, or until the cheeses have warmed through and the Parmigiano-Reggiano has melted. Keep covered until serving.

POTATO CROQUETTES

MAKES ABOUT 1 DOZEN CROQUETTES

Another favorite recipe from my grandmother Mary, and another good way to use day-old mozzarella. You can serve these in marinara sauce or add a little truffle oil to the croquette for a Northern Italian twist, but they are also great just plain, sprinkled with sea salt or a little lemon juice. My mother also likes to add a little chopped prosciutto crudo.

5 large Idaho potatoes, peeled and boiled until soft

1/2 cup fresh parsley, minced

3 tablespoons grated Pecorino Romano

Salt and freshly ground black pepper to taste

2 large eggs, beaten

2 cups seasoned breadcrumbs

3/4 cup fresh mozzarella, diced

Extra virgin olive oil

Sea salt for finishing

Marinara sauce or lemon wedges, optional

1. In a large bowl, mash potatoes with parsley and cheese until the mixture is almost smooth, and add salt and pepper to taste.

2. Make the batter: place the eggs in a small bowl and the seasoned breadcrumbs in another.

3. Form the croquettes: Line a baking sheet with waxed paper. Using your hands, form about 1/3 cup of potato mixture into an oval about 2-1/2 inches long. Make a small indentation lengthwise in the center of the croquette with your finger. Place two or three pieces of mozzarella in the indentation, then cover with more potato mixture. Pat the croquette into shape, making sure all the mozzarella is covered. Dip the croquette into the beaten egg and then roll in the breadcrumbs, making sure all sides are well covered. Place on the prepared baking sheet and repeat until all the croquettes are formed.

4. Prepare another baking sheet with paper towels. In a medium-sized skillet with deep sides, heat about an inch of olive oil over medium-high heat until it shimmers. Fry the croquettes in batches until they are lightly golden all over, being careful not to crowd them. Place on the paper towel–lined baking sheet to absorb the excess oil, and sprinkle with sea salt. Serve while still hot with marinara sauce or lemon wedges.

PECORINO

When people talk about the king of cheese in Italy, they usually mean Parmigiano-Reggiano. But in the early years of our store in New York, we didn't sell much of it, if any. That cheese came from Northern Italy, and we—and our customers—were Southern Italians. Parmigiano-Reggiano really started to take off in the United States in the 1960s. Before then, when our customers wanted a nice piece of cheese to grate over their pasta, they reached for an aged pecorino.

In Italian, *pecora* means "sheep," and *pecorino* means any type of cheese made from sheep's milk. In the far north of Italy, sheep are mainly kept for wool and meat, because the cool hills and plains around the Alpine and Apennine mountains are perfect for pasturing cows, which give a lot more milk than sheep do. But Italy gets hotter and more hardscrabble the farther south you go. There's less shady grassland, just rocky, rough Mediterranean terrain, and so the vast majority of Italians traditionally milk sheep, which is why there are many, many kinds of Italian pecorinos—aged, young, hard, soft, sweet, washed-rind, truffle-coated, wrapped in chestnut leaves, layered with whole peppercorns or saffron or pistachios or whatever grows in abundance in a particular region. Di Palo's has offered more than a hundred varieties of this important cheese.

When many customers come in and ask for a nice piece of cheese to take to a dinner party, they'll balk if I offer them a pecorino. "Oh," they'll say with a look of distaste, "that's too salty." That's because most Americans, and even many Italian-Americans, think of pecorino as Pecorino Romano. Students of cheese consider Pecorino Romano the first cheese in Italy, or at least one of the oldest with an official name and process. Centuries before Christian monks were developing the technique for what would become Parmigiano-Reggiano, Pecorino Romano was a defined art and the cheese of choice for the ancient Romans. Not only did they take it with them on military campaigns around Europe, they also took along the shepherds and their sheep for milk, meat, and wool.

Today thousands of pounds of Pecorino Romano are made each year, and probably even more of the generic, mass-produced, often dry version of it is sold at American supermarkets under the name "Romano." Real Pecorino Romano is salty, but it should also be moist, rich, and flavorful. It's a complex, wonderful, robust cheese, full of personality, and its intensity is the heart of many Roman dishes like *bucatini all'amatriciana,* made with *guanciale* and tomatoes; *spaghetti alla carbonara,* made with guanciale and egg yolk; or *cacio e pepe,* which, when made in the traditional manner, is just skinny Roman *tonnarelli* pasta, crushed black pepper, and a lot of Pecorino Romano, melted and bound to the tonnarelli with a little pasta water. Genuine Pecorino Romano is so rich that it requires no butter, oil, or cream.

Pecorino Romano is now also produced in Sardinia from cross-bred flocks, but originally it was made only from the milk of Italian sheep—the *Sopravissana*—that grazed on the especially fertile flat grasslands around Rome in what is now the region of Lazio. These sheep have curly hair and chubby bodies and faces, and the rams have curly wide horns. Sopravissana give only a few liters of milk a day, which make their milk even more valuable. Today the majority of Romano producers crossbreed their flocks with Sardinian or Sicilian sheep, which look almost emaciated and bony, and have a much longer face. They produce much more milk than Sopravissana, though in my opinion the milk is not as rich. Sardinians make wonderful, delicate cheese, fantastic aged cheeses in particular, but the richness of Sopravissana milk adds a more robust, almost barnyardlike flavor.

Pecorino Romano is cured hand-packed with lots of salt and aged for at least eight months. The best ones are aged for at least a year. In ancient Rome Pecorino was prized not just for its rich flavor derived from Lazio's mineral-rich soil and Roman sheep, but also its saltiness. To the ancient Romans, remember, salt was currency, hence our word salary; it was valued because it preserved food and thus life. The saltier the cheese, the more valuable.

Pecorino Romano notwithstanding, the vast majority of pecorinos are not salty at all. Sheep's milk cheeses tend to be more intensely flavored than cow's milk cheeses, or even most goat's milk cheeses. Sheep's milk is high in fat, higher than even the richest cow's milk and many times more than low-fat goat's milk. Fat carries flavor, which is why sheep's milk cheeses are richer and feel more luxurious on your palate and in many ways more satisfying. Many of the original sheep's milk cheeses—made well before Pecorino Romano—were celebrated for other attributes like sweetness, richness, creaminess, and sharpness. They were developed by the Etruscans, another ancient shepherding civilization that predated the Romans. The heart of the Etruscan state was just north of Rome, which is why the region is now called Tuscany: the Romans called their forebears "Tusci."

The sheep's milk cheeses from Tuscany have been celebrated for centuries—the rounds of whole milk *Pecorino Toscano,* eaten after a few weeks or well-aged, were among the original DOP cheeses designated in the 1950s. Pliny the Elder recorded the art of their making for his ancient Roman readers is his *Naturalis Historia,* an encyclopedic work of Italy's foodstuffs and natural wonders, published around AD 77. By 1400, the famous *Marzolino d'Etruria* was made with the first sweet spring milk in March, or *marzo.* It was the only cheese Michelangelo would eat all year and has always been celebrated along with the original Parmigiano from Parma as one of Italy's great cheeses.

After Sicily and Sardinia—where there are literally more sheep than people—Tuscany is one of the largest commercial producers of sheep's milk cheese. My favorite makers of Tuscan pecorino—really one of my favorite *caseifici* in Italy, period—is a thirty-six-year-old company called Il Forteto in the area known as Mugello, just north of Florence. When people talk about the rolling green hills of Tuscany, Mugello is what they mean. Il Forteto is a stunningly beautiful place: an old Renaissance estate on a small mountain. As you can imagine, the local nobility had good taste.

The forested hills make for truly great sheep's milk cheese. Il Forteto started out following the area's tradition of handmade pecorinos from the pristine milk of sheep that live among the old stone farmhouses and steep hills. Today Il Forteto is known around the world for its Pecorino Toscano DOP, the famous marzolino and small pecorinos that age in tomato paste, hay, and ash according to Tuscan tradition. All are made from sheep that free-graze the green hills nearby. And I mean free: they often use the roads to travel between hill and pasture, and have the right of way. When a hundred Tuscan sheep—they are often shaggy Apennine sheep, named after the nearby mountains—come down the highway guided by their shepherd and a sheepdog, you have no choice: you stop your car to let them pass.

Il Forteto functions as an Italian *coop agricola,* an agricultural co-op, where farmers and producers join together to produce a product under one name. But it is more than a co-op—it is technically a commune, or an Italian kibbutz. My good friend Stefano Sardi, a founder of Il Forteto, was one of sixteen students who joined together with their former professor in 1977 to reclaim this land, rebuild its old farmhouses and live there together with their families. They make their own olive oil, wine, and bread, brew beer with their own grain, and raise Tuscany's famous white *Chianina* cattle for meat. (Their products, along with honeys, nuts and beans, and countless other products from their region are all available at a large supermarket they now run on the property, where you can buy a round of Pecorino and a Chianina steak or eat a Tuscan breakfast—focaccia and mortadella—with an espresso at the bar in the morning.)

The founding families still live together, work together, and take their meals together—big family-style affairs on gingham-topped picnic tables, loaded with endless plates of vegetables, roast meats, sausage, and cheese produced on the farm. While Il Forteto now hires paid employees—and works with outside shepherds to source much of their milk—a lot of the work is still done by the extended families: somebody is responsible for making the cheese, somebody takes care of the horses, somebody bales the hay, somebody makes breakfast, somebody runs the farm shop, and somebody runs the little hilltop suites of the *agriturismo,* where tourists can stay on the property for weeks at a time.

Today Stefano is one of the more respected makers of pecorino in Italy. Under his guidance, Il Forteto has grown from a heartfelt little caseificio to a major maker of cheese. In the beginning Il Forteto was about as artisanal as a place gets. Stefano remembers milking sheep by hand and toting the milk in big urns to the dairy in the basement of an ancient barn. They still source the finest-quality milk, have a full lab and state-of-the-art dairy and aging rooms where they enhance their pecorinos with new flavors or techniques, often found by researching old recipes. Today they might soak their *brillo* cheese in wine, bury the *fossa* in nearby caves, mold-ripen soft young rounds, and even produce high-end cow's milk mozzarella and burrata for supermarkets. Today you'll find Il Forteto in cheese shops literally around the world, though most have no idea of the story behind these rounds—they just love the cheese. I do know the story, and love what Il Forteto is all about: blending true traditional wisdom with the best modern cheese-making technology.

This approach is increasingly common when you visit the best producers of almost anything in Italy these days. I appreciate what they do—it's what I do in Little Italy in my own shop when I make mozzarella and ricotta. But on my first few visits to Italy nearly forty years ago, I was interested in visiting the little farmers, not factories.

On an early trip to Sicily I wanted to see pecorino made the traditional way—by the small Southern Italian *pastore,* or shepherds, who still tended and milked his own sheep, somebody who was making a little bit of fresh ricotta, the month-old young cheeses called *primo sale,* and a few wheels of the basket-aged pecorinos that change in name and flavor from village to village. I have always loved real shepherds like these—and how they care for their animals like children.

In Sardinia and Sicily, especially, you still find these peasant farmers who live off the land but also sell a few rounds of their regional versions of pecorino. So on one of my first trips to Italy I went to visit a Sicilian family who had a flock of sheep and a tiny caseificio. I got out of the car to meet them, and was immediately surrounded by sheep—I was a little worried about going into the cheese-making room, since I was walking through sheep droppings. The farmer didn't seem to mind, so we went into his dairy, which couldn't have been much bigger than my own dairy room at Di Palo's. He had one kettle in which he made sheep's milk ricotta, and another one where he made his pecorino, and nearby was a little old, worn wicker stool, where he sat to milk his sheep by hand. The pecorino he had just made was in the vat maturing in the acidic whey, and his fresh ricotta was sitting out too. There were thousands of flies—and you know where those flies were just before they were in the room with the ricotta.

Believe it or not, I had been brought to the caseificio by the region's minister of health, who didn't mind the flies, and gave me some fresh cheese to eat. It was absolutely delicious: creamy, rich, warm, sweet. It was the best, the top product, and the semi-aged wheels of pecorino were wonderful too. Afterward the shepherd asked us to come with him for a ride. We got into our car and drove a few hundred yards or so, down a hill, up a hill, and finally we reached this brand-new building under construction, where everything would be clean, monitored, computerized, ready to pass inspection for export. He looked at me, and he said, "Me, I am old, I am happy. My son, he loves the business, he wants to continue it. Soon we can't do it in the old way anymore, so I built this place for him."

A PECORINO PRIMER

THERE ARE HUNDREDS OF PECORINOS MADE THROUGHOUT ITALY, mainly from the south up to Tuscany and Emilia-Romagna. Sardinia is the biggest producer, followed by Tuscany: many Tuscan shepherds are Sardinian expats, who moved there in the 1950s and 1960s as the industry started to expand. The majority of Italian sheep's milk cheeses were traditionally salted and pressed, though today you do see more young or soft fresh cheeses made around the country, often with a mix of milks from sheep, cows, and goats. While many pecorinos, especially in Sardinia and Sicily, are made in much the same way, there are at least seventeen different types of sheep in Italy, and many different climates and terrains. As a result, even cheeses made in an identical manner can be very different from maker to maker, region to region. Here are a few traditional styles of note—and remember this list does not include fresh ricottas, which when made with sheep's milk are technically pecorinos too.

PECORINO ROMANO DOP: This salty, aged cheese is not meant to be eaten out of hand, like Parmigiano-Reggiano or other aged cheeses, but as an accent or grating cheese. The best Pecorino Romano is aged at least a year; the more aged the Pecorino Romano, the saltier and sharper it will be. While it was made famous in ancient Rome, today Pecorino Romano can also legally be made in the regions of Tuscany and Sardinia, and very little of it is made in Lazio, its original home. My favorite Pecorino Romano is "genuine," meaning it is still made in Lazio.

PECORINO TOSCANO DOP: Made from the western coast to the Florentine hills, Pecorino Toscano must be made with Tuscan milk and aged at least thirty days, but can be aged as long as a year (*stagionato*) or year and a half (*stravecchio*). All wheels are branded with the seal of the DOP consortium. Some, like Il Forteto's stravecchio, are rubbed with olive oil, adding a glossy sheen. Aged between three and six months, Pecorino Toscano has a great balance of texture and flavor and is fantastic with a Chianti wine. The younger ones I like to pair with fresh fruit—especially pears—while I often put a few drops of honey on the older ones. You can even use the well-aged rounds as a grating cheese, like Parmigiano-Reggiano or Grana Padano.

PECORINO FIORE SARDO DOP: The small island of Sardinia produces more sheep's milk cheese than any other part of Italy, and a lot of it is Pecorino Romano. They also produce unique pecorinos of their own, like *sardo,* a rich, well-aged pecorino, good for grating, with fruit and mixed with Pecorino Romano and Parmigiano-Reggiano in the famous Ligurian basil pesto called *alla Genovese*. This cheese is what I call shepherd's cheese: rustic, once originally made by peasants. In some cases, after it is made, the rind is coated with melted lard and vegetable ash and given a slight smoking, which gives it an earthier flavor.

PECORINO SICILIANO DOP: Like Pecorino Toscano and Pecorino Romano, this aged cheese is one of the oldest in Italy, recorded in *Naturalis Historia* by Pliny the Elder. Like canestrato, it is made in a basket, aged for a few weeks to eighteen months, and varies in flavor by region. It must be made with the raw milk of the local sheep free-grazing in the area, following centuries-old traditions. It's sometimes crusted with other ingredients like peppercorns, chili flakes, Sicilian olives, walnuts, pistachios, lemons, and oranges.

PECORINO DI FOSSA: In eastern Emilia-Romagna and the region of Marche, there are warrens of underground rock formations—little caverns, or *fossa*—where the peasant farmers would hide their food and other valuables from bandits, who would show up during the harvest period. When the first snows arrived, it was safe to take the cheese from the hiding place. Because of the unique environment of the underground cave, the flavor would intensify and the color would darken. Because they piled the cheese one on top of the other into sacks, by winter the cheese would be molded into different shapes and sizes. Today producers still bury the cheese in caves in August and bring it out in November. *Pecorino di Fossa* is earthy, musty, and very strong. It's best served with a sweet wine like a *passito,* or a little honey. In that region salamino di fichi is made: fig salami, made with figs, nuts, and a very dry liqueur called *aniche* blended together and wrapped in a fig leaf. A slice of that is fantastic in combination with this cheese.

CANESTRATO: In the southeastern regions of Basilicata, Abruzzo, and Puglia, pecorino is aged in baskets traditionally made of woven reeds, though today it's often plastic. The basket gives the cheese its woven shape and its name. *Canestri* means "basket" in Sicilian dialect, and in English what we often call canestrato is a country cheese, whose flavor and age vary from town to town. It is also often made with cow's milk or a mix of goat's or cow's milk with sheep's milk. Incanestrato, made in Sicily, is essentially the same thing.

PRIMO SALE: Sicily and Sardinia, especially, make very young pecorino in early spring called *primo sale,* or "first salt," which refers to the early stages of cheese-making, when the rounds are salted in their molds. It's eaten fresh, and is soft, bright white, and very milky in flavor.

MARZOLINO: This is the Tuscan pecorino made in the month of March, when early spring grasses and flowers give the milk a special sweet, floral flavor. In Italy today it's meant to be consumed just after it's made—preferably in March. As it is made with unpasteurized raw milk, we often don't get it in the States until May, because by law, raw milk cheeses have to be aged for at least sixty days.

CROTONESE: The province of Crotona in the region of Calabria is famous for sheep grazing, and their milk is used to make small rounds of cheese aged in baskets.

MOLITERNO: A historic pecorino from a small area of Basilicata, where my great-grandfather grew up. Today it's made with 10 percent goat's milk and is usually aged anywhere from thirty days to eighteen months. It takes its name, and its unique flavor, from the area where it's produced.

PIACENTINO OR PECORINO ENNESE: This famous pecorino cheese has been made since the twelfth century with black pepper and saffron near the city of Enna in Sicily. The saffron gives it both a unique flavor and yellow color.

———

BUYING PECORINO

ECORINOS RUN THE GAMUT OF THE CHEESE WORLD: THEY INCLUDE EVERYTHING from soft fresh cheeses, young rounds good for slicing into sandwiches, to well-aged versions with aggressive flavors that can be grated onto pasta. If you're in Italy, eat the pecorinos made where you are visiting. Outside of Italy, the important thing is to find a cheesemonger you trust, someone who will tell you about the different varieties in stock, and let you taste before you buy.

It's also important to know that sheep, unlike cows, don't produce milk all year round. Their best milking season is between October and June—when they naturally give birth and raise their young—and if they do give milk in summer, it's not much and of poor quality. Some producers in the United States keep their sheep indoors and fool them into giving milk all year round. But 75 percent of sheep's milk cheese production occurs in spring, between March and June, when the milk is of excellent quality: the animals eat fresh spring grasses, and the milk is very sweet, fragrant, and flavorful. The very best fresh product—primo sale, the ricottas and caciottas, the cheeses aged just a few weeks or months—is seasonal and disappears by the end of June. Then the young cheeses appear thirty, sixty days later, and so on. A really good cheesemonger will usually have a rotating stock of different pecorinos throughout the year, so be sure to ask what's in season. There are also many DOP pecorinos from all over the country, for those interested in trying a cheese from a particular region.

Buying Pecorino Romano also requires some attention to detail. It's not all the same quality or even the same thing. In the United States and Canada, domestic, or non-DOP cheese made in the Pecorino Romano style can be sold as Romano cheese, but it is not made according to the same guidelines as real Pecorino Romano. It isn't made with Italian sheep's milk from Lazio or Sardinia, and sometimes is even made with cow's milk. It is often found precut and wrapped and can be very dry and salty, and won't provide the same sharp complexity or richness of a real Pecorino Romano. It can be grated onto pasta or pizza, but for a dish like cacio e pepe, which is built upon this cheese, it's important to get the best quality. If you buy it grated, also make sure it was grated to order. Like all cut cheeses, exposed to air it loses its aroma, flavor, and moisture very quickly. It's also available in several ages; as it ages, the drier, saltier, and more complex it becomes. If your cheese shop stocks more than one age, you can ask to taste them to find which one you prefer.

STORING PECORINO

FOR PECORINO, AS FOR ANY CHEESE, MY ADVICE IS ALWAYS TO BUY ONLY WHAT YOU need for a short period, and avoid storing it much longer altogether—a week or two at most for aged cheeses, and a day or two for fresh cheeses. For grating cheeses like Pecorino Romano, you might be tempted to buy more to save a little money per pound, but it won't be the same quality cheese after a few weeks. While many pecorinos are meant to be aged, that doesn't apply to pieces sitting in your refrigerator. When cheese is cut and wrapped, it is exposed to air and to humidity. Taking cheese in and out of your fridge wears on a cheese even more—it warms up and cools down; it's exposed to humidity, which causes mold. Good cheese should breathe, which means a good wrapping in plastic is preferable to ziplock plastic bags, but if kept for more than a week or two, even a well-wrapped cheese will take on odors, the edges will harden, and it will develop an off-taste and texture. The younger cheeses like primo sale, on the other hand, are often vacuum-packed so they will make the trip to the States, and they really need to be consumed as soon as possible once they are opened, as they turn quickly.

SERVING PECORINO

WHILE PECORINO ROMANO AND OTHER EXTRA-AGED PECORINOS ARE USED PRImarily as grating cheeses—we use them in our meatballs—most pecorinos are table cheeses, excellent for a cheese plate. A spring specialty in Roman enotecas is chunks of Pecorino Romano with fresh raw fava beans, because the sweetness of the beans balances the saltiness of the cheese. You could also use a soft, young, mild Pecorino Toscano or marzolino in a sandwich. For a pecorino cheese plate, you could try three different styles of cheeses made from sheep's milk—for example, fresh, semi-hard, aged—cheese from three different regions of Italy, or three different styles from one producer such as Il Forteto, or even three DOP cheeses. The younger primo sale cheeses are best with a little olive oil and black pepper as a first course, or, for a simple dessert, paired with fruit.

If you're unsure whether to use Parmigiano-Reggiano or Pecorino Romano, look to the recipe's regional origin. Southern Italian dishes—Sicilian meatballs, classic pasta dishes like amatriciana or carbonara, or even a classic Ligurian pesto—usually call for Pecorino Romano, and these dishes were built upon the cheese's salty flavor profile. You wouldn't want to use Romano (or a similar extra-aged pecorino) on a cheese plate, but instead as a grating cheese or an ingredient on pasta or pizza. Overall, Pecorino Romano adds salt and sharpness, while Parmigiano-Reggiano adds sweetness and a general enhancement of flavors, because of its high level of natural glutamates, or what food scientists call umami. Butter is mainly used up north, so dishes with butter tend to call for Parmigiano-Reggiano too.

TONNARELLI CACIO E PEPE

(Roman Spaghetti with Cheese and Black Pepper)

SERVES 4 AS PART OF A MULTICOURSE MEAL,
OR 2 TO 3 AS A MAIN COURSE

In many central Italian dialects, cheese is *cacio*, so Tuscans and Romans called their cheeses "cacio" instead of pecorino. This is why this famous Roman pasta dish is called cacio e pepe: it is literally pasta with pepper and Pecorino Romano cheese, which melts into the dish and reveals the richness of the sheep's milk. Today you'll see many recipes from well-respected chefs that add butter, olive oil, cream, or cheeses like Parmigiano-Reggiano. But traditionally, the only ingredients are pasta, very good quality genuine Pecorino Romano from Lazio, and freshly ground black pepper, which is tossed with the long square Roman thick spaghetti noodles called *tonnarelli*. You can substitute good quality spaghetti if you can't find tonnarelli, but what you can't do in the original recipe is substitute the pecorino with Parmigiano-Reggiano, because as good as that cheese is, it doesn't have enough fat. This dish is very simple, but like so much of Italian food, it's the ingredients that make it fantastic.

Coarse sea salt
1 pound of tonnarelli or thick spaghetti
1 tablespoon freshly ground black pepper, plus more to taste
1/2 pound genuine Pecorino Romano cheese, freshly grated

1. Bring water to a boil in a tall spaghetti pot, and add a pinch of salt. Normally you want the water to be very salty when making pasta—almost like seawater—but avoid that here because you will add the cooking water to the final dish and Pecorino Romano itself is very salty. Add the pasta and cook to al dente.

2. As the pasta cooks, heat up a large serving bowl either on top of the boiling spaghetti pot or in the oven. This will help your sauce become creamy. Drain the pasta but save at least four cups of the pasta water, which now has starches from the pasta that add body to the sauce and help to emulsify it.

3. Add the black pepper to the bottom of the bowl and then add the drained pasta. Working quickly, stir in 1/4 of the grated cheese and about 1/3 cup of pasta water, tossing to melt the cheese and incorporate it into the water, then repeat two more times until you've added almost all of the cheese. You want to mix it aggressively— tongs work nicely—so that every piece of pasta is coated with a creamy sauce and plenty of black pepper. If the sauce is too wet, add in more cheese, mixing well; if it is too dry, add in more pasta water, tossing well. Season with several more grinds of black pepper and toss well again before serving.

RICOTTA

When you make fresh ricotta at a latteria like ours, you have to cool it down right away or it will begin to spoil and ferment. But in 1910, when my great-grandfather Savino was making ricotta in Little Italy, there was no refrigeration. Instead he relied on hundred-pound blocks of ice, delivered by icemen with horse-drawn carts. I've already mentioned that even on a good day Savino wasn't pleasant—he was a hothead, a burly man who didn't take nothing from nobody.

One very hot summer afternoon, when my great-grandfather had finished making his fresh ricotta, he went outside and saw the iceman just standing there with the ice in tongs on his back. The iceman happened to be a young, muscular guy from the Italian city of Bari—just east of where my grandfather grew up in Basilicata. Immigrants from Bari owned the ice delivery trade in Manhattan, and they also had a notorious reputation as ladies' men, real Casanovas. Instead of bringing the ice in to my grandfather, the Bariese iceman was outside talking to a couple of girls on our front stoop. Typical, thought my great-grandfather.

I can picture him standing in the door of the shop with his arms folded over that big belly of his, slowly growing angrier as he watched two things happen: his ricotta was starting to turn, and the ice he was paying for was melting. He finally ran into the street, yelling and waving his ice pick at the iceman, who responded by taunting and mocking my great-grandfather. They eventually started to chase each other around the horse and the cart—a fat old man in an apron running after a young, virile iceman in the crowded cobblestone street full of pushcarts, in front of our store. Finally Savino—frustrated and out of breath—took his ice pick and poked the behind of the horse. It took off clattering down the street, the cart trailing behind it spilling ice, and the iceman couldn't catch up with it until Canal Street, two blocks away.

Thanks to refrigeration, we no longer have to worry about amorous icemen at Di Palo's. That's not all that has changed in making ricotta over the years. *Ricotta* means "re-cooked." Traditional ricotta was made from re-cooking the whey left over from cheese-making. Long ago, cheesemakers found that if you heated up the remaining liquid, the enzymes that coagulate the milk would go to work again, and the little stringy dry bits of leftover fat and protein would bubble up to the top. If you collect that, then you have true ricotta. I've made it many times, but in my opinion, that ricotta is dry, gritty, and crumbly. The way ricotta is made today—and the way they have made it in Italy for nearly a century—is with whole milk from sheep, cows, or goats, and sometimes a touch of cream. The flavor and texture are vastly better, and even though you still don't get huge yields—twenty quarts of cow's milk will provide you only ten pounds of ricotta—it's a big improvement. So today ricotta isn't re-cooked, but instead it is what Italians call *formaggio fresco,* a "fresh cheese," and it is one of the best.

From Tuscany south, dairies milk more sheep than cows—and so most Italian ricotta was traditionally made from sheep's milk, especially in the south, where my family is from. *Ricotta di pecora* has a bright, tangy complexity, and most of the time I prefer it. We sell sheep's and even goat's milk ricotta imported from Italy when it's available; our ricotta is from cow's milk, which is most readily available. Americans usually raise sheep for meat, not milking. We make fresh cheese from cow's milk from local farms that keep their animals on pasture, and we always have. When my great-grandfather Savino was alive, the herds were in upper Manhattan and Queens; now they're in Upstate New York. As the Northeast artisan dairy movement has grown, there are more sheep being kept for milk, but the industry is small enough that most good farms use the majority of their product for cheese and yogurt, so there isn't enough to sell commercially.

HOW TO MAKE FRESH
RICOTTA AT HOME

•————————✖————————•

MAKING RICOTTA FROM SCRATCH IS EASY, BUT THE KEY IS PATIENCE. You have to heat the milk—it can be any kind of milk or mixture of milk and cream, depending on how rich and thick you like your ricotta—slowly, gently, moving the liquid the entire time with a wide spoon or spatula so it doesn't scald on the bottom. You want to stir it like paddling a canoe. We use the same stainless-steel paddle for ricotta that we use to stretch our mozzarella. It's also best to use a deep saucepan or pot with a very heavy bottom—a large Dutch oven would also work for a small batch at home. I heat my milk to 180 degrees, just before a simmer. Without a thermometer, my great-grandparents probably let it simmer and then cool down a bit, but that gets the milk too hot, the ricotta ends up hard and dry. (It's not as easy to be patient when you have a kettle with twenty gallons of milk: it can take hours to rise to 180 degrees, and you have to be there the entire time.)

When your milk is almost to temperature, about 170 degrees, add a small amount of white vinegar—two tablespoons per gallon, diluted with equal parts water. You keep slowly, gently agitating the milk with your spoon or paddle, waiting for the reaction when the protein and fat separate and rise to the top. They usually do it in one large mass that rises very fast and makes a sound almost like a little explosion—you'll often hear a loud "whoompf." (If you've ever burned milk or egg yolks, it's a similar experience.) Wait just a little longer, so that more little bits of leftover fat and protein rise to the top and your curds tighten up just a little more. If you take them out too soon, the ricotta will be too soft. Instead of simply pouring the whole vat over a strainer, you scoop out that fluffy ricotta—at that point Italians call it *spuma*—with a slotted spoon by hand, which helps keep the curds soft and fluffy. We scoop it into a metal tin with tiny holes in it, but you can use a cheesecloth-lined colander.

The goal is to have the curds continue to expel whey, which is an acidulant that will eventually ferment your ricotta. Refrigerate the colander set over a sheet pan or bowl, and pour off the whey as it gathers to keep your ricotta from spoiling. Ricotta also needs a little bit of time to set. If you taste ricotta right out of the pot, it will be creamy, soft, and sweet. But if you taste it again the next day or after at least three or four hours of refrigeration, it tightens and develops—in my opinion, it's even better.

———

Today cow's milk is the flavor profile most Americans still prefer. But if you read the label of a commercial container of ricotta at your grocery store, you will find all kinds of additives in addition to milk: nonfat dry milk, skim milk, stabilizers. That kind of ricotta can last for six weeks if you don't open it—I don't want to know how they do it, to be honest. Our ricotta at Di Palo's is made the old way, by slowly heating whole milk to 180 degrees with a little salt, breaking the milk into curds and whey with plain white vinegar, and then gently scooping out the curds into slotted metal containers. That's it.

The real skill with any ricotta is in the details, in the way you approach each step. For starters, source good milk the same way cheesemakers in Italy do. Another important consideration is the way you separate the curd from the whey. We use an acid to curdle the milk rather than enzymes to coagulate it—that way you get a softer, fluffier texture. Ricotta-makers can choose any kind of edible acid: lemon juice, buttermilk, white wine vinegar, fermented whey left over from the day before—Italian farmers traditionally used the sap from some fruits or members of the thistle family, like artichokes. I've even made it with the sap from unripe figs from my mother's Brooklyn backyard.

Each acid will give you a different flavor—you get a little citrus from the lemon, a little sour from the buttermilk or the whey. It was my father's cousin Henry, whose family ran a latteria around the corner from Di Palo's called Santomauro's until the 1970s, who came up with the idea of using plain white vinegar. With that, you taste just the milk—and in my opinion, that's what good ricotta should taste like. It's clear, plain milk flavor is also the best all-purpose ricotta for filling ravioli or lasagne or baking desserts.

Di Palo's ricotta uses a pinch of salt, though that's still a subject of some debate in our family. My son, Sam, doesn't approve. When he made wonderful sheep's milk ricotta after college at Il Forteto in Tuscany, they didn't use salt, he told me, because they wanted to keep the true expression of the milk. They do, however, add salt to the ricotta they export to the United States, which we sell. Like us, they found that just a little salt will help ricotta last a week, rather than a few days. So it's not just about flavor—though I actually prefer a little salt—but preservation as well.

I am proud of the cow's milk ricotta at Di Palo's. But ultimately, as Sam points out, good ricotta is about the flavor of the milk. The very best ricotta I've ever tasted—and I've tasted a lot—is made by my good friend Cesare Lopez, whose family has been making some of Italy's best sheep's milk cheese for generations, less than an hour outside of Rome, in the region of Lazio. When you taste his ricotta—made only from fall through spring, because sheep don't produce good milk in the summertime—you take two steps back. This is the best ricotta in the world, with a wonderful rustic richness and smooth texture like custard.

Cesare's sheep graze in Lazio's famous flat grasslands. Formerly known as Latium, Lazio was founded on volcanic soils near the Tiber River and what were once mineral-rich marshes called the Pomptina Palus. Sheep will notoriously eat anything—Southern Italian sheep's milk can be pale, because there isn't much grass. But in Lazio, sheep's milk has an almost greenish hue from all the chlorophyll in their grass-rich diet, and this is the region where Pecorino Romano, Italy's most famous sheep's milk cheese, was born. Cesare's windswept ranch is not far from Rome's Leonardo da Vinci airport; so if your plane goes a certain way, you can look down and see his green, open pastures just off the *autostrada,* dotted with nearly eight hundred sheep and a few fluffy white sheepdogs that look just like them.

One reason Cesare's ricotta is so much better is that his sheep are the ancient Roman variety called *Sopravissana.* They're "Little Bo Peep" sheep: they have fluffy wool and chubby bodies and faces, and the rams sport majestic, curly wide horns. Today Cesare is one of my good friends in Italy, and because he and his wife, Stefania, live in Rome, I see him often. Cesare is a true shepherd as well as a cheesemaker, and those are both difficult jobs.

Roman ricotta made in Lazio is so good it's actually been made a DOP product. Unfortunately, Cesare makes his without salt. After a few days, that rustic sheep's milk flavor starts to taste and smell like a barn, and by the time it gets to me—it's brutal! I can't get Cesare's ricotta here to the States fast enough to be able to sell it. So we bring his other cheeses—genuine aged Pecorino Romano; young pecorinos like *Crema Roma* that are just thirty days old. When it's available, we bring in salted sheep's milk ricotta from Tuscany and Sardinia and from another producer in Rome, and of course we always have our own cow's milk ricotta made fresh every day. But for the very best ricotta I've ever tasted, you'll have to go to Italy.

ONE CANNOLO,
TWO CANNOLI

CANNOLI ARE ONE OF MY FAVORITE DESSERTS, AND IF MADE TRADI-tionally, one of the best ways to showcase good ricotta. Sicilians fill fried cannoli shells—the word means "little tube" in Italian—with sheep's milk ricotta, whose gaminess stands up to the sugar in the filling. As a result the cannoli are balanced and rich and interesting, rather than overly sweet. (Sheep's milk ricotta is actually in almost every Sicilian dessert—traditional cakes, doughnuts, and even fried pastries that look like ravioli.)

The *cannolo*—if you want just one, you ask for a cannolo—was originally created near Palermo, on Sicily's western coast. They were originally made during Carnevale season right before Lent. They are a year-round staple in the rest of Italy now, but in Sicily you typically won't find a cannolo when the sheep aren't giving milk—you can get them only from October to June.

The very best cannoli that I've ever tasted are from a tiny shop in the dusty village of Dattilo in Sicily, east of Palermo. In this part of Sicily, cannoli are massive, about nine inches long and extra wide too. I found the closest thing to it in Brooklyn, at Villabate Alba Bakery on Eighteenth Avenue in the Bensonhurst neighborhood, where I grew up and my mother still lives. Villabate is one of the best Sicilian pastry shops in New York. True to tradition, their sheep's milk cannoli are filled with real Sicilian ricotta di pecora made with whey, whole milk, and cream—and very rich. You usually have to know to ask for it, and of course, it's only available when the ricotta are made, from late fall to late spring.

At Di Palo's we've printed postcards with the recipe for our cow's milk cannoli cream for decades. In America, most cannoli are too sweet, because store-bought ricotta absorbs more sugar than fresh ricotta. While this isn't as good as sheep's milk cannoli filling, it is good enough to eat on its own. Here's how to make it: Blend one cup sugar and one teaspoon vanilla into three pounds good quality, fresh whole milk ricotta and check for sweetness. Add more sugar to taste, then whip the ricotta until it is creamy and soft. Add two tablespoons of sugar to one-half pint of good quality heavy cream and whip until soft peaks form, then fold into the ricotta mixture. Stir in a few chocolate chips and/or chopped candied citron, if desired, and keep covered in the refrigerator for at least one hour before serving. This makes enough to fill two dozen cannoli shells, but try it with cake or fruit, too.

———

BUYING RICOTTA

LIKE OTHER LATTERIAS, WE SELL RICOTTA IN SEVERAL SHAPES: IN TALL PERFORATED metal tins with a mound of ricotta piled up on top to keep it pressing down, or in squat woven baskets made of plastic. The former are drier and better for cooking or baking, the latter are best when you want to serve ricotta sliced on a plate, drizzled with honey or jam. We also stock imported sheep's milk ricotta when sheep are giving milk. It is at its best in the spring, when the grass is new and sweet—if you see imported sheep's milk ricotta in the summer, it's likely not very good.

You'll also sometimes see *ricotta forte,* or "strong ricotta," a specialty from Puglia that got its start as a way to use up older product. What vinegar is to wine, ricotta forte is to ricotta. It smells and tastes like a strong gorgonzola. It's simply fermented ricotta, or ricotta turned a little sour, with a little fresh ricotta added for balance. (We usually don't eat it fresh, but add it to calzones or stir in a spoonful of tomato sauce.)

When ricotta is salted and pressed, over time it becomes a solid cheese with a much longer shelf life, though it still retains its fresh, milky flavor. There are two versions, both called *ricotta salata,* or salted ricotta: One is very dense, dry, and salty and is typically grated onto pasta. The other is more of a table cheese—it's moister and less salty and very good with slices of fresh tomato or drizzled with olive oil. The funny thing is that they usually go by the same name, so you have to ask to make sure you are getting the right one. Sicilians also bake ricotta into a mild cheese called *ricotta infornata,* which is firmer, with a more caramelized flavor. We make it at Di Palo's too, sometimes baked with acacia or chestnut honey.

In addition to ricotta, one of the most common formaggio frescos made in Italy is called *caciotta,* and we also make that daily at Di Palo's. It's made like ricotta, but we use rennet to break the milk rather than vinegar. The milk is heated to a lower temperature, and then it is also pressed a little more intensely into a basket shape and aged for a day or two. It's similar to American "farmer's cheese" and is a little drier and more solid than ricotta. There is also *cacioricotta,* which is a dry, denser caciotta made at the same high temperature as ricotta and then salted. It's usually shaved or grated over pasta.

STORING RICOTTA

RICOTTA—EVEN RICOTTA SALATA—SHOULD BE CONSUMED WITHIN A WEEK IF NOT A few days, or it will begin to ferment. At Di Palo's we prefer to send you home with ricotta in perforated containers wrapped in plastic bags. If you refrigerate them, and keep the whey draining into the bag or a pan or bowl, the ricotta will last for about a week. But you want to keep pouring off the whey each day, because its acidity eventually will spoil the cheese. All forms of formaggio fresco are exactly that—fresh cheeses, and that's why they should be eaten as soon as possible.

SERVING RICOTTA

AT DI PALO'S WE BAKE RICOTTA INTO MY GRANDMOTHER'S CHEESECAKE, FRITTAtas, and lasagne; we use it as the savory filling for pasta like *manicotti,* and as the sweet filling for cannoli. At home I love to toss it fresh into spaghetti with black pepper and olive oil, or fry slices of it when it gets a little older. In my opinion, however, good ricotta is really best by itself, served on a plate or a piece of bread topped with a little bit of olive oil or honey. Many people tend to mash it to make it easier to spread, but the flavor and texture are better if you keep it whole and simply cut or spoon out a slice, especially if it's made with sheep's milk. Eaten this way, it's also better chilled; ricotta is the one cheese I prefer cold.

Caciotta is nice sliced and drizzled with honey or extra virgin olive oil. You can shave or grate ricotta salata over salads, or any kind of pasta. A traditional way to use ricotta salata is in *pasta alla norma,* where you toss pasta, typically *rigatoni,* with tomatoes, chilies, and shreds of eggplant cooked in olive oil until soft. It's often served as part of an antipasto with sliced tomatoes or olives and peppers—it's really too milky to eat after the meal. I like to serve baked ricotta, or ricotta infornata, for dessert. You can glaze it with honey and bake it in a low oven until a golden crust forms on the outside, then serve it by the slice with fruit.

CONCETTA DI PALO'S MEATBALLS

SERVES 4

My grandmother simmered her meatballs in her sauce, but her real secret weapon was our ricotta. It keeps the meatballs incredibly moist, and adds a little richness. Because she was from Basilicata, she actually used a mix of caciocavallo, or whatever aged pecorino she had on hand, rather than provolone or Pecorino Romano, but good quality versions of these two cheeses are much easier to find. Whenever we make these in our store, they go quickly.

1 pound of ground beef, about 20 percent fat to 80 percent lean

1 egg

1/2 cup seasoned breadcrumbs

1/4 pound grated aged provolone

1/4 pound freshly grated Pecorino Romano

1 clove garlic, minced

1/4 cup fresh chopped parsley

1/2 pound fresh, good quality, whole milk ricotta

Extra virgin olive oil

1 quart marinara sauce

1. In a large bowl, mix meat, egg, breadcrumbs, cheeses, garlic, and parsley well with your hands.

2. Roll into small meatballs, about two and a half inches wide, and place on a sheet pan.

3. In a large saucepan, heat the marinara sauce over low heat.

4. Heat an inch of olive oil over medium-high heat in a large skillet. Add meatballs, cooking them in batches, if necessary, and pan-fry until browned on all sides.

5. Place meatballs in marinara sauce and let simmer for 20 minutes.

CONCETTA DI PALO'S RICOTTA CHEESECAKE

MAKES 1 9-INCH CAKE

This recipe from my grandmother Concetta is a good example of our cooking philosophy: let the ingredients speak for themselves. This cake is rich, moist, and less sweet than traditional American cheesecakes—a little more complex. We've been handing out this recipe since at least World War II—you can tell by the zwieback cookies the original recipe called for. The current version is on a postcard with a caricature of my father scowling from the back of the store, drawn by SoHo artist Jacob El Hanani, who has been shopping with us for decades. We had the same photo screen-printed onto a tile that we placed in our dairy when we renovated a few years ago, so my father could still watch over us as we made the ricotta, just like he used to.

Butter for greasing the pan

2 cups sugar, divided use

1/2 cup crushed zwieback cookies or graham crackers,
    plus extra for garnish

3 pounds good quality, fresh, whole cow's milk ricotta

6 eggs

1 teaspoon vanilla

4 teaspoons orange blossom water

3/4 cup of heavy cream

1. Preheat the oven to 350 degrees and butter a 9-inch springform pan.

2. In a small bowl, mix 1/2 cup of the sugar with the cookies, and then evenly coat the bottom and sides of the buttered pan with the mixture.

3. In a large bowl, beat the remaining sugar and the ricotta, eggs, vanilla, orange blossom water, and cream together until very smooth.

4. Pour mixture into springform pan. To prevent the cheesecake from cracking, place into a larger pan or ovenproof dish and fill it halfway up the side with water.

(continued)

5. Bake for about one hour or until a toothpick comes clean when inserted in the middle of the cake. Remove from the water bath and let the cheesecake cool on a baking rack before removing sides of springform pan and serving.

SEA SALT

Years ago I was invited to visit Italy by the chamber of commerce of Trapani, a rugged and remote province on the western coast of the island of Sicily. The *Comune di Trapani,* or the capital city of the province, is so far west it is actually closer to North Africa than the Italian mainland. That should give you an idea of the semi-arid climate in this part of Sicily, which includes both medium-sized mountains and very blue seas: It's hot, sunbaked by early June, and by August it can be nearly desertlike.

The city of Trapani itself was founded on a thin crooked finger of land, an ancient sickle-shaped harbor that's lapped on all sides by the Mediterranean. The port is so old there are myths explaining the shape of its harbor, where today little hand-built wooden fishing boats still bob along in the water. In the Roman version, Saturn went after his father, Uranus, with a sickle, which fell into the water and became Trapani. In the Greek version, the city was born when Demeter, looking for her daughter, Persephone, who'd been kidnapped by Hades, dropped her sickle into the sea.

The Greeks—whose decaying temples sit on the hilltops of western Sicily—are just one group that has owned Trapani's productive harbor over the centuries. Like most waterfront cities, Trapani has changed hands many, many times since it was colonized around the eleventh century B.C. by early Sicilian tribes. Trapani is 150 miles or so from Tunisia—and ancient Carthage—and by water isn't that far from Athens, Tripoli, or Beirut either. The people and food of Trapani are influenced by many cultures—at any type of *ristorante* you'll find that perfectly steamed couscous topped with seafood is as prevalent as pesto-topped *busiate,* the long curly strands of telephone-cord twisted pasta that are made all over the province.

Though it's been through many periods of boom and bust—and was practically wiped off the map during World War II—the area has always been extremely fertile. Among the rocky cliffs that glow orange in summers, there are farms with almond and pistachio trees, caper bushes, ancient gnarled olive trees, wild fennel and oregano, wine, tomatoes and eggplant, and famous pink Nubian garlic. Below is the water itself, still Trapani's main source of income and its most valued asset—and not just for tourism. The three almost untouched Egadi Islands off Trapani's coast, for example, are still the heart of the Italian tuna trade, and there were once so many bluefin, fishermen would simply corral them in nets, ripping them out of the water with wooden-handled spears.

Today we sell many products from Trapani, but on my first trip in the mid 1990s, the province didn't have much of a presence in the States—there weren't many people importing artisanal products from most parts of Sicily, which is still a thirty-minute boat ride to the Italian mainland at its closest point. But I had been chosen by the Trapani chamber of commerce to tour the region and its purveyors, and I felt it was important that I go not just to learn where things come from, but because a lot of times in these more far-flung parts of Italy—all of Sicily—you really have to meet families face-to-face and spend some time with them breaking bread in order for them to work with you. Only then will you be able to do business with the very best people, and more often than not, that's how you find them in the first place.

La Pasticceria Maria Grammatica

People say the original village of Trapani may have been founded by bands of native Sicilian settlers hundreds of years before Christ. The story is that they most likely launched the city as a port for Erice, a beautiful town teetering high above Trapani on Monte San Giuliano. Erice—it's pronounced ER-ee-chay—looks like it did in the Middle Ages, complete with a castle and medieval architecture. There's now even a little tram, or what Italians call *funicolare,* that will take you right to the top from the center of Trapani. I always make a point of driving up not just because it's beautiful, but because my friend Maria Grammatica owns a pasticceria where she makes amazing Sicilian sweets. Her specialties include tiny *cassata* filled with ricotta and candied fruit; warm, sweet fried ravioli-shaped stuffed pastries called Genovese; and berry *granite* all from the ancient recipes used in the cloistered Erice monastery where she went to live for fifteen years after she was orphaned as a young girl.

The nuns were known for their pastries, but Maria wasn't a nun, so the story told is she spied on the sisters as they worked and learned their secrets. No matter the source of her recipes, in my opinion this woman makes the world's best *pasta di mandorle*—what Italians call *marzipan,* made from flour from the almonds that grow nearby. Technically Maria makes *frutta martorana,* slightly sweeter marzipan shaped into perfect mandarins or husks of corn or blushing peaches or prickly pears, which grow all over Southern Italy. They come in a beautiful wooden box, and for years my customs broker advised me not to bring them in—they'll hold the sweets too long for inspection and they won't be good by the time you get them, he warned me. But they hold up just fine, and we finally started importing them into the United States last year.

One of the things I was most interested to see on my first trip to Trapani was "The Salt Road," or *La Via del Sale,* from Trapani to Marsala. Hundreds of shallow ponds on either side of this roadway slowly evaporate in Trapani's sweltering summer, and the result is the area's famous *sale marino,* or sea salt. Throughout all my previous visits to Italy, anytime I'd meet a pasta maker or stop in a latteria or see prosciutto being made, or visit nearly any other food artisan, they'd always claim they had a secret ingredient. When they finally showed it to me it would always be sea salt, and almost always from Trapani. At that point I didn't really understand how salt could be so important—so I wanted to go to Trapani to find out more about how it was harvested, and also to find the very best *salina,* or salt house.

Salinas have been a respected part of Trapani's history for almost as long as it has been a city. The first real record of Trapani salt pans was in 1100 by an Arab geographer, but it probably started with the clever maritime traders the Phoenicians—who ruled Trapani after the Greeks but before the Goths, the Arabs, and the Romans. The Phoenicians were fantastically smart folks who ran a vast trading empire from 1550 B.C. to 300, made up of city-states like Trapani along the Mediterranean. According to legend, they were the first to realize that this sickle-shaped harbor had a unique potential for salt production and first came up with the system to tap it for money—thus cementing Trapani's position on the culinary world map for centuries to come. Not only was the Mediterranean Sea around Trapani high in salinity, the land around the ports was low and flat, and Trapani's long, hot, windy, and dry summers were ideal for stress-free evaporation. On top of that, the unpolluted Mediterranean seawater was very pure, with just a trace of the minerals we need, like iodine, fluorine, potassium, and especially magnesium, which handily makes Trapani salt dissolve a little faster in water.

It's hard to describe just how important *any* salt was at that time in history. We need salt to survive, and it makes food taste better. But before refrigeration of any kind, salt preserved food, and therefore life. It was like gold or oil or diamonds—a real commodity, traded, tracked, and valuable. In fact the word "salary" itself comes from *sale,* the Roman word for "salt" because it was once so rare and valued—making salt involved wooden pumps, windmills, and lots of backbreaking work before technology made mining underground deposits efficient—people were paid in salt, and a lot of it came from Trapani. By 1572, at least according to Sicilian historians, Trapani was the biggest supplier of salt to Europe.

In the years after the world wars, Trapani's salt industry almost disappeared, replaced by dozens of other regions with more infrastructure to make salt more cheaply than by the mining of underground salt mines all over the world. Today the Trapani saltworks are growing again, kept alive in recent decades by a growing artisanal market and a few dedicated folks who realized salt's place in history. (The area would have likely been totally dismantled if it hadn't been designated a wetland preserve by the Italian government.)

On the day I was scheduled to go to see one of the oldest, most pristine salinas, I also had an appointment to appear on the local television station. So that morning, I wore a suit and tie and my brother, Sal's, brand-new shoes, which I'd borrowed for the occasion. They were Bruno Magli—$500 Italian-made shoes, a big deal for my brother who, like me, rarely wears anything fancy. We work with food all day, every day for twelve hours—so we usually wear sensible shoes that can take a slosh of salty mozzarella water—on top of that our shoes are almost always hidden behind our counters. When I was leaving for Italy, I didn't even have a good pair of shoes, and I didn't have time to shop. I'm usually in the store until the last second, working the counter, taking care of orders or getting shipments from our warehouse or whatever, running around frantically until I had to leave for the airport. "Lou," Sal said to me, knowing I was pressed for time and that we wore the same size, "just take my shoes already!"

So I did, and when we got to the salinas, there I was dressed in a suit, a tie, and Sal's $500 shoes he hadn't even worn yet . . . and it was raining. Salinas are essentially acres and acres of huge, square, open pools of seawater built right up along the sea. Those are called salt pans, and that's an accurate description—they are flat as can be, totally exposed to the elements. The only vegetation surrounding most of them are thick, red-stemmed plants called samphire that look like chunky seaweed and miraculously survive the intense sun, salinity, heat, and winds.

Salt pans are set apart from the sea and from each other by low stone or mud walls—and here and there, surprisingly, old battered Dutch-style windmills—*mulini a vento*. Before electricity, they helped pump water into the pans and to grind down huge chunks of salt into finer particles. (Today they are just for show.) From above, the salt pans look like a patchwork quilt of white, pink, and brown—and they are scattered around the little stumps of windmills, many on top of old stone buildings that used to be the offices for the salinas.

Each salina has four pans, connected by little ditches and canals. In March, the water is brought in from the sea to the first large pond, called a *fridda,* where a few remaining salt crystals in the mud help seed the operation. The water is then pumped from the *vasu cultivu* pan to the *ruffiana.* At each step, the pans are smaller and shallower, the ecosystem changes, the water evaporates a little more, the salt in the water gets a little more concentrated, almost pinkish in color. By the final pan, which is called the *casedda,* there is a thick crust of pure salt, which the workers—salt farmers, or *salinari*—wade through with long-handled rakes, gathering the salt into plastic baskets. They do it again and again over the months as the year progresses, making beautiful huge mountains of white salt, piled over the roads and around the salinas. Later it's crushed down into fine or coarse salt for grinders, or even pressed into pellets that are sold for boiling pasta.

The very first harvest, usually raked carefully into baskets and packed in mid to late June, is the best of all, the most valuable. The French call it *fleur de sel,* and Italians call it *fiore di sale,* both of which translate as "the flower of the salt." The flower is the top of the plant, and fiore di sale is just that—the very top layer, the most pristine. The rest is simply sale marino. Fiore di sale is the one you save to sprinkle on top of a dish you're proud of, right before you serve it. It tastes pure and clean, is white as snow and just as finely textured, and is a little moist, almost soft to the touch. It's very expensive: a small bottle can cost $10. But it's the best of all the sea salt you can get.

There are dozens—maybe hundreds—of salinas along La Via del Sale, but the one we buy from, called Sikelía Srl, after the old Greek name for Sicily, is just a few miles from the southern edge of Trapani's port, an area used for salt production for centuries. It's set deep inside the salt pans—protected from any fumes from boat traffic or any exhaust from the cars of the road by a handful of other salinas. Even better, it's just inside a mostly untouched wetland nature preserve run by the Italian branch of the World Wildlife Fund, or WWF, which was set up in 1995 to protect the species that thrive around the high-salinity environment of the first fridda pan and the *canale*—the canals—that separate the salt pans. These include the bright yellow blooms of the maritime calendula, a new species of grasshopper, and flocks of flamingos, who actually get their pastel-pink tones from the tiny crustaceans that thrive in the waters. In fact, you aren't even supposed to drive to Sikelía unless you work there and have a special pass, though plenty of tourists on bikes make the trip. Between the windmills, the blinding white salt mountains, and the flocks of pink flamingos that thrive on fish trapped between salt pans, the place is unlike any other part of Italy.

For most of the long Sicilian summer there is no rain in Trapani. The earth around the salinas is covered in a fine mist of shiny, almost silvery salt where it crunches in the dusty orange dirt beneath your feet like you're on the surface of Mars. But my first trip to see them was in winter, when it rains. To protect the salt, they cover the growing mountains with what look like clay roofing tiles. Salt still washes down into the pathways and roads, turning the place into a saltwater bath, which is what I was walking through at Sikelía, all dressed up in my television suit and Sal's brand-new shoes. Most of the salinari wear jeans and rubber waders all day long even in the summer. I, on the other hand, was trying to walk as delicately as I could, perching on my tiptoes in those fancy shoes. And the man that was taking me around finally noticed. "Luigi," he says, "che fai?"—*What are you doing?* In what little Italian I knew at the time, I said to him, "Le scarpe di mio fratello!"—*The shoes of my brother!*

He looked down at my feet and started to laugh. Because this pair of shoes, well, I had already ruined them. It was hopeless. When I got back to New York I bought another pair for Sal, and took the old ones to the shoe repairman, but he just laughed too—they were destroyed, just as the salt on New York's streets in winter eats away at the paint of your car. Luckily Sal told me not to worry about it, because we could now describe to our customers how even a simple thing like salt can be multifaceted, detailed, and complex. And we now tell them, with the same pride as those artisans had when they told me, that our secret ingredient—in our mozzarella, and in nearly anything else we make—is sea salt from Trapani.

SICILY'S BEST ANCHOVIES

VERY MONTH TRUCKLOADS OF TRAPANI SEA SALT ARE SHIPPED DOWN the coast to a company called Scalia in a small port town to the southeast called Scaccia, which is known for anchovies and sardines. Scalia sells me little jars of anchovies so good—tender and almost sweet, they're never fishy or mushy—my customers go nuts when they are out of season. The company was started by Benedetto Scalia. His father was a struggling Scaccia fisherman—you pronounce it SHAK-ah. But in the 1970s, Benedetto decided the more lucrative business would be to start canning the fish, rather than catching them. A friend gave him some anchovies for free, and a few weeks later Benedetto went around tiny Scaccia, selling them door to door. Soon, he outgrew his waterfront location—steps from where his mother lived right on the water—and was processing in a new plant a few miles away.

Since then his children have joined him, but his basic products are still made almost exactly the same way they've been made for centuries. The fish come in and are left to soak under loads of Trapani salt brine for a short spell to clean them. They are then beheaded, cleaned, and sorted—anchovies go here, sardines there—all by hand, every worker with a tub of sea salt in front of them at all times. All over the little fish packing room of the factory—essentially a big garage—there are tubs of Trapani sea salt. The workers dip a hand into the salt every few minutes, covering the fish and their tables to keep them clean: fish in one hand, salt in another. The anchovies and sardines are slathered in dry salt, a preservative, and then when they are packed into cans and tubs one by one, they're layered with even more salt. When the cans are first filled, the layers of fish tower inches above the top of their container. They're covered with plastic weights, stacked feet high on a pallet, then left to cure covered with a 150-pound cement slab. The salt cures the fish, and the liquid runs down the drain, and then eventually the fish are so flattened the cans are easily cleaned and sealed. The bigger tubs, meanwhile, are headed for the more expensive jars of anchovy fillets. The fish are taken out of the tub, filleted by hand, then packed into small glass jars and covered with olive or sunflower oil. And even though he doesn't pack them himself anymore, at nearly every step, Benedetto Scalia is still there on a little stool, watching as the cans are packed and weighed. If you ever wondered why good anchovies are so expensive, that is why. Just as with the salt itself, even the simplest products take effort and time, hard work and patience.

———

BUYING SEA SALT

Y OU CAN NOW EASILY FIND MANY HIGH-QUALITY SEA SALTS FROM AROUND THE world in good supermarkets or specialty food stores—there's even a store that sells only salt called The Meadow in Manhattan. Along with salts made along the Mediterranean, Adriatic, or the Baltic Seas, there are black volcanic salts, pink Hawaiian salts, and of course, the famous French sea salts from the other side of the Mediterranean from Italy—there is even sea salt from the tip of Long Island in New York where I fish for tuna. Each has a slightly different flavor or texture; as you know by now, I prefer the taste of salt from Trapani.

These days if you go to any specialty food store with a decent selection of Italian products you'll likely see a bag of Trapani sea salt. There are dozens of salinas—or saltworks—to choose from along La Via del Sale to Marsala. I prefer Sikelia because of its protected environment. And you only have to touch and taste their fiore di sale to know it's special—it's so moist, so pure. Just by looking at it you can tell that it's different from regular sea salt.

For that reason, before you spend a lot of money on an unknown sea salt, see if you can see it or even taste it first, and see if the shopkeeper knows anything about the story behind the salt in the bag. Also remember the first rule of buying specialty food products: if it seems like the price is too good to be true, it probably is.

You should also know what type of salt you should be buying. There is sale marino—regular sea salt; and then there is fiore di sale. The former is for cooking, the latter is more delicate, and it's what you use as a finishing touch. If you want to cook with your salt but don't have a grinder, you need to buy *sale marino fino,* or finely ground salt. If you have a salt grinder or mortar and pestle, you can opt for less expensive, coarser salt. (Both fino and coarse salt tend to vary from producer to producer—some is more fino than others.)

STORING SEA SALT

O NCE YOU'VE SEEN TRAPANI SALT PANS IT'S ALMOST LAUGHABLE TO WORRY ABOUT storing sea salt. It sits in the open air and harsh Sicilian sun until it's packaged. It will last forever, provided you keep it away from direct contact with water. You can easily keep an open saltcellar by your stovetop to use when you're cooking. In fact, a jar with a wide enough lid for your fingers or a spoon is the best way to store salt, which you want within arm's reach as you're cooking. If you buy it in bulk, it is best to keep it safely sealed, away from moisture and any smells it might pick up. If you do buy really expensive fiore di sale, common sense dictates you should take a little more care with it: keep it in a sealed jar, away from spills or other food.

SERVING SEA SALT

I USE REGULAR SALE MARINO FOR EVERYTHING—SEASONING MY PASTA WATER, MAKing the brine for mozzarella, for anything I cook at home or make at the store. The bulk boxes of coarse sea salt are not that expensive, and in my opinion, the food tastes better—sea salt also dissolves more quickly than mass-produced salt.

Use regular sale marino for most dishes, and save fiore di sale for finishing. You should really think of it as an element or ingredient: the crunch and minerality is just as important as what's underneath. If you look at it that way, it's not that expensive. One thing the Sicilians do that really shows off the salt as an ingredient—and something I love to eat—is very simple. It's just good bread—and Sicily has excellent bread, thick crusted with a moist crumb, thanks to the semolina flour—basted with Trapani's fantastic olive oil, and sprinkled with its sea salt.

The coarse salt, on the other hand, you'll want to grind or crush in some way before you cook with it so it will be absorbed evenly, unless you're using it to make something like Trapani's famous salt-crusted fish.

TRAPANI-STYLE SALTED
SEA BASS

SERVES 2 AS A FISH COURSE, 1 AS A MEAL

This is the dish I had in the salt museum, prepared with the Mediterranean sea bass that grow up right in the salt flats of the old salina. The recipe is inspired by one that appears in the beautiful cookbook published by the Trapani chamber of commerce. Luckily sea bass are found all over the world, even though the flavor of those in the United States won't be as intense as the ones that thrive in the saline environment of the salt flats. In Trapani they serve most seafood with sliced lemons and olive oil, the perfect way to season a whole fish; this would be a great summer meal. I recommend using a Trapanese *Biancolilla* olive oil, which is gentle and mild and won't overpower your fish.

1 to 1-1/2 pound whole sea bass, gutted and scaled

Freshly cracked black pepper

1 clove of garlic

1 sprig fresh thyme or oregano

4 cups of sea salt

Fresh lemons and extra virgin olive oil,
    preferably from Trapani

1. Preheat oven to 400 degrees F and cover a sheet pan with parchment paper.

2. Wash the sea bass, pat it totally dry with paper towels, and place it in the middle of the parchment-paper-covered sheet pan. Sprinkle each side of the fish with black pepper and insert a garlic clove and thyme or oregano inside the cavity.

3. In a large bowl, blend the sea salt and 1/2 cup of water until all the salt is moistened and the mixture feels like a thick paste. If it's too wet, add more salt; if it's too dry, add a little more water, stirring to mix.

4. Cover the fish completely with a thick layer of the salt paste, making sure there are no holes at the head, tail, or sides. Let it dry for 10 minutes.

5. Bake the fish for 15 minutes. Bring the platter to the table and gently remove the crust from the fish, and serve as you would for any whole fish, being careful of bones.

6. Season to taste with fresh lemon juice and extra virgin olive oil.

GRANA PADANO AND PARMIGIANO-REGGIANO

Like most things, the history of two of Italy's most famous cheeses—Grana Padano and Parmigiano-Reggiano—is debated. The story I like to tell starts with the Po, Italy's longest river. It runs eastward across the base of the country's crown, from France to the Adriatic just outside of Venice. Around it is a huge plain, four hundred miles of valley that stretches to the foothills of the Alps, and south below Modena. It is one of the country's distinctive geographical features. "Of the Po" is *padana* in Italian, so this area is called *pianura padana*—the plains of Padana. Northern Italy is considered anything from the Po River valley and above.

Immediately north of the river is the breadbasket of Italy, Lombardia—whose land is rich and fertile, and produces the best rice for risotto and cereal grains for flour, with plenty of grasslands left over for cows. It's been coveted for its potential throughout history. There are two reasons for its fertility: this land between the Adriatic and the Mediterranean was completely flooded millions of years ago, and second, just north are the mineral-laden Alps. As the rains came and snow melted in spring and summer, those rich minerals filtered down and settled into the Po River valley grasslands. Portuguese explorers came here; so did the ancient Romans, the Gauls, the Goths, and the Celts—everybody wanted this part of the peninsula.

Around the year 400 another raiding group of *barbari,* or barbarians, harassed the farmers who were tending the land, literally chasing them up into the mountains. Over the next six to seven hundred years, the lush area was destroyed, the barbarians were pillagers, not farmers. Without careful attention, yearly rains and overflowing river-banks turned the valley into swampy marshlands. But eventually Cistercian monks moved down from Switzerland and France to recolonize the land, turning it to fertile grasslands with the help of cows and oxen. The cows gave milk twice a day, but you can only drink so much before it sours.

Above the Po the milk was so rich, goes the legend, that monks would let the urns from the evening milking stand overnight so the fatty cream would rise to the top for making butter. But with the remainder of the skimmed milk—not fat-free skim like ours today, but skimmed of just some fat—they made cheese. Over the years, they figured out that if you broke the curds into very small pieces the size of a wheat berry or rice grain, then pressed it, salted it, and aged it in large forms, it would last for years. That kind of cheese was called *grana,* or "grain," and it was sweet, caramelly, crystalline, and wonderful. Today, we use the word *grana* to refer to the family of cheeses made in this same way, Grana Padano and Parmigiano-Reggiano being the best-known types.

According to legend, the technique for making grana cheese traveled across the river to a smaller, less fertile area just along the southern border near the city of Parma. Parma made grana too, but there was less milk and what was there had less fat, so they added some whole milk from the next morning's milking to the skimmed milk, blend-ing the two together. Because the resulting cheese now had more fat than the cheese made above the Po, it was richer and thus more intensely flavored.

In the fourteenth century, a French poet took note of a wonderful grana from Parma. He called it *Parmesan,* or "of Parma." To Italians, it was *Parmigiano.* This cheese was sweet and delicate, aged but never dry, punctuated by tyrosine, those little white lines and circles of calcium deposits and crystals of protein, which give it that special grainy crunch and punch. It turns out that Parmigiano-Reggiano contains more clusters of amino acids that turn into protein, or umami, than any other cheese and most other foods. It's good grated atop pasta, cooked into polenta, grated and baked into thin crisps called *frico,* and best of all, eaten in whole chunks out of your hand. As my friend Jeffrey Steingarten put it in "Decoding Parmesan," his essay on the product, it's the only cheese that "forms the basis of an entire cuisine."

At first, however, Parmesan just meant the grana cheese made near Parma. Every village made its own grana: In Reggio, the next town over, they made Reggiano. In Emilia, they made Emiliano. Above the river you had Montovana from Montova, Trentingrana from Trentino near the Alps, and Lodigrana from Lodi, and those are just a few examples. Lodi, by the way, claims to have been the site of the very first monastery to make a grana cheese. For centuries, every region made its own local grana, but by the 1950s, the Italian government began identifying certain regional products as having special characteristics, so they could be both protected and marketed to the rest of the world. The first thing they did was standardize the way products were made and what they were called.

The mixed-milk cheese from south of the river was made in only five zones: the area around Parma, Reggio Emilia, Modena, Bologna, and a small part of Mantova. They named it Parmigiano-Reggiano, after the best-known versions. But north of the Po, the zone for the skimmed milk version included twenty-eight provinces across the Po Valley, an area that stretches across five regions. They called it Grana Padano, or grana of the Po. Grana Padano is less expensive than Parmigiano-Reggiano because so much more of it is made. Parmigiano, "The King of Cheeses," may get more accolades, but Grana is still the most widely sold cheese in Italy.

Many small, regional granas are still made in Northern Italy that are neither Grana Padano or Parmigiano-Reggiano. Trentingrana, for example, is still produced way up north in the mountains of Trentino between fall and spring. And even though Grana Padano and Parmigiano-Reggiano cheeses are governed by a consortium that sets rules for production—that the milk come from cows in the proper region, that they graze in certain places, that certain kinds of rennet are used to curdle the milk, that the cheese is a certain size, and of course that the cheese is correctly named, but there is still room for variation within these products.

Like any product, there is a vast range of differences between the largest grana producer and the smallest. There are several thousand farms that supply milk to several hundred cheesemakers, and these farms and businesses continue to consolidate. Today many companies are cooperatives, meaning dozens or hundreds of regional farmers provide milk to one central cheese-making house. They are shareholders in the cooperative, and their pay is based both on the quality and quantity of the milk they supply. On the other side of the scale, there are still a few small, family-run caseificios. I once visited one that bought milk from just seven farmers, who brought their milk right to the *casaro,* or cheesemaker, himself. It was just one man and his wife and son, and had only enough room and equipment to make eight wheels a day, which they didn't export to the United States. By contrast, some of the big factories produce hundreds of wheels of grana a day!

Whatever the size of the operation, Grana Padano and Parmigiano-Reggiano are made in a nearly identical process—with skimmed evening milk for grana, and a mix of skimmed evening and whole fat morning milk for Parmigiano-Reggiano. All types of grana cheese are made in a giant copper kettle called a *caldaia,* and each batch produces two wheels of cheese. Like the pasta, these two wheels are known as *gemelli,* or "twins"—they are bound together. But even those two might not be exactly the same, depending on where they sit in the aging room, or if one is slightly bigger than the other.

In the big cheese houses, the cheese-making room is huge, with high ceilings and suspended lights that looks like a cross between a giant cement-floored gymnasium and a scene from *Willy Wonka.* All the workers are dressed in white T-shirts and baggy pants tucked into big white waterproof boots and use several giant-sized whisks, pot scrubbers, or blender attachments that fit over the side of a kettle to keep it agitating. There are rows and rows of caldaias, and teams of two burly men—they have to be strong—tackle several at a time, pacing themselves so one pot is always heating, curdling, or being cleaned.

First the milk is heated to 97.7 degrees Fahrenheit, to which a little fermenting whey from yesterday's cheese-making and calf's rennet is added. In a few minutes, the milk starts to coagulate, separating into curd and whey. Workers with big whisks break the curd into tiny rice-sized pieces, while the mixture is gently brought up to temperature again, then the heat is turned off while the curd forms into a big mass at the bottom of the kettle. Using a large wooden paddle, cheesecloth, and brute strength, two men hoist that massive round of curd from the whey, slice it into two rounds with a giant wire cutter, and wrap each piece in cheesecloth.

Each round of cheese is put into a wooden or Teflon mold beneath a heavy weight for a few hours, to drain more whey. The rounds then go into plastic molds decorated with the famous pinhole markings that spell out Parmigiano-Reggiano or Grana Padano, the government-issue number of the factory, the number of the dairy where the milk came from, and the month and the year when it was made. The mold is removed and replaced with a steel girdle, which gives the cheese its classic curved shape. A few days later the steel is removed and the cheese gets a three-week dunk in a room-sized tub filled with a brine—so that the tub looks like a public swimming pool filled with thousands of cheeses—and then a brief dash of sunlight before it goes into the aging room for the rest of the year.

The cheese is kept with thousands more wheels in huge aging rooms on the factory property for a year. Each wheel is rotated and cleaned of mold every week, usually by giant robots that go from aisle to aisle, working down the wall of aging cheese one row at a time. After eleven months, the cheese has its first visit from a consortium inspector—the *battitore,* similar to the Italian word for drummer. That's because his main tool—other than his eyes and nose, is a tiny little metal hammer, which he uses to tap away at several parts of the wheel, listening carefully for hollow sounds that might reveal fissures or soft spots. If all is good, the whole wheel gets marked with an ID number and later fire-branded with the seal of the consortium. With bad cheeses—of which there are several out of every hundred made—the name is scraped off and they are sold to food processing companies. Though Grana Padano can be sold after one year, most of it is aged at least sixteen to eighteen months. That's when the cheeses with the highest marks are fire-branded with another seal to certify they are of high enough quality to be aged even longer, which is known as *riserva.*

Parmigiano-Reggiano is often aged up to thirty-six months, but is usually sold when it is between twenty-four and thirty months old. (Parmigiano-Reggiano or Grana Padano aged at least two years is called *stravecchio.*) Like some other cheese sellers, I will often age wheels of Parmigiano-Reggiano myself once I get them: I open one up, see how it is, then let it age a little longer if need be. I prefer my wheels to be at least two years old, even a little older—some wheels can even go up to three. That is a phenomenal age for a cheese—like wine, it's the very rare cheese that can stand the test of that much time. As grana cheeses age, peptones, peptides, and amino acids form and then crystallize; they give good Parmigiano-Reggiano that crunch, that crystalline texture. These massive golden wheels must be at least 30 kilograms to be approved, though I prefer mine at least 37 kilos (about 82 pounds) for proper aging, so that the outside doesn't age too quickly before the interior is at the right stage. I wait until I have the full range of flavor in the wheel, the best calcium and protein development, a cheese that is well aged but not yet dry. That's what I work for in every individual wheel.

Retailers can buy grana cheese through distributors, but I try to work directly with Parmigiano-Reggiano producers themselves and with what Italians call a *staginatore*. These are people skilled at picking the best wheels from the hundreds in an aging room, and bringing them to the peak of maturity. They usually inspect the wheels early on, and buy the ones they are interested in, marking the wheel with their own brand or insignia. Once cheeses pass inspection the staginatore brings them to their own aging rooms, and then sell them to their clients. I prefer the smaller staginatores who turn the wheels by hand, clean them by hand, and can literally inspect every wheel daily.

Being a staginatore is a very respected and difficult job. Staginatores have to buy a lot of expensive cheese up front, and have a relationship with producers to get the best wheels. They spend a lifetime learning to care for this cheese. One of my favorites is the Cravero company, just outside the city center of Bra, in the region of Piemonte. Cravero is actually in the Grana Padano zone, but the family has been aging Parmigiano-Reggiano for generations. I work with Giorgio Cravero, who learned to nurture a wheel to perfection from his father, Giacomo, who learned it from his father, Giorgio, who learned it from his father, Giacomo. You know you're in the right place, because when you pull up at the gate there's a giant copper caldaia used as a planter.

To find the best selection of Parmigiano-Reggiano for Di Palo's I visit farms and factories and aging rooms. It's important to track down the source, to trace the steps back to the dairy, the actual cows, the sub-regions and their *colline,* or hills, where cows have more diverse feed and crisp air. Luckily it's all on the rind: the dairy, the producer, and the month it was made. Today I buy from about twenty-five producers—some direct from cheesemakers and some from staginatores like Cravero—and I am always searching for specific months from specific years and from my favorite zones. I also buy bigger wheels that are usually between 37 and 42 kilos (or 82 to 93 pounds). Although they take longer to mature, they age more consistently and the inside doesn't get too dry before the cheese reaches its peak.

Between these steps, there is room for variance, for making ordinary cheese or excellent cheese: how you source and store your milk, how much fat you skim, how well you clean your facility. Do you dunk your cheese in a full brine, or do you dip it carefully for a limited time? Do you dutifully clean and turn your wheels? How much clean air gets into your aging rooms?

Some people believe that the most important factor with grana cheese is the cow— that older, indigenous types of cows make the best cheese, like the Reggiana or *la vacca rosa*—the Red Cow. That used to be the grana cow in Reggio Emilia, because it gives very good quality, rich milk, but too little of it. Like other indigenous Italian breeds, the *bruno alpino,* the *Modenese* white cow and the *razza rendena*—these cows are harder and harder to find in Italy.

Today the majority of cows giving milk for grana cheeses are a common cross between European and American breeds called Holstein-Friesian. They are the black-and-white cows you see all over the countryside, which were introduced to Europe after World War II to help farmers get back on their feet—they give a lot of milk. Occasionally I will see some wheels made from vacca rosa—but after years of experience with granas I find that all cows make good cheese. What's more important is whether the cheesemaker takes care at every step of the process. If he does, then you can get really great Parmigiano-Reggiano from the milk of those postwar black-and-white cows.

What also matters is where the herd lives, and what it eats. Every region contains micro-regions, with *colline,* the hills, and *pianure,* or plains, and you even have real mountains. Regions vary: some have more sun or shade, more rain or snow, more heat or frost, and different soils, flora and fauna, which affects the color, flavor, and the texture of the cheese. I have my favorite zones, my preferences: I've spent years visiting the regions and tasting granas. I prefer higher altitudes and hills for all grana cheeses—the air is more pristine, the grasses are greener, the cheese is more intense.

With Grana Padano, the main consideration for a cheese buyer is this diversity between regions, but with Parmigiano-Reggiano, there is also seasonality. What the cows are eating, as well as the natural cycle of birth and nursing over the year greatly affect the flavor and consistency of their milk. Seasonality is less pronounced in Grana Padano because it has less fat, which carries flavor.

Seasonal changes were traditionally so noticeable in Parmigiano-Reggiano that previous generations of Italians had different names for the cheese. The spring began in April and was *testa,* the head or beginning; July and August were *agostano* or *di centro*—the middle—and then the fall, which ended in November—was the *coda,* the tail or end. Winter was *invernengo.* That's why among the various important pieces of information imprinted on the massive edible rind of Parmigiano-Reggiano—the government-given number of the Italian dairy farm, the official seal from the consortium that certifies it as Parmigiano-Reggiano, and the code for the plant where the cheese was made—the month is always clearly legible.

I still remember the first time I learned what a complicated cheese Parmigiano-Reggiano really is. By now I have cut open thousands of wheels of Parmigiano-Reggiano, and sold hundreds of thousands of pounds of it. At Di Palo's we can go through several wheels in a day, and each of them is at least 37 kilos, or 82 pounds of cheese. But decades ago, when I was in my teens and my father ran our little family store, we didn't sell much grana, as we were still primarily a Southern Italian store. My father had just gotten in a shipment of cheese from one of the most reputable Parmigiano-Reggiano staginatores in Italy at the time. But when I cracked it open with my grana knife I thought something was wrong with it. It was a pinkish white instead of the yellow gold I was used to, it was drier, and it had a flowery smell and taste, unlike any Parmigiano-Reggiano I'd ever had. "Dad," I asked my father, "what happened to this cheese?" Nothing, it turned out. It's just that the wheel had been made in April, when the spring flowers had just begun to bloom.

PARMIGIANO BY THE SEASON

TRADITIONALLY, EARLY SPRING MILK IS LOW IN BUTTERFAT WHEN cows give birth, then builds in richness as the year progresses, which affects both the flavor and mouthfeel and also the texture of the cheese: less fat and the cheese will be drier, more and it'll feel softer, a little moister. With more butterfat in the milk, the crunchy pockets of calcium and protein take longer to form or don't form in quite the same way.

While most American cheese shops don't sell Parmigiano-Reggiano with distinct seasonal differences like we do, if you are lucky enough to find one here's what to expect, and how to pair them.

SPRING: This was once the year's first Parmigiano-Reggiano. April is the start of the testa, when the cows first go outside, when the grass is vibrantly green, almost emerald in color and laden with yellow flowers and tender herbs that grow wild around the Po River. This is when you are going to find the most herbaceous floral notes in your grana cheese. Spring cheese has an almost pinkish hue, because of the carotene in the flowers. April cheese is the least rich—the casein count, or butterfat in the milk, is at its lowest because the cows have just given birth—so it is a little drier. But it is also more complex, because of all the vitamins and minerals stored in the ground throughout the winter.

I think spring Parmigiano-Reggiano is the best choice for pairing with a glass of wine, especially a lighter lambrusco or a sparkling wine, which seem to work especially well with this very flavorful but less rich cheese. I also like a *Dolcetto d'Alba*. Spring Parmigiano-Reggiano is also really good shaved over steamed asparagus—which you broil until the cheese just starts to crackle on the edges. The herbaceous notes in the cheese from early spring flowers complements the asparagus—the first vegetable of spring.

SUMMER: By summer the cows are stressed by heat, and the partially dried grass has a different, sharper flavor. The cheese is a little richer because there is more fat in the milk, and it is more yellow from the intense carotene and color of summer blooms. Summer cheese was preferred by older generations of Italians, because it was the most aggressive and had the biggest bite. A century ago milk was more sour, usually almost fermented, and so that flavor was what people liked.

Today we like more delicate flavors, and summer grass is usually cut before it burns and the cows are kept out of the heat and away from flies, so they're not so stressed. But the summer cheese is still the most intense and best for cooking. Use it in pesto, on top of a rich *ragù* or in stuffed pasta, or baked into a frittata with onions and peppers. It's a good grating cheese, with a strong flavor. Eaten on its own, I like to balance it with a mild honey, such as acacia, or pair it with a big wine like *Barolo* or *Barbaresco*.

FALL: By fall, when the grass is dry, the cheese is absolutely golden and the richest in flavor because the milk is so high in butterfat. But there is also a lot of sweetness and complexity, too, because of the grass. Fall cheese is a balance of fat, flavor, and sweetness, a blend of both richness and crystalline crunch. To me, this is the best season. I love the flavor: sweet, yet intense, best for eating in chunks. It's the easiest cheese to sell because of its delicious-looking color. October and November are really the peak time for making this cheese. Pair it with a really good true *Balsamico di Modena*—the expensive aged balsamic vinegar made nearby. The two great flavors are so simple but so elegant in combination. If you want to pair this cheese with a wine, I like *Chianti* or a dry *Lambrusco.*

WINTER: I always liken the color of Parmigiano-Reggiano to the seasons: Spring has always been pink; summer bright yellows; then golden colors in the fall, just like the cheese. And what do you see in the winter? Snow.

By midwinter, the cows are usually inside, feeding on sweet dried grass, hay, and alfalfa from the region, and the milk of the cows is sweeter with the least amount of herbaceous notes and color. This Parmigiano-Reggiano is strikingly pale, snow white, with the sweetest, mildest flavor and a rich mouthfeel. It also has the most butterfat, which means you see fewer crystals of protein and calcium and experience less crunch, because it takes more time for them to come through and develop.

It's really best eaten straight, by itself, so you can taste its unique characteristics. You can also slice it thin over cured *bresaola* with arugula and olive oil—that's a classic pairing, or with prosciutto, baby greens, and figs. Winter cheese is good with a *prosecco* or a Friulian *pinot bianco.*

————

Years ago, you couldn't legally sell the mild winter *invernengo* as Parmigiano-Reggiano. Originally, true Parmigiano-Reggiano could be made only from April 15 to November 15—while the cheese made between December and March was sold as invernengo. At that time early spring cheese wasn't as coveted either. But then world consumption for Parmigiano-Reggiano exceeded expectations and the consortium changed its mind and decided to make it and sell it all year long! That's why when I do a tasting of different seasons, I always like to start with the spring, because originally, that's where it started.

That's all in the past, however—in recent years that kind of seasonal distinction is harder than ever to find, especially as most large-scale dairies no longer keep their cows primarily on pasture. Farms that don't pasture their cows have started adjusting the mix of naturally foraged grasses and flowers with dry feed all year so that the milk is more consistent season to season, meaning the cows give the same quality milk all year long. In summers, for example, farmers cut the grass before it burns, as it naturally would, which is what helped to give summer Parmigiano-Reggiano its traditionally strong flavor.

The consortiums are going to hate me for saying this, but I've always felt that striving for consistency is not always the best approach—although I understand it. If you're making three million wheels a year, you don't want a million of them to be subpar. Over the years, farms and factories have become more efficient, and little by little, the small farms are being eaten up by the big guys. There are fewer than a hundred and fifty factories of Grana Padano in five regions and four hundred or so producers of Parmigiano-Reggiano, which are usually smaller. I remember when it used to be one thousand. Most of them are technically cooperatives, which source their milk from dozens of farmers who all have a share in the company. Some giant cheese-making plants now run their operations like pharmaceutical companies. I understand why, but there's such a thing as overkill for perfection, and sometimes cheese is at its best when you let nature take its course.

Today there is less diversity in texture, flavor, color, and aroma, and for Grana Padano there is also less regional diversity. There is also less diversity in quality: there may be less and less badly made grana, but there is also less grana made on the very highest level too—the wheels that surprise and delight you. Today there is much more very good Parmigiano-Reggiano, but the type of cheese that excites me, that draws me in, is the kind that is increasingly hard to find.

So while the Grana Padano and Parmigiano-Reggiano we sell tastes good and our customers appreciate it, I am more critical. I very rarely open a wheel and feel that I've found magnificent cheese. But if you seek out cheese made from farms where the cows are left to graze on open pasture all year long, as I do—and fewer and fewer do, these days—if you're lucky, you are occasionally rewarded. You can literally taste the seasons of the Italian countryside—those pale yellow flowers and fresh grass, or the sweet winter dry alfalfa baled up in big bundles along the Po. What better record of a place and time could there be, what more delicious way to mark the seasons in one of the most fertile, most respected growing areas of the world? That, to me, is what makes this cheese so special.

As a lifelong owner of a latteria, my first passion is cheese. We sell more than three hundred kinds of Italian cheese, from every region and every province. I still seek out new flavors, new rounds, and I am always excited by the arrival of my favorites. One week it might be *squacquerone,* a soft, creamy yogurtlike cheese produced in the foot-hills of Emilia-Romagna, or it might be the pungent wheels of extra-aged *Bitto,* made in the far north near Switzerland, so robust only the local wine balances its sharp flavor. But the most interesting cheese to me, the one I never tire of eating or talking about, is grana. If you look at the thousands of pieces sold shrink-wrapped in supermarkets, or the sheer number of identical-seeming wheels you see stacked almost everywhere in the world that sells cheese, it might seem like all Parmigiano-Reggiano and Grana Padana came from the same factory, tastes the same, and isn't all that special. Nothing could be further from the truth.

BUYING GRANA CHEESES

T'S FAIRLY EASY TO KNOW YOU ARE GETTING REAL PARMIGIANO-REGGIANO OR REAL Grana Padano as long as you can see the rind. It's a natural rind, but the entire wheel is marked with the name of the consortium spelled out in little pin dots. If you can see the whole wheel, you should also be able to spot the brand of the consor-tium—if any part of the wheel is rubbed off or has an X, then the wheel was rejected and isn't real Parmigiano-Reggiano. In the United States, cheesemakers can sell their cheese as "Parmesan"—French for *parmigiano*—if they want to. But it's not real Parmigiano-Reggiano—it might be made similarly, it might taste very good, but it won't be the real thing. Much of it is made here or in South America, and there are actually very good grana-style cheeses made in both Wisconsin and in Argentina but not in Europe since it's illegal for anyone to use Parmesan in branding except real Parmigiano-Reggiano.

Even if the cheese is genuine, it isn't necessarily great quality. You can tell a little about that by looking at the outside: is it moldy, very dry, cracked? But my primary advice is the same I give for almost anything I sell: ask to taste a piece. Remember that spring and summer cheeses are slightly drier and better for grating, while fall is the best, in my opinion, for a cheese plate. I sell Grana Padano by age—we have twelve month, fourteen month, sixteen month, and then twenty months, which is known as *Riserva*. Like Parmigiano-Reggiano they get drier and more crystalline and develop more flavor and more aroma as they age—you should taste the different ages to see what you like. As a general rule, the older the cheese, the more grainy and crunchy—but it should never be dry. Most cheese shops might stock only one or two Parmigianos, and usually of a similar flavor. One might like richer and fattier cheese, or cheese that's more crunchy and dry. Some might have one of each. In a really good shop, one might find more than one season of Parmigiano-Reggiano. If so, ask if you can taste both.

I don't recommend buying grana cheeses shrink-wrapped or precut, unless you really trust the store to have cut it recently. The cheese dries out, takes on off flavors, and decreases in richness and intensity. Of course many companies cut it and shrink-wrap it in Italy, packaged for sale to supermarkets. The cheese essentially goes to sleep and stops aging—but it's not as good as having it cut to order. I also doubt that cheese-makers would precut their very best wheels.

You should buy your grana from a cheese shop that takes care of its stock and sells a lot of cheese quickly. As soon as a wheel is cracked open, it begins to oxidize. You should watch to make sure the store knows how to open and cut a wheel of grana cheese; it isn't sliced, but cracked open with a kind of dagger, almost like chipping away at a piece of stone, so you can experience the true grainy texture of the cheese.

I never buy pre-grated cheese, unless the date stamp shows it was grated that day. You want to be sure cheese was grated freshly, and you want to be sure it's 100 percent real Parmigiano-Reggiano or Grana Padano, so ask to have it grated for you. It'll give you much better flavor.

STORING GRANA CHEESE

BUY ONLY WHAT YOU'RE GOING TO USE IN THREE WEEKS, OR ONE WEEK FOR GRATED cheese. After that, the flavor starts to change. So it doesn't pay to buy a huge piece or big tub of grated cheese. As soon as Parmigiano-Reggiano and Grana Padano are cut and exposed to air, oxygen starts to change the character, and form a crust around the edge. This is what you want to prevent, through careful wrapping and refrigeration. You might see them sitting out on our counter after they've been cut, but they usually don't last a whole day, even though our store is also very cold.

To maintain the integrity and the right moisture level in a piece of grana, the easiest thing to do is to use plastic wrap, which keeps the cheese from breathing. For a day or two that's fine, but if you are going to keep it any longer, the surface will start to taste stale—you should change the wrapping at least once a week. Parchment paper and an outer layer of aluminum foil are much better at protecting the cheese than plastic wrap. You should change the wrapping every time you take the cheese out of the refrigerator because the change in temperature will cause condensation on the surface of its wrapper. It might be so little you won't be able to see it, but eventually it causes mold. So when you take out the cheese, let it breathe for a few minutes, then put on fresh plastic wrap or paper.

SERVING GRANA CHEESE

PEOPLE OFTEN ASK ME ABOUT THE DIFFERENCE BETWEEN GRANA PADANO AND Parmigiano-Reggiano. Many think Grana Padano is less expensive than Parmigiano-Reggiano, because the area where it can legally be produced is much larger, and there is more milk produced, and so much more of it is made. Both cheeses are made nearly the same way, with the difference that Parmigiano-Reggiano uses a blend of whole and skimmed milk and Grana Padano is all skimmed.

They are both delicious, complex cheeses, and can be used in similar ways or often interchangeably: chunked onto a cheese plate, grated onto pasta or in any other dish. The major difference is that Grana Padano is more delicate than Parmigiano-Reggiano, with a lighter mouthfeel and flavor. This is often preferable in making a dish like a risotto with spring peas or a polenta that will be paired with strongly flavored foods. We use it in our cheese-stuffed *arancini,* or fried rice balls, because unlike Parmigiano-Reggiano, it won't overpower the other cheeses. We also often make a salad of thin shavings of it over arugula and thin slices of bresaola, the delicate Alpine air-cured beef. You layer them on a plate, sprinkle on the arugula and then the cheese, and then season the dish with very good, mild extra virgin olive oil, sea salt, and freshly ground black pepper.

Overall I prefer to pair the cheese of a region with the food of that region—if you are making a dish from a region north of the Po, use Grana Padano; if you are making a dish from the regions below it, use Parmigiano-Reggiano. But the best thing to do is to taste them side by side, so you can really see the differences.

Most Americans eat Parmigiano-Reggiano or Grana Padano only grated into a dish or on top of pasta—there are thousands of recipes for cooking with a little grated or shaved grana cheese: risotto, polenta, frittatas, pasta sauces, melted into an omelet, and so on. But if you do that, you are missing out on the best attributes of these cheeses. Grana cheeses are best eaten as a table cheese. Cut a chunk about an inch wide, and take a bite—you'll know why it is one of the best cheeses on earth. It's salty, sweet, crunchy, complex, and tangy all at once—it has an incredible texture and so many facets, but you'll miss out on most of them if you only grate it onto your spaghetti. It is great by itself, but goes very well with a drizzle of honey or balsamic vinegar and slices of figs, pears, and apples.

To get the best flavor, you have to cut it properly: it should really be cracked open, rather than cut. Otherwise you flatten out the cheese, and the experience is diminished. You need a grana knife with a squat triangular blade, usually with a wooden handle. It looks like a tiny spade. With that knife, you get the real craggy, grainy texture of the cheese. To cut a piece of grana correctly, you insert the pick, and bend it forward and then toward you so that you create jagged craters. If you're serving it for a party you can prepare bite-sized chunks yourself or buy a large hunk and let your guests do it themselves.

The best way to serve grated grana is to grate it yourself. In my house we use an old-fashioned box grater to grate our own cheese over our pasta, or any dish that calls for it. As the cheese is warmed up by your food, its aroma rises and your appetite awakens. Grana cheeses are also excellent shaved into giant curls with a vegetable peeler: shave it over salads and steaks, or layer the shavings over steamed asparagus and run it under the broiler for a minute or two until the cheese starts to crackle.

Hang on to your grana rinds, or the last inch or so of cheese that's too dry to eat or cut. It's a natural rind, and has great flavor. Because the cheese has been aged for two to three years, you should either scrape it well or wash it under running water before you use it. Then add it to any broth or poaching liquid, to polenta or risotto, to minestrone or any soup or stew, or to a pasta sauce instead of a bone. You can either fish it out and eat it, or cut it into smaller pieces and put it back in the pot.

But my very favorite thing to do with a grana rind is to grill it for about ten minutes per side, or put it in the broiler or toaster oven. It will be soft and chewy, and you can eat it between bread like grilled cheese. In a microwave, it'll bubble and crisp, like a cheesy chip.

ASPARAGUS WITH PARMIGIANO-REGGIANO AND EGGS

One of my favorite simple recipes with Parmigiano-Reggiano is asparagus covered with cheese shavings and a runny egg. It is broiled until the egg is still soft but has a light crust on top. This gives you two textures of the cheese: it's crispy and crusty where it's exposed but soft and melted under the egg. I like to use spring Parmigiano-Reggiano with asparagus, because its intense flavor matches that of the bright green spring vegetable.

> 1 pound medium asparagus, trimmed and washed
> 1/4 pound Parmigiano-Reggiano, preferably made in the spring
> 4 large eggs
> Extra virgin olive oil, sea salt, and freshly ground black pepper

1. Preheat your broiler. Blanch the asparagus or steam it until it is just barely tender.

2. Cover the bottom of an ovenproof baking dish with the spears. Shave the cheese over the asparagus—it should fully cover the spears. Neatly break four eggs over the top of the dish, being careful not to break the yolks. The eggs should not overlap but instead cover each quadrant of the dish.

3. Broil the asparagus until the cheese begins to crisp and the whites are cooked through but the yolk is still runny, about 5 to 7 minutes. Remove from the oven, top with salt, pepper, and olive oil to taste, serve hot.

In 1994 I got a call from Illy coffee, whose headquarters are in Trieste, way up in Northern Italy near Slovenia, along the curve of the Adriatic. We were doing such a good job selling their coffee beans at Di Palo's that Dr. Ernesto Illy invited me to lunch.

Like Italians, Americans have grown to treasure great espresso and coffee. We admire the nuances of flavor and aroma, the complexities of the bean itself, and the skills of the *barista*. But in 1994 most Americans barely knew what espresso was—it was the year the very first Starbucks opened in New York City's Upper West Side. Coffee was something most people still bought according to price, rather than artistry, and at that time Illy coffee was *very* expensive. So even though our customers bought a lot of espresso, I thought I'd sell more if Illy cost a little less. So when I met Dr. Illy at Il Cortile, a fancy Northern Italian–style restaurant around the corner from Di Palo's, I planned to ask that he lower his prices.

I had barely greeted Dr. Illy before he began to talk. He was already nearly seventy at the time, slim and elegantly dressed in his fashionable gold spectacles and swell-made suit. Dr. Illy was sophisticated, very well-spoken with a PhD in food chemistry. When he died in 2008 at eighty-two, leaving the company to his son

Andrea, *The New York Times* called him a "scientific perfectionist" of coffee, an "evangelist of espresso," and that's exactly what he was. It was Dr. Illy who first introduced many Americans to espresso, and in Italy he was a celebrity.

Italy has had a love affair with the drink ever since Venice gave the world its first European coffeehouse in 1645. And it was already popular well before then thanks to Venetian traders who brought coffee beans along with spices and gold for the *doge*. But unlike Americans, who drink big mugs of coffee loaded with milk and sugar, coffee in Italy has always meant espresso, and so at Di Palo's beans roasted and ground for espresso are mainly what we sell. (If you want a regular cup of coffee in Italy, you order a *caffé americano,* or a shot of espresso topped off with hot water.)

Espresso itself—the word in Italian roughly means "fast, for one"—was created in 1903 when a Milanese tinkerer created a steam-driven machine to make coffee in minutes using very finely ground beans. The resulting drink was smaller than a traditional cup of coffee and had less caffeine, but its flavor and aroma were much more concentrated. Better still, it came topped with a little cap of reddish-brown froth called *crema,* which results when air combines with the oils that rise to the surface of roasted beans. If you don't see that crema when you get your espresso, either the beans are old, or your blend or your barista is bad.

Today the art of espresso in Italy is as all-important as wine or pasta, and good espresso is literally everywhere: For as long as I can remember, you could get a good one even in the *aeroporto,* where true baristas craft wonderful *cappuccini.*

One reason good espresso is found everywhere in Italy is the Illy family: they've always been innovators. Ernesto's father, Francesco, who founded Illycaffè in 1933, was a Hungarian refugee who moved to Trieste after World War I. If you trace the northern curve of the Adriatic Sea, Trieste sits just east of Venice, where Italian coffee culture was born; by the late 1800s, its port had also become a coffee hub, a place where beans arrived from Ethiopia or Brazil before heading to the rest of Europe. Francesco worked with coffee and cacao roasters, and he was the one who invented the method for perfectly preserving freshly roasted coffee with pressurized gas in a can so that it no longer had to be roasted on-site.

After getting his doctorate, Ernesto joined his father and took over the company in 1956. It was much more than love of chemistry that kept him improving his family business, which became clear to me during our lunch at Il Cortile. This man was passionate about perfecting his product. He didn't sell his beans for home coffeemakers until 1965, when he invented the first automatic home espresso machine, which used pressurized water instead of steam. Before that, he wouldn't have trusted anyone but a real barista to make his espresso. Dr. Illy eventually became not just a proponent of applied science, building a high-tech lab to perfect Illy espresso at every step, but a traveling espresso ambassador who spent his life on a 747 in pursuit of what he called "the Four M's," the four factors for making great coffee.

Today when I talk about espresso I talk about Dr. Illy's Four M's. First is the *Miscela,* or the blend, the foundation for any espresso: the quality and types of beans, whether two varietals or ten, and how long and deeply each bean in the blend is roasted. A good espresso, for example, may use nine different types of beans from four different continents.

It's common in the United States for fancy coffee shops to focus on single-varietal or estate-grown beans, to reveal the natural *terreno*—the Italian word for "terroir"—of beans grown in tropical regions around the world. But for the best espresso producers, a consistent and unique blend of beans is the real secret to their espresso.

Blending is a complex task. To begin with there is all that terreno: beans from different parts of Ethiopia, Brazil, Guatemala, or Hawaii. But there is also the type of bean. The two main species of coffee beans are *robusto* and *Arabica*. The robusto bean is cheaper, faster, and easier to grow, has more caffeine and fewer natural oils, which are largely what give roasted beans their aroma. Arabica beans tend to be milder and more delicate, and because they contain more oil, they have more aromatic properties—the aroma of banana or blueberry, of orange peel, chocolate, or cinnamon. For that reason, it's Arabica beans that most modern American coffee shops tend to focus on, often at a lighter roast than Italians so that their unique notes and aromas come through.

But with 100 percent Arabica in your blend, you'll find less of that wonderful crema—the little cap of *spuma,* or foam, that is caused by forcing pressurized water through the coffee grounds. The more oil there is, the less foam you're going to get. Try dropping a little oil in a sink filled with soapy water, and you'll see the foam immediately disperse. That crema is very important to Italian coffee drinkers and to espresso makers, so Italian blends tend to use robusta beans with less oil.

Northern Italians prefer a more delicate roast than the southern varieties, which can and should be a little bitter. Typically, the farther south you go, the stronger the coffee. In most parts of far Southern Italy—where poverty meant cheaper beans were dark roasted for better flavor—the bitter, heavier intensity of darkly roasted 100 percent robusto espresso is still their preference today.

The second M is the *Macinato,* or the grind of the beans: are they coarsely ground into papery chips as for a press, or almost to a fine powder, as for espresso? The answer depends on the third M, the *Macchina*—the machine you use to make your coffee, whether it's an American drip coffeepot, an Italian stove-top *moka* espresso maker, a real espresso machine, or a French press. The grind has to fit the coffeemaker.

And then, the fourth M—and the most important of all—is the *Mano,* the hand. That's the person making your coffee, who understands how to apply heat and pressure and water, who puts together the first three M's—the right blend with the right grind with the right machine used the right way. That person is going to make the difference between a great cup of coffee, a decent cup of coffee, or a terrible cup of coffee. You can get the first three right, but without the fourth, it won't matter a bit.

All this Dr. Illy told me in great detail as we ate beneath the Roman columns and greenery at Il Cortile. By the time our plates were cleared, I'd changed my mind about asking him to lower his prices. My customers understand why a particular round of cheese might cost $20 a pound. As Dr. Illy spoke, I learned what the true value of coffee was. "Dr. Illy," I found myself saying, "you don't charge enough for your coffee!

"Now I want to tell *you* a story," I said to him. "My one hobby is fishing for giant bluefin tuna," I explained, "and my friends and I will drop everything to chase that fish from South Jersey to Maine." I told Dr. Illy about the time my friend Michael and I tracked a school up the Atlantic Ocean from New York City to the tip of Cape Cod. After a long, exhausting day of deep-sea fishing, we docked Michael's boat, cleaned ourselves up, and set into town for dinner, at a crowded place right off the marina. As we were waiting I pointed out the cans of Illy coffee stacked up behind the bar. "Mike," I proudly told my friend, "I don't know about your meal, but you're gonna have a great cup of coffee."

The food, I told Dr. Illy, rivaled the best seafood you'd find in Manhattan, pristinely fresh fish, perfectly cooked. But then came the coffee: I took one taste, and I put the cup right back down. It was the worst I'd ever had. So bad that as I got up to leave, I had to speak to the owner. "I was so impressed with your food," I told him, "but you might as well save your money and buy the cheapest coffee you can find." It was the mano, I told Dr. Illy, that I now realized was missing.

Dr. Illy didn't waste a second. "Tomorrow," he instructed an assistant who had joined us at lunch, "I want somebody to go to this restaurant in Cape Cod and teach them to make our coffee. I don't care if you have to buy them a new machine: I want my coffee in that restaurant, but I want it to taste good."

As he was making plans, here came the chef of Il Cortile himself with a cup of Illy coffee for each of us. When I was younger, I loved espresso. In Italy I used to drink it four times a day. In New York, I'd do business over a double at my de facto business office, aka Ferrera Bakery and Cafe across the street from our store. But that was until I realized that coffee was what was causing my persistent stomach problems. Skipping it altogether, I found, was the only way to keep them at bay. By that point, when I was sitting across from Dr. Illy and a freshly brewed cup of his life's work—I hadn't had a drop of coffee in years. But instead of explaining, I pretended that I was going to drink it: I lifted the cup up, I put it to my lips, and then I put it back down. But the chef is standing right above me, and he's paying attention to my reaction. "Lou," he asks, "what—you don't like the coffee?"

"Well, to tell you the truth," I sheepishly admitted to them both, "I don't drink coffee anymore. I drink tea."

To my surprise, Dr. Illy just lifted up his head and laughed. "So do I!" He started the day with espresso, but after that one cup, the most important man in Italian coffee drank tea.

HOW TO ORDER COFFEE
IN ITALY

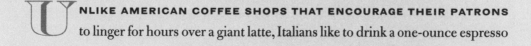

UNLIKE AMERICAN COFFEE SHOPS THAT ENCOURAGE THEIR PATRONS to linger for hours over a giant latte, Italians like to drink a one-ounce espresso four or five times a day, usually from coffee bars with a constant turnover—where you can be in and out in ten minutes. Often coffee bars don't have seats, just a high counter where customers stand to drink an espresso—that's why they're called bars, rather than shops or cafes. And they function like old-fashioned bars, too, in that you often see men gathered around shooting the breeze at the bar in the afternoon when everyone else is at work. (There are also *pasticceria,* or pastry shops, which are more like our cafes— they may have waiters, chairs, alcoholic drinks, gelato, and wonderful Italian sweets, but they are nothing like American coffee shops where all the customers have laptops.)

Ordering at an Italian coffee bar can be confusing the first time you try. To buy an espresso, you first go to the attendant at the register and pay for your drink, then take the receipt to the barista behind the counter. (For one cup or "shot" of espresso, you say *un espresso per favore;* for a double it's *uno doppio*.) You can also order one of many espresso-based drinks, the most common of which are the *macchiato,* which is an espresso topped with a small amount of foamed milk (the name means literally "marked" or "stained"), or a *cappuccino,* made by topping espresso with hot milk and then foamed milk, named after the Capuchin friars, whose light brown and cream habits look like a cappuccino. But if you order cappuccino in Italy in the afternoon, you'll mark yourself as an American! Italians don't drink anything with foamed milk after two.

————

BUYING ITALIAN COFFEE

E USUALLY SELL AT LEAST TEN DIFFERENT COFFEES FROM ALL OVER ITALY: TRIeste, the Veneto and Piemonte up north, then Rome, Naples, and Sicily to the south. Some of the difference in their beans come from how the producer selects and roasts his beans, but the majority of it is regional preference—as I mentioned before, a general rule of thumb is that in the north the coffee is usually less intense, while in the south, it's bitter, strong, and heavy. Overall, Italian coffee will be stronger tasting and more bitter than American coffee. With three sugars and lots of cream, you might prefer a dark Southern Italian roast; if you take yours black, maybe you would like a less intense blend. We also sell barley coffee; by World War II, Italians were so taken with coffee that when wartime rationing reduced supplies, they got their fix by brewing roasted barley, which has a nutty, toasty flavor and is still sold as Orzo Bimbo.

For Americans—and even some Italians—coffee is really more than just a pick-me-up; when we drink one, even quickly, we linger. As a result, it's one of those foods that can easily invoke memory, so we often buy it not just for flavor, but to reconnect to our past or a favorite moment. That's one of the reasons why we sell beans from wonderful Italian coffee bars all over Italy. One of my favorite stories is about the pregnant woman who rushed into Di Palo's, literally in labor en route to the hospital, to buy two yellow cans of coffee from Sant'Eustachio, an eighty-year-old, wood-roasted-coffee bar in Rome. Sant'Eustachio still wood-roasts the beans in the back of the store the way it's been done for decades. As a result their coffee is very frothy, very delicate, with a smoky aroma and a sweet finish. And the baristas themselves are so proud of how they make the coffee, dressed in their sunflower yellow jackets, that they hide the process behind partitions along the counters. So here was that woman going through a life-changing experience the birth of her first child—but she had had that wonderful espresso on her honeymoon in Rome and loved it so much she made her husband stop the car when she saw the cans in the window.

At Di Palo's we sell only beans that are already roasted and packaged in special cans or bricks. We have some whole beans and some coffee grounds for drip pots, but the majority of what we sell is pre-ground for espresso. Unroasted green beans could probably sit around for years, but once you've toasted those aromatic oils, it's downhill from there. Over time the aromatic oils that give coffee so much of its flavor and aroma dissipate and grow more and more mild, and can become stale and rancid. Roasters in Italy can work around this and send roasted beans to the States by vacuum-sealing the can or bag and filling it with nitrogen gas to keep beans fresh. In my opinion, coffee beans in the can are fresher tasting than those sold in a brick; they seem to hold up a little longer. If you do buy a brick, make sure it's as hard as a literal brick, not soft and loose, which means it has lost its seal. Most packages are around 250 grams; there are also bulk kilo bags, which cost less. If you buy one of those to save a bit of money, unless you have a large family, you will probably lose a little freshness by the end of the batch.

STORING ITALIAN COFFEE

ONCE A SEALED BAG OR CAN HAS BEEN OPENED, YOU SHOULD TRY TO USE IT WITHIN a week or so because it will begin to lose its intensity after just a few days. Once you open a brick or can, the nitrogen that kept the roasted beans fresh disappears, no matter where or how you store your beans, and it's exacerbated in beans that are already ground. (Kept sealed in the bag or can with the gas, they are good for about a year.) In addition to using your beans quickly, you also want to keep them in a can or airtight container in a place that's cool and dry, away from the heat put out from your stove or refrigerator. Some people say to store open bags or cans of coffee *inside* the refrigerator or the freezer, but in my opinion that's not a good idea because of the humidity, and the condensation that results when you open and close the door can ruin the flavor of coffee beans. As I mentioned before, the key is to buy smaller bags or cans.

SERVING ITALIAN COFFEE

THE REAL KEY, NO MATTER WHAT TYPE OF COFFEE YOU SERVE OR POT YOU USE OR what you put in it or what liqueur you plan to add, is to remember Dr. Illy's Four M's. Buy fresh beans and store them well before you serve them; make sure they are ground appropriately for your coffeemaker; and use your coffeemaker correctly, applying the proper temperature, time, and ratio of water to grounds. A lot of companies like Illy now sell fully automated espresso machines that work with portioned "pods" of ground coffee. That way you don't have to worry about any of the M's, because the macchina does it for you. Overall, because Italian coffees are more bitter and intense than American coffees, you might find you prefer Italian roasts with more sugar and milk than you take normally—most Italians add sugar to their espresso, and so many blends are designed with that in mind.

If you prefer making espresso at home, there are several traditional Italian options. While we don't usually sell coffeepots or espresso machines, Italians generally make espresso at home using one of two devices, a dedicated espresso machine that can usu-

MOZZARELLA

Technically the mozzarella we form by hand every day at Di Palo's is called fior di latte, *as it is made with cow's milk. Fior di latte means "the top of the milk" or "the flower of the milk"—in other words, the very best part. True mozzarella— mozzarella di bufala—is made from the milk of the water buffalo.*

RICOTTA

*Ricotta, which means "re-cooked," was
traditionally made from heating whey left over
from cheese-making. It's now made with whole
milk and even a touch of cream: the flavor
and texture are better, but it's technically
formaggio fresco, a "fresh cheese,"
and it is one of the best.*

SEA SALT

One of the things I was most interested to see on my first trip to Sicily was "The Salt Road" from Trapani to Marsala. Hundreds of shallow seawater ponds on either side of the road slowly evaporate, and the result is the area's famous sale marino, *or sea salt. This is* fior di sale, *which is both hand-harvested and the most pure.*

PECORINO

Pecorino Romano *from Lazio was originally prized not just for its rich flavor derived from the area's mineral-rich soil and special Roman sheep, but also its saltiness. To the ancient Romans, salt was currency, and the saltier the cheese, the more valuable.*

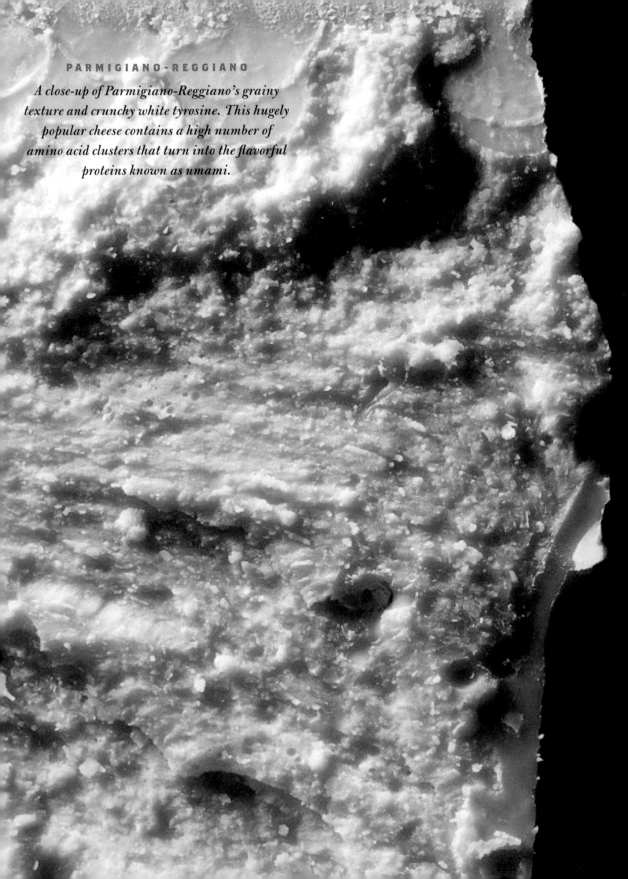

PARMIGIANO-REGGIANO

A close-up of Parmigiano-Reggiano's grainy texture and crunchy white tyrosine. This hugely popular cheese contains a high number of amino acid clusters that turn into the flavorful proteins known as umami.

OLIVE OIL

We've been selling Italian olive oil at Di Palo's since my grandparents ran the shop, when it came in big drums and our customers would pay by the ounce or the gallon. This is Sicilian extra virgin, new harvest olive oil, now produced and bottled with the perfect blend of tradition and technology.

Please see page 211 for the captions and credits for each picture

COFFEE

Northern Italians prefer a more delicate roast with the aromatic notes from arabica, while in Southern Italy, the bitter, heavier intensity of a darkly roasted blend of robusto and arabica is still the preference. Pictured here is a blend of robusto and arabica beans.

BALSAMIC VINEGAR

The traditional balsamic vinegar—Aceto Balsamico Tradizionale—is aged for a very, very long time in a series of wooden barrels called a batteria. Barrels can be made of juniper, chestnut, acacia, mulberry, ash, oak, or cherry—each of which imparts a different flavor.

PROSCIUTTO CRUDO

Prosciutto crudo *can be sold with or without the bone, but I believe bone-in legs have the best quality. To slice it to proper paper thinness, you must either do it by hand with a knife using an old stand called a* morsa, *or you have to debone them before you can use a mechanical slicer.*

PASTA

There are hundreds of pasta shapes in Italy. Many may be similar to something you know— strands, tubes, filled pockets—but they have a slightly different shape or name based on regional dialects or traditions. This is usually called penne rigate, *so named because it resembles the tips of old-fashioned quill pens.*

PIAVE AND OTHER MOUNTAIN CHEESES

Later in life I finally realized the importance of the mountains— their purity, semi-isolation, and diversity—to Italian cheesemaking. This is a selection of mountain cheeses including (top to bottom) Crucolo, Caciottone Pepe, Vento d'Estate, Caprino Foglia di Noce, pecorino aged in hay (leaning), and Piave Vecchio.

Thousands of years ago there were two basic ways to preserve meat: You could salt it where it was warm, or smoke it where it was cold. The Alpine villages of Alto Adige–Südtirol are where these two ancient methods meet in a product called Speck Alto Adige Südtirol.

ally foam milk for cappuccinos, or a cheap stove-top coffeemaker usually known in Italy as *la moka,* or the poor man's espresso maker. The moka was invented by Alfonso Bialetti in 1933, and its flat-sided aluminum body, shaped almost like a vertical bow tie, is ubiquitous in Italy. It's really three pieces that screw together: You fill the bottom with water, and the middle band with finely ground coffee and screw on the top part. When you put it on a hot stove, the water steams up through the grounds into the top chamber. Mokas—also called Bialettis—create a dark, intense brew that's very close in intensity to real espresso. Newer versions of the moka also let you foam milk at the same time—though few home cooks are as skilled at making espresso drinks as trained baristas.

Around Naples there's another ingenious stovetop espresso maker called the *caffettiera napoletana.* It has two little aluminum pots one on top of the other, each with a handle. The top pot has a little screw-in filter compartment, which you fill with dark, bitter Napoletana espresso grounds, like Pasa Aqua or Kimbo. The bottom pot has a spout, and that's where the water goes. You fit them together, heat the pot, and the water goes up through the grounds and back into the bottom compartment. When it's done, you screw off the top part and serve it Neapolitan style with a short clear glass and a lemon peel. You rub the lid of the cup in lemon, dip it in a bed of sugar, and pour in the coffee. That's how Neopolitans drink espresso; the hint of lemon and the sugar balance out the intense bitterness of the coffee.

Italians serve coffee after dinner, but not like Americans, who serve it with a piece of cake or a slice of pie. To Italians, espresso is the final course all by itself at the end of the meal, perhaps taken with a little *sambuca* or another sweet *liquore.* Northern Italians wisely call that a *caffè corretto*—it sets you straight after a long night.

The alcohol Italians add varies from place to place. In the Veneto or Trentino where it's colder, you could add wine-based *grappa.* In Marche along the Adriatic Sea, it's an anise-flavored liqueur called *anice.*

SAL'S TIRAMISÙ

At almost every family function, Sal uses a favorite espresso to make an excellent tiramisù by soaking *savoiardi*—the Italian ladyfingers originally from the ancient Northern Italian region called Savoy—in espresso and layering them with a rich mixture of mascarpone and eggs. The word *tiramisù* means something like "pick or pull me up," as in, "make me happy." Sal's combines caffeine, cocoa, and Grand Marnier.

2 cups freshly brewed espresso

1/4 cup Grand Marnier

1 cup sugar, divided use

6 large pasteurized eggs, separated

1 pound Italian mascarpone cheese at room temperature

1 7-ounce package savoiardi or other ladyfinger cookies

Bittersweet cocoa powder for dusting

1. In a bowl, stir together the coffee and Grand Marnier. Taste for sweetness, whisking in sugar if desired.

2. In a separate large bowl, beat the egg whites until stiff peaks form.

3. In a large bowl, beat the egg yolks with 3/4 cup of the sugar. Whisk in the mascarpone until the mixture is smooth and spreadable, then gently fold in the beaten egg whites.

4. Dipping each ladyfinger in the coffee mixture, make a neat layer of cookies on the bottom and sides of an 11-inch brownie pan or glass baking dish. Cover the layer of cookies with about 1/3 of the egg and mascarpone mixture. Add another layer of coffee-dipped cookies, and then another third of the mascarpone mixture. Repeat a third time, ending with a layer of mascarpone. Dust the top of the dessert with cocoa powder.

5. Refrigerate for at least 6 hours before slicing into squares and serving. The cake can be refrigerated overnight, but will begin to get soggy after 24 hours.

O L I V E   O I L

Today nineteen of Italy's twenty regions produce olive oil. But in Sicily, olives are everywhere—providing six DOP olive oils, more than any other region. The island is covered with rows and rows of olive trees, and it has been for centuries. Most experts trace the birth of the domesticated olive to Turkey. To Sicilians, olive trees are as common as maples, oaks, and pines are to Americans, and most can point to their backyard to show you a gnarled, split trunk that's two hundred, three hundred, sometimes five hundred years old. It's usually still producing that wonderfully intense Sicilian oil, known for its grassy notes and the sharp peppery finish you feel in the back of your throat. Italians call it the *pizzica*, or "the little pinch."

Sicilian suppers almost always start with antipasto, based on their excellent oil. Little toasts slicked with salt, chopped tomato, and a wash of olive oil; thin rounds of poached eggplant delivered in a pool of oil and splash of vinegar, long broad beans dressed with oregano and oil, the sweet-sour mix of roasted peppers, onions, and eggplants called *caponata*, or little fritters of leftover minced meat, egg, and bread, fried in even more extra virgin oil. One reason Sicilians cover their food with their fantastically flavorful oil is that they can't afford much else. My maternal grandmother, Mary, was from a small town just south of Mount Etna, in eastern Sicily, and this is the way she cooked and ate—it wasn't until I visited the island as an adult that I finally realized why.

If you look down the rows of trees in Sicily in the summertime, the soil around those weathered, twisted roots is dusty, hot, dry, and rugged. In the green mountains in Umbria above the old city of Trevi, where I buy some of my favorite fruity green oil from the fourth generation of Checcarellis, the soil is like a forest floor, often green and mossy, with the smell of wild mint. Farther north around the pristine waters of Lake Garda, where the oil is delicate and buttery, the fog along the shore acts as a warm blanket to keep the Alpine chill from hurting the fruit. Both of these regions produce great oil, but it's nothing like Sicily's, whose seacoast climate may be tough on people, but it is great for producing copious quantities of grassy, peppery, intense olives.

This is why I went during the olive harvest in late fall on one of my first Sicilian sourcing trips to the province of Trapani on the far west coast. Twenty-five years ago, we were just beginning to bring in very high-quality oils, special bottles representing various provinces and regions, their *terreno,* or terroir. In addition to its salt flats, Trapani was known for its olives and oil, thanks to the Mediterranean sea breezes and very rich soil. The olives here are larger than those from inland Sicily, where the soil is harsh and the oils are much more intense. But in Trapani the trees are loaded with olives, which provide a gentler, more elegant oil. I wanted to find my ideal Trapani *frantoia,* or press, which is today more often used to mean the larger companies that press olives into oil.

There are hundreds of frantoias in Sicily, and dozens in the province of Trapani alone. On this trip I must have visited at least fifteen of them before I found what I was looking for. The first frantoia I went to was a giant wholesaler, where the oil comes from many farmers who bring their olives to a huge modern press. The patriarch of the business was an older man, with a lit cigarette permanently wedged between his lips, and the ash just grew and grew as we talked. His office looked unchanged from the 1930s. "I'm here to buy some olive oil," I told him. But instead of quoting me a price, he asked me how much I wanted to pay.

At first I didn't understand what he meant. "It depends on what you want to buy," he explained to me. "Do you want to buy this year's oil, or maybe last year's or the year before? Or maybe you want a blend: fifty percent this year, fifty percent last year? If you spend a little more, you can get seventy-five percent this year and twenty-five percent last year. You tell me how much you want to pay," he said to me, "and that's the oil I will give you!"

Legally you put the expiration date on your olive oil only after it's bottled; by Italian law olive oil expires eighteen months after bottling, which is about when its flavor starts to disappear. In Sicily, there's an abundance of older oil in storage facilities like the one I was visiting, held in big stainless-steel tanks like those at a winery. You can buy blends of new and older oil, shuffling the flavor and the price point till you get what you need for your business. So for new oil—which is all I sell—you need to know when it was harvested. The best, most flavorful olive oil is the newest. *Vino vecchio, olio nuovo,* as my grandmother used to say: Old wine, new oil.

Many Americans have yet to taste fresh extra virgin oil, and its rawness, its bite, is unexpected. We are so used to the mild, sometimes stale taste of commercial extra virgin olive oil that it can take a while to get used to the really good stuff—the type of oil that is not a cooking medium but an ingredient to respect and appreciate. The first pressing of the year's olive oil that is bottled immediately—usually around October 15—is called *olio nuovo,* or *novello,* and there is just one batch per year. It has so much pizzica it can literally burn your throat if you swallow it the wrong way when you're tasting it. But in a few weeks the oil softens a bit, and particles settle to the bottom or are filtered out. Frantoias will then often blend the early part of the harvest, the October oil, with the later November oil to reach a desired balance of flavor and intensity.

You can actually store good quality extra virgin olive oil for up to four years, by keeping it away from heat, light, and air. It will slowly lose its intensity, flavor, and aroma, but it won't necessarily be bad. Freshly pressed olives have the best aroma, flavor, and character of the specific olive, and that's what we look for, not just in Sicily, but in Umbria, Liguria, and Tuscany. The big company's novello oil, when I tasted it, was very good. But I wasn't in Trapani for very good, I was in Trapani for very special.

Finally, I came to a farm called Fontanasalsa. I tasted the oil from their frantoia and my eyes opened wide. The fragrance was of fresh cut grass, the flavor of a tart green tomato, with a slight pepper finish at the end. "This," I said, "this is the oil I want."

It was owned by a contessa by the name of Maria Catarina Burgarella. Maria was a trained physician who inherited the land from her father. She'd lived in Milan, Saudi Arabia, and Tripoli, but without her father there was no one to run the farm, so she decided to come back to Trapani to do it herself. "I had no brothers," she said, "so I had to take over." When Italy was unified the nobles lost their power and most of their land. The Burgarellas had owned a lot of land, and the 1,400 hectares of Fontanasalsa— about 3,500 acres where her family had raised citrus, grapes, and tons of olives for centuries—is the last of it.

The heart of the property is what Italians call a *baglio*—an old set of stone buildings in a square surrounding an enclosed central courtyard, which is surrounded in turn by meandering groves, gardens, and fields, and finally by another stone wall. Centuries ago the property was used solely during the olive oil harvest, then later it housed the family and the farm director. Today it's a beautiful agriturismo—a farm that opens itself up to guests—where each room is named after an olive. You can stay in Cerasuola or Nocellara and take your meals communally with fellow guests—simple, homey food, vegetables and roast pork loin and fresh ricotta, drenched with the contessa's olive oil and served with her wine. On warm days you sit under the shade of the grape arbor in the stone courtyard, and watch the contessa's many lazy dogs splayed out in the sun.

In most regions of Italy people tend to cultivate the same types of olives, which have usually been growing in their region for centuries. Umbria, for example, makes fresh, fruity, green oil from *Frantoio, Leccino, San Felice, Pendolino, Moraiolo,* and *Dolce Agogia* olives. Ligurian oil is sweeter and more delicate, mainly from the *Opalino* and *Taggiasca* olives. And in Puglia growers press a nutty, fruity oil from olives called *Coratina, Provenzale,* and *Ogliarola.* In Trapani everyone grows the same three olives: the bitter, herbaceous and spicy *Cerasuola,* the more delicate, fragrant, and fruity *Biancolilla,* and the *Nocellara,* a round green olive very rich in flavor, with the traces of artichoke, tomato, and almond—all of which grow well in Trapani. These oils are typically blended, and at Fontanasalsa the first thing I tasted was their Trapani DOP blend, with olives grown and pressed in Trapani and a flavor representative of this region.

The contessa also bottles oils from her individual varietals, or *monocultivare.* Those were really special to me. When you taste the oils separately, you learn what makes each one different, what each brings to the blend. Even more exciting to me, you can use them like a spice, a condiment. I have many olive oils in my pantry for that reason. You reach for an intensely green and peppery bite for a rustic slab of toast, but I want a delicate, buttery oil on grilled fish or on a *caprese* salad, so the flavors of the basil, the excellent summer tomato, and the milkiness of the fresh mozzarella come through—enhanced, not overpowered. Blends provide a more consistent oil, a little sweetness, a little pepper; but with monocultivare, you get the true expression of the olive.

The contessa's best oils are expensive, even in Italy, but I wanted to sell all of them—the blend and each of the varietals. At first my friend Cesare Gallo, who was with me on this trip, didn't want me to do it. Cesare is a food importer, and he would have been the one to sell the contessa's products to other stores. Cesare and I have spent years traveling together. He's a native Calabrian who moved to Pennsylvania and worked for an Italian food distributor. He is very knowledgeable about Italian food products from all over the country, and you can tell by looking at him that he loves food: he is a big, big man. Like me, he's also totally passionate about visiting producers in Italy, and our trips to Italy were what recharged our creative batteries. But now he was thinking about all his other clients, the ones who balk when prices are high—this was twenty-five years ago, remember, most Americans weren't ready to spend a lot of money on olive oil. "Luigi," he groaned, "she wants too much money for her oil!" But I told him to buy less expensive oil for everybody else. I had to have the contessa's.

The contessa and I have worked together for years, and I know how dedicated she is to her family business, to her land. More than once she insisted I drive through her groves to see her trees: All of them. So we piled into a jeep with her manager at the wheel. "Vieni, Deepaallo," she would say in her high-pitched voice: "Come with me!" There was no real road, so we bumped over the rocks and the roots, flying every which way in the car. Almost every five feet she'd yell, *"Alto! Alto!"* She'd make us all get out of the car. *"Guarda le mie olive!"* she'd sing. "Look, look at my beautiful olives!" The contessa would hold up the ripe olives so tenderly in her hands: they were big, perfect fruit, ready to be harvested, and she was showing them off as if each bunch was one of her own children. You could see that she had so much passion for her land, and also that she was so happy to be there. This is why we need to know the people who produce the products we sell, to see their land; it's how we determine what's good enough to sell at the store.

The contessa is exactly the owner I look for—she cares about her product, she's proud of it, she wants it to be perfect. But she also has the help of a Trapanese man named Alberto Galufo, who when I first met him was a young olive oil maker with curly hair that he's managed to keep over the past three decades. He is very, very good at making olive oil. Today he works on research projects with the Italian university system, and is hired out as a consultant wherever people make olive oil, from Spain to Japan. When I first met Alberto, he was the *direttore* at Fontanasalsa, responsible for everything from the fields to the labels on the bottle. For a while he left the estate to produce his own oil, with olives grown by his cousin in nearby Trapani, and now today he's doing both jobs. The oils are so good, we buy oil from both Alberto and Maria.

OLIVE OIL FRAUD: THE OLDEST TRICK IN THE BOOK

WE'VE BEEN SELLING OLIVE OIL AT DI PALO'S SINCE MY GRANDPARENTS ran the shop. Then it was mostly Italians who bought olive oil. It came in big drums, and our customers would pay by the ounce or the gallon. During World War II olive oil became very expensive, about $20 to $30 a gallon—with inflation, that's more expensive than it is now. One day a pushcart vendor my grandmother had never seen before showed up across the street from the store peddling olive oil for just $10 a gallon. People went crazy for it, my grandmother told me, including all her regular customers. She was so angry—she wondered how that price could be possible, or how this vendor could be making any profit unless he'd stolen the oil.

It wasn't till the following day when this truck was long gone that one of her regulars told her the barrels contained only 20 percent oil! The rest was water: the oil rose to the top, and the water sunk to the bottom, but you didn't find out till you got it home.

They must have been pulling the same stunts back in Roman times. And there is still plenty of fraud, because good Italian olive oil is valuable. The two biggest problems in Italy for many years were false claims of extra virgin and oil labeled as being from Italy but actually from places with larger production like Spain, Africa, or Greece. Companies would bring in the oil to Italy, bottle it, then say it was Italian. International labeling laws now take care of the first problem, and the Italian government now makes sure even if the product was bottled in Italy, and is labeled accordingly.

———

A good olive oil director is like a good winemaker. There is the place where the fruit is grown, the soil, and weather for the year—was it too hot, was it too rainy? There is the type of fruit, whether it's blended and at what proportions. Also like wine, there are human factors: how the olives are grown and fertilized, picked and pressed. These details are what make one olive oil different from another, and from one year to the next.

In the old days, growers harvested by hand, which took months. They'd crush the olives into a paste with a huge stone wheel pulled by a donkey. The paste would rest for a few minutes while the oil droplets merged—a step today called "malaxing"—and then you'd press the paste further. The resulting liquid flowed into an old clay pot, which acted as a decanter where water and sediment settled to the bottom, and oil rose to the top, which you'd scoop out with a big wooden ladle. After so much exposure to air, light, and heat, and with olives that were by then so overripe, it must have tasted pretty bad.

Time, air, light, and heat are the "four enemies" of olive oil. Today technology, cleanliness, and attention to detail defeat these enemies, so that olive oil tastes better than it ever had before. Olive trees are pruned, mulched, and inspected for mold, insects, and other diseases, but what happens during the harvest is most important. The contessa told me she remembers when the harvest and pressing would start in September and last until March—now it's done by November. For the best oil, olives must be picked when they're just beginning to ripen, and then pressed and protected from light and air as soon as possible—two hours maximum. A whole year's work, the contessa likes to say, hangs on just a few crucial hours.

The contessa has a *tenuta,* or a single-estate operation, which helps to keep the quality of the oil high. The olives are grown, picked, pressed, bottled, and stored all in one estate. Big firms can buy olives from many different farmers stacked in bins, and it might take a while to get them pressed. But the contessa's olives don't travel or sit in a warehouse, but are pressed right away when the flavor is best. These smaller estate oils are some of my favorites.

As the fruit ripens on the tree or sits waiting to be pressed, the sweetness and the acidity rise. The higher the acidity, the poorer the quality of the oil, with less complexity; fewer antioxidants, vitamins, and minerals; and a shorter shelf life. To be legally classified as extra virgin olive oil in most of the world, the acidity of the oil must be 0.8 percent or below. However the really good-tasting, costly extra virgin olive oil is probably going to be far less than 0.8 percent—more like 0.1 or 0.2 percent. The acidity level isn't really something you can taste; instead you have to test for it in a lab. Until recently, it wasn't added to the label, though some of the top producers are so proud of their results they've started adding it.

Today methods for harvesting and pressing olives and fruit vary from hands-on to high technology and everything in between—the key is finding the right balance between technology and tradition. Really large-scale farms, for example, will plant their trees in perfect wide rows so that harvesting machines can drive right down them, shaking the olives into nets laid on the field. As farms get smaller and more artisanal like Fontanasalsa, they pluck olives by hand or use electrically powered rakes with gentle moving "fingers" that shake the olives down into nets. Some are truly fastidious, and hang the nets from the trees so the olives never touch the ground.

The olives are then washed to remove dirt and leaves, stems, rocks, and other debris, then crushed into a paste. A few leaves in your olive oil are marginally acceptable, and in sloppy frantoias may result in that bright green color, as most olive oil is more yellow than green. The paste is blended for a half hour or so, and finally the oil itself is "extracted"—or separated into waste, water, and pure oil.

In a traditional press, the paste is spread on multiple layers of filters and squeezed; the result is then decanted to separate the oil. More often today this is done by fancy centrifuge systems known in the industry as "continuous cold cycle," which is a more accurate term than "cold press." They spin, and the various weights of the water, waste, and oil send each material off into different pipes. Fontanasalsa uses reverse-osmosis machines as an extra step to extract the water from the oil even more efficiently. The words "cold press" or "pressed by mechanical means" no longer means anything distinctive on a bottle of extra virgin olive oil, as all of it must be made without heat or chemicals.

I'm not an expert on all of the above, but Alberto is. He's worked for years with the nearby University of Italy at Palermo to perfect his own technique, and after testing thousands of bottles, he designed a special press recently installed in Fontanasalsa. Most of the best frantoias use giant metal-toothed discs or multipronged hammer mills to press olives. Discs provide a little less heat and intensity, resulting in oil with higher antioxidants and lower acidity, so it lasts longer. (What protects the oil from aging also protects us. Those antioxidants are why nutritionists recommend olive oil over other fats.) Hammermills, on the other hand, yield oil that degrades more quickly but has more aroma and more flavor.

Alberto's machine incorporates both. With the flip of a switch, he can change between hammer or disc as he's pressing, thereby getting the exact ratio he wants for every olive he presses, depending on its ripeness and variety. As a result, his oils have both better shelf life and ultra-low acidity—characteristics of good extra virgin oil—but also the best flavor and aroma. Alberto's oil is so respected, he's a rock star in Japan; he sends his bottles to the country with a cartoony label featuring a tiny image of his face.

I've visited Alberto several times, and he's visited me in Little Italy and even had lunch with my mother in Brooklyn. Like the contessa, Alberto is proud of his Trapani olives. His own groves—on his cousin's land—are as wonderful as those as Fontanasalsa, and I always stop and visit them. We sell great quantities of his excellent olive oil. To reach the estate, Alberto leads me through a dust-colored village with laundry hanging out of windows and dogs lying in the middle of the streets. But then Alberto stops at an unmarked driveway; two big doors swing open onto rows of olives, as well as oranges, pistachios, and pomegranates, leading up to a mansion with a lush lawn of artichokes, fig trees, bird feeders, and flowers.

I am often asked why my olive oil is so expensive. And I always picture Alberto leaning over the press that took him years to perfect or the contessa cradling her olives like the precious gifts they are. Like everything in life, you get what you pay for. Behind these wonderful oils are world-class modern technology and the passion of a true *maestro,* and his ancient art.

BUYING OLIVE OIL

THE MOST IMPORTANT CONSIDERATION WHEN YOU BUY GOOD QUALITY OLIVE OIL IS to be sure you get what you are paying for.

Unless you are buying a brand you already know, I recommend that you avoid supermarkets and instead buy high-end olive oil from a shopkeeper or store you trust. It should be a place where they know their products and where somebody can answer your questions about where the oil came from, or how it's pressed or what it tastes like before you spend $25 to $30 on a bottle. Most important, you should taste the oil before you buy it.

Most places will put out bread for customers as part of an olive oil tasting, as we do. Bread, oil, and salt are traditional Sicilian peasant foods. When there was nothing to eat they'd have homemade bread made from Sicily's great semolina flour, topped with their own oil and their own sea salt, all provided by the natural environment. It's a fantastic way to serve really good olive oil. But it is not a good way to *taste* it, to evaluate its quality. To do that, you have to taste the oil itself.

The way I taste oil when I decide whether to buy it—and the way true olive oil professionals taste it for a competition or a rating—is to take a sip, to drink it. Most sampling glasses are about the size of shot glass, and a shot's worth is about what you taste. Grip the bottom of the cup with your palm and cover it with your hand, then swirl it vigorously to warm the oil a bit, which brings out the aroma and flavors. Next, take a sniff, and then a small sip. When professionals take this first taste, they really slurp it—pull their mouths taut to the sides and make a sharp hissing, slurping sound. It sounds ridiculous, but what they're doing is circulating air and oil around their palate and into the start of the nasal passages, since aroma makes up so much of what we think of as flavor.

At home or in a store, if you want a real tasting, the best thing to do is compare three—from different regions, producers, or olives. For most of us, it's really hard to discern any differences after tasting three to four oils. But professional judges can taste dozens in a single day, searching for both bad flavors—mustiness, mold, burnt oil, rancidity—and for positive flavor attributes like grassy, green tomato, vegetal, buttery, green tea, hay, pine nut, cinnamon, almond. (There are olive oil flavor tasting wheels that list most of the vocabulary, which you can easily find online.)

The glasses in professional blind tastings are usually blue, so you can't see the oil. Color is not really a factor you evaluate: olive oil naturally ranges from pale straw yellow to green but the color is not connected to the tastes. Years ago frantoias added lots of leaves to make the oil greener, to suggest good quality. I didn't know otherwise until I started visiting frantoias in Italy.

At Di Palo's we also have spoons and cups for those who really want to taste olive oil. Try it, the next time you have a chance to sample some, and you'll see how complex good oil can be.

Beyond tasting, it also helps to understand what the labels mean. You already know that the baseline for extra virgin—the highest quality oil—is 0.8 percent acidity. So if you see the acidity listed and it's lower, that is a very good sign.

"First cold press" or "pressed by mechanical means" doesn't really mean much these days: all extra virgin is typically from the first press of an olive, without heat or chemicals. Some large-scale frantoias may still heat the paste or add hot water during this process to increase their yield, but the oil wouldn't be extra virgin.

Today it's more important to see words like "single-estate," "organic," and especially the harvest dates—the best olive oil is bottled as soon as it is harvested. You should also look for an expiration date, to make sure the oil has not been on the shelf for a year. By law, oils expire eighteen months after bottling, though many oils are bottled well after they are harvested. Because time, light, and heat also affect oil, I'd avoid buying oil in clear glass bottles, or oil that is left in direct sunlight or in a hot place. A store that keeps oil like that doesn't care about its products.

Many oils will carry a DOP seal or other regional certification, which is also a sign of good quality. And there is also the label of olio novello—the very first pressing of oil for the season—or unfiltered, which is a sign it's a hands-on operation. I tend to think unfiltered oil—whose tiny particles are left in the bottle—is a little more intense in flavor. I like the rawness of oil just off the press—in my opinion, oil can't be fresh enough, so I always try to get a little novello after the first harvest in October. By the time I get my shipment of new harvest oil, of course, it's usually January, as it is shipped by boat. (One time I really wanted to have it for Christmas so I flew it in. I had to go to the airport a few days before the holiday and pick it up myself. The shipping added $4 more a bottle, but as soon I walked into the store I was selling cases of it.)

After extra virgin, there are lesser quality oils. By law, virgin oil is 1.5 percent acidity or less, then "olive oil" is around 2 percent acidity. "Pure" oil is refined olive oil blended with a little virgin oil, and finally there is pomace, which is chemically washed and made into a usable food product for large-scale food service. None of these oils should demand a high price—they are cooking oils. If you're worried that you didn't buy 100 percent olive oil, one sure way to know is to put it in the refrigerator. At 45 degrees F, olive oil turns thick and cloudy.

And of course there is country of origin. By law, if the oil is bottled in Italy but actually comes from Spain or Greece or another country, the label must say so. The more information on a label, the more you know the frantoia cares about their product.

A good rule of thumb is that if it seems too cheap to be true, it probably is. Good oil is expensive.

STORING OLIVE OIL

FRANTOIAS MIGHT STORE EXTRA VIRGIN OLIVE OIL FOR SEVERAL YEARS, BUT THAT IS not what I recommend you do at home. Once you open a bottle of extra virgin olive oil, you want to use it up quickly, ideally within six weeks or so. Almost immediately, oxygen enters the bottle and the quality of the oil begins to deteriorate. In two to three months, you'll notice a change in flavor. Unopened, it will usually have an expiration date of eighteen months after its bottling date, which should be about the same as the harvest date for good oils. I recommend using it within a year, as the flavor will diminish over time. For that reason, buying extra virgin olive oil in bulk is generally a bad idea unless you use a lot of it.

The same rules apply to storing olive oil as to pressing it: Keep it away from oxygen, heat, and light at all times, which decrease the quality of the oil you spent so much money on—destroying its flavor and aroma and health properties—and can even turn it rancid. Rancid olive oil tastes waxy or like stale nuts. It is still very common in large-scale oils; other common olive oil defects are mustiness and staleness, both of which are easily perceptible once you know what good olive oil tastes like. That's also why you should usually buy olive oil in a can or a bottle that's dark, or comes with foil wrapped around it to protect it from the light, and keep it in a cool place, around 50 to 52 degrees F is ideal, but the main point is don't store it near your stove.

While olive oil can withstand cool temperatures, it's best not to keep it chilled at home because taking it in and out of the cold repeatedly shocks it. If you do put it in the refrigerator or a cold room it will cloud and thicken at 45 degrees, but that's normal— just let it come back to room temperature.

If you have an unfiltered oil, you might also see particles by the end of the bottle— they are edible, but you should avoid cooking with unfiltered oil as those particles will burn more quickly than the oil.

If you make any kind of flavored olive oil—such as lemon, garlic, or basil—you should refrigerate it and use it up within a few days.

SERVING OLIVE OIL

XCELLENT QUALITY EXTRA VIRGIN OLIVE OILS SHOULD BE USED LIKE A SPICE OR A special salt to enhance the flavor of your food, or to complement it, or add a touch of bright herbaceousness or pepper. Some oils are buttery and light, others are aggressive and spicy. A good oil can also make something very, very simple—Tuscan white beans, for example, or plain grilled vegetables—savory and delicious. For these reasons I recommend having at least two different high-quality extra virgin oils on hand. A buttery, nonaggressive one for fish and vegetables and other delicate dishes, and a bright, aggressive peppery oil for finishing strongly flavored dishes like grilled steak, tomato sauce, or maybe a bean soup that needs a spark. You might want an in-between, balanced oil too. To me, extra virgin olive oil is like wine—you don't drink the same wine every day. Just make sure you don't buy so much you can't use it before it loses its flavor.

It's also helpful to think regionally; for example, if you are planning a Sicilian meal or want to make pesto Genovese with your basil. There are at least forty DOP oils, each with the unique flavor of their region. As a general rule, oils of the region are good with dishes of the region; they were created together, after all.

When it comes to cooking with olive oil, I use extra virgin for all kinds of recipes— not a high-end finishing oil but a lower cost, higher production extra virgin. Then I finish the dish with a drizzle of more expensive oil. There is a common belief that you can't really cook over high heat with extra virgin olive oil because of its low smoke point, but that's not true—you can roast with it, saute, even fry with it. Heat will affect its aroma and flavor and some of its beneficial properties, but that's why you don't use your best oils for sauteeing or poaching. Olive oil does have a lower smoke point than other oils, meaning it will burn and smoke faster—so keep a close eye on it when cooking over high heat.

A lighter-flavored oil or a blended oil—an actual blend of olive and another seed or vegetable oil—is also useful if you are making a flavored oil, a dressing, mayonnaise, anything where you don't want the final result to be overpowered by the flavor of olive oil. You could also cook with pure olive oil, which has an even lower price point, and doesn't burn as easily, but still offers some health and flavor benefits.

GRANDMA MARY'S SICILIAN CAPONATA

This classic antipasto from my mother's mother is similar to *agrodolce*, the sweet-sour vinegar glaze Sicilians apply to almost every vegetable, with the addition of a lot more olive oil. In Sicily, where there is a strong Arab influence, raisins and pine nuts or other locally grown nuts like pistachios or almonds are often added to caponata. The trick we use at the store to make sure the celery and onion retain a little crispness is to cook the eggplant in a separate pan. We usually serve with toasted bread, as a condiment on a sandwich with salami or ham, or even mixed in with tuna salad.

1 large eggplant

Extra virgin olive oil for sauteeing

1 medium-sized white onion, cut into medium dice

1/2 bunch celery, washed, trimmed, and sliced 1/2 inch thick

1/4 pound large green olives, pitted and cut into quarters

1 teaspoon salt-packed Italian capers, well-rinsed

6 tablespoons white vinegar

2 tablespoons sugar

1/2 cup marinara sauce

1. Peel the eggplant lengthwise, leaving about an inch between peelings, so that half the eggplant still has its skin, then roughly chop into cubes about 1-1/2 inch wide.

2. In two heavy-bottomed skillets, heat 1/8 of an inch of olive oil over medium heat.

3. In one pan, saute the eggplant until it is completely soft and almost broken down, about 15 minutes, stirring frequently with a spatula or wooden spoon to make sure it doesn't burn. Add a drizzle of oil or turn down the heat if necessary to keep it from sticking to the pan.

4. In the other skillet, saute the onions, celery, olives, and capers for a minute, then stir in the white vinegar. Once the vinegar begins to simmer, stir in the sugar until it is incorporated. Cook, stirring frequently, for another 3 to 5 minutes or until the onions and celery are softened but retain a bit of firmness. Remove from heat.

5. When the eggplant is fully cooked throughout, turn off the heat, add the celery and onion mixture and the marinara sauce to the skillet, and stir with a spatula or wooden spoon until everything is evenly mixed.

6. Chill for several hours and serve cold or at room temperature, drizzled with a little good quality extra virgin olive oil.

BALSAMIC VINEGAR

Nearly forty years ago, my brother, Sal, and I went to the opening of the Meadowlands racetrack. I'd never been to the track before, and I was so excited cheering on my horses that I lost my voice. The next day at the store, I could barely talk. So when I started to serve a young man, he politely asked me if it was okay if someone else took care of him. "I hope you don't mind," he said; "my son was just born with a heart condition. I'm going to the hospital to see him, and I don't want to take any risks."

"I don't have a cold," I reassured him, "but to put your mind at ease, someone else will serve you."

Years later, a boy came into the store. He was so small he looked no older than six, though I later learned that he was nearly nine. One of the younger girls in our family working with us at the time started serving him, and I overheard him asking her about the cheeses—their ages, what they tasted like. So I took over, and an hour and a half later he left with his purchases. I was amazed at how much he wanted to learn. Eventually I found out he was the little boy with the heart problems! His name was Max, and his parents, Tony and Rena, were regulars who lived around the corner—he'd been growing up eating our cheese, learning about each one.

Over the next few years, he would come in to shop and buy cheese, or some good balsamic vinegar or olive oil—and I always served him, because he was so eager to learn. We became friends. But one day, around the time Max was sixteen, his mother, Rina, came in, and I could tell that something was wrong. "Max is in the hospital," she told me, "and it doesn't look good." Later I called him at the hospital and told him that I had set aside something really special, and that when he was able, he had to come into the store to get it. Many months later he was strong enough to make it in, but he was so frail he carried an oxygen tank.

What I gave Max was a bottle of balsamic vinegar, a one-hundred-year-old, private stock *aceto balsamico* from Giuseppe Giusti in Emilia-Romagna—with a letter explaining my gift. I wrote that this balsamic vinegar had been started by a great-grandfather, nurtured by a grandfather and a father, and then bottled by a son. It had been cultivated, aged, and transferred from one barrel to another to improve its flavor over a century. This balsamic vinegar was not for using in salads or on fruit—although you could use it like that—but was a vinegar that you would use to toast your best friend, taking one sip at a time. To me, and other Italians, this vinegar represents a true friendship that should last the test of time, that will develop and ripen, that will become thicker, richer, more complex and sweeter as the years go on, like the vinegar itself—and the bond between Max and me.

Italians have been making vinegar as long as they have been making wine: Vinegar means "soured wine," from the old Latin words *vinum* (wine) and *aigre* (sour). It occurs naturally when wine is exposed to air—in fact, winemakers spend most of their time trying *not* to make vinegar. Naturally occurring bacteria in the air ferment nondistilled alcohols like cider, beer, and wine, producing acetic acid, which gives vinegar its tart, sour taste. Not all bacteria make vinegars that taste good: The best *acetaia*—vinegar makers—typically use a carefully selected "mother," or clump of bacteria that forms in existing batches of vinegar. When you add it to wine, *presto*: you get vinegar.

Acetaias make good wine vinegars all over Italy: *Barolo* wine vinegar from Piemonte, *Negroamaro* wine vinegar from Puglia, and *Zebibbo* vinegar from the tiny island of Pantelleria, to name but a few. But real balsamic vinegar, the aceto balsamico I gave Max, is no ordinary wine vinegar. It is not made from wine, but from grape must—the juice, skins, stems, and seeds of the freshly pressed fruit. It can be made only in two provinces of Emilia-Romagna south of the Po River—Modena and Reggio Emilia, which each have a consortium—and only from local grape varieties like white Trebbiano and red Lambrusco. The must from ripe fruit is simmered until reduced by at least half into a thick syrup called *mosto cotto,* or "cooked must." That thick sweet liquid is then left to oxidize, ferment, acidify, and darken in a wood barrel with a balsamic vinegar mother for a year.

That is where the real work begins: the traditional balsamic vinegar—*Aceto Balsamico Tradizionale*—is aged for a very, very long time in a series of wooden barrels, each resting on its side with a small hole in one side to let air in. The group of barrels is called a *batteria;* the wood is juniper, chestnut, acacia, mulberry, ash, oak, or cherry— each of which imparts a different flavor. It may have been out of necessity at first, but today those different woods are what enable vinegar makers to define or subtly change their own unique stamp, by leaving the vinegar in some barrels longer than others, or finishing with one type of wood or another. Oak may give you vanilla notes, cherry will be sweeter, while juniper, used less and less often, is more aggressive. The age of the barrels also matters: the wood mellows and is flavored by the vinegar itself.

Managing the batteria requires patience and skill; it's not always easy to determine the results of your choices until years in the barrel. Makers must inspect the condition of each one to make sure the environment is free from infection, fungus, and especially fruit flies. To keep flies out of the barrels, the old tradition is to keep the hole covered with a tiny lace doily—you still see ancient black barrels one after the other wearing their little lace hats.

What is even more important is the amount of oxygen in the barrels. The vinegar has to be at the right level—about 75 percent full—to maintain evaporation at a slow but steady rate. Batteria are made up of a series of increasingly smaller barrels, almost like Russian nesting dolls. Once or twice a year, balsamic vinegar makers transfer the vinegar from one barrel to the next. The largest barrel holds the newest vinegar, while the smallest holds the oldest. (Some people keep their own at home on a smaller scale, and those look almost like toys—by the time you get to the end, the barrel is the size of a piggy bank.) You start by filling up the smallest barrel with the oldest vinegar to 75 percent capacity from the second-smallest barrel with the second-oldest vinegar, and that barrel from the third smallest, and on and on up the line till you get to the newest vinegar in the biggest barrel, which is topped off with new vinegar. The smallest barrel is never emptied, either: you must leave at least 40 percent of what was there for the next year. By the time you bottle the vinegar, then, the true age of the vinegar is almost impossible to determine, as one generation mixes with the next. Some drops could be hundreds of years old, some just twelve, the minimum number of years an Aceto Balsamico Tradizionale must be aged. Most of the best are at least a quarter-century old.

The resulting liquid isn't anything like normal wine vinegar, but is very thick and concentrated, dark as night, sweet and complex—each drop holds so much flavor. Sweeter and thicker is not necessarily better with balsamic vinegar. In my opinion, what you really want in a good balsamic is what has been there since the start: the proper balance of what we call *agrodolce,* or sour and sweet. If balsamic vinegar is too sweet, then it doesn't have the true characteristics of a vinegar. Good balsamic will almost be pruney, with a long finish you can really savor. One or two tiny drops will be enough on ice cream, pears, strawberries, asparagus, cheese, a veal chop. It's costly, and it should be cared for and applied not as a condiment but in the same way as other expensive ingredients. True balsamic vinegar on a steak is as important as the flavor of the beef itself.

Balsamic vinegar was developed more than two thousand years ago in Italy's northeast corner, in the steep mountains of Friuli-Venezia Giulia. The ancient Romans knew a good thing when they tasted it, so they moved its production nearer the center of Italy. They soon realized the cities of Modena and Reggio-Emilia had ideal conditions, with hot summers and cold, humid winters. The constant extreme change of temperature was what the vinegar required to develop the best texture and flavor. In summer it would ferment and reduce—when the warm weather encouraged both evaporation and bacterial activity—and then rest in the winter. My friend Luciano, who runs Giuseppe Giusti in Modena, which has been making balsamic vinegar in almost the exact same way since 1598, always says balsamic vinegar "makes love in the summer, and sleeps in the winter."

Today there are vinegars in this style in many places: they still make it in Friuli-Venezia Giulia. They're made in Puglia and Piemonte and even in our own Pacific Northwest. But because balsamic vinegar is now a DOP product, none of them can legally be called Aceto Balsamico Tradizionale. There are other rules too: the vinegar must be made with 100 percent must, aged twelve years at minimum—though typically it's aged for at least twenty-five—and pass an inspection from a team of tasters who evaluate every batch. Those that pass the highest muster are not sold in your supermarket as "balsamic vinegar"—that is usually a lesser-quality product called *Aceto Balsamico di Modena IGP*—but are the tiny bottles with special caps that cost up to $125.

READING THE LABEL: WHAT ARE YOU REALLY BUYING?

TODAY THERE ARE TWO TYPES OF TRUE BALSAMIC VINEGAR MADE IN Emilia-Romagna: Aceto Balsamic Tradizionale DOP from the provinces of Reggio-Emilia and Modena, and Aceto Balsamico di Modena, which is IGP.

The first is the real deal, and the DOP certifies that it is made following the old traditions as I've described and that every batch approved by a panel of highly trained inspectors who grade each sample and give it points for texture, aroma, flavor, and so on. The more points it receives, the higher its status. The most prized, most expensive vinegars are not necessarily the oldest, but those that are very highly ranked. In fact because balsamic vinegars are essentially an aged blend of many different ages, in recent years new rules say producers are not allowed to declare a specific year or age on their regular products.

Tradizionale di Modena is sold as either *affinato* (aged a minimum of twelve years) or *extra-vecchio* (aged a minimum of twenty-five years), which typically is bottled with a gold cap. Tradizionale di Reggio-Emilia have three levels. The affinato gets a red label, and then there is silver and then gold, the latter of which is also labeled extra-vecchio. It is points, not age, that determine whether a bottle is given a gold label. A silver could be older than a gold, but score fewer points overall.

The younger Tradizionales are typically a little less sweet, thick, and complex. Like winemakers, balsamic producers usually make special private stock bottles, too, where they've aged their best extra-vecchios for many years, sometimes decades longer than required. There are also extra-special, extra-aged bottles makers set aside as private stock, which are above and beyond the Tradizionale DOP certification and are very expensive. (By 2015, Di Palo's will have the first release of its own Tradizionale private stock. In 2003 we started working with an acetaia in Reggio-Emilia called San Giacomo, who now watches over a special batteria just for our stores, which uses barrels in seven different types of wood.)

Tradizionale is only a very small fraction of balsamic sold around the world. A step down in quality and intensity is Aceto Balsamico di Modena IGP. This is what most people buy when they are buying "real" balsamic vinegar to put in their salad dressing, not Tradizionale. It imitates the traditional product, but is created in larger quantities by many makers—and like all things made on a wide scale, quality varies. Just like Tradizionale, it must be made in Modena from local grapes. Some is actually made like the DOP but just didn't meet standards. But IGP makers are allowed to use wine vinegar, use color, caramel, or even thickeners, and they need only to age it for two months, and typically use huge barrels made of just one type of wood, so it becomes a little less expensive, and with a little less complexity.

On the higher end of the scale, makers blend good wine vinegar with fermented grape must and age it in large wood barrels. If you see *invecchiato* on the label, that means it has been aged for at least three years, and if you see *botte antiche,* that means "old barrels," or an assurance that they don't use any flavorings or additives. It can be very good vinegar, but even at its best it is nothing like the texture and flavor of a Tradizionale. It is, however, much more affordable for daily use—$40 instead of $140.

There are different degrees of aging with all of these IGP products, and like wine, there are many different tastes and price points. Most companies have their own ranking system or labeling conventions. Giusti uses a coin system, which ranges from five coins to one coin—their prized IGP vinegar is the five coin, and is often about $50. It's aged between fifteen and twenty years with a little red wine vinegar added. Two coin is the most commercial type—it's less expensive, very vinegary, good for marinades and salad dressings. I like to say the current three coin is the vinegar of the twenty-first century: in previous generations we liked things that were a little more sour. For modern palates, Giusti started cooking the must a little longer and using barrels made of sweeter woods like cherry, so the resulting product is sweeter too. They also make a *banda rossa,* which to me is their most complex and balanced IGP product. It's my recommendation for a great all-purpose everyday balsamic vinegar from Modena.

Even farther down the scale, you will find bottles labeled *aceto balsamico di Modena* without the IGP, or even "balsamic vinegar" made in other regions or countries that have no rules about its production. Italians actually call it *condimenti*. Some condimenti may be excellent quality. But much of it is not even good quality wine vinegar; it's acetic acid plus sugar, flavor, and color.

Also, even though you'll see bottles labeled as such, there is no such thing as "white balsamic vinegar." It is really a product Italians call *agrodolce*—technically "sweet and sour," but here meaning a sweeter white wine vinegar. It's often made from sweet Trebbiano white wine vinegar, and usually in the area where real balsamic is made. If it were aged in barrels, it would turn black, too, like balsamic vinegar, which is made mainly from white Trebbiano grapes as well. It's a great vinegar, and I sell and use it frequently. There are also many kinds of thick balsamic vinegar glazes and cremas and other products that are made by respected companies and very popular in Italy—you see the glazes out on the table at Italian fast food restaurants all the time. (I sell them, but I don't use them myself.) Lastly, I also sell *saba* and *mosto cotto*, which are thick reductions of fruit vinegars and grape musts that make excellent sweeteners or flavorings for all kinds of dishes, as well as many other types of excellent Italian vinegars from all over the country.

———

Giuseppe Giusti in Emilia-Romagna is the oldest company making balsamic vinegars. Before the 1600s, only royals could have it—they hired families like the Giustis to make what they called "black gold," or *oro nero,* just for them. In 1605 the duke of the region finally authorized Giusti to sell balsamic vinegar commercially so that he could collect taxes on it. The old store, the first *aceteria,* still exists in the arcades in *centro* Modena, though the company sold the building years ago when they moved to a bigger facility. Giusti is still one of my favorite producers—they preserve the old traditions and also keep up with modern tastes. They create new products that Italians embrace—balsamic cremas, or thick glazes, *bianco* vinegars made with a blend of white wine and must from white grapes.

As the oldest producer, Giusti set the standard for modern balsamic vinegar production. They wrote the first recipe for the production of aceto balsamico in 1863, which in 1929 earned them a patent from King Victor Emmanuel III. Giusti has been in business for seventeen generations! How many companies can make that claim? Though the last person named Giusti to run it recently died, his nephew Luciano now runs the company with help from his son Claudio and the rest of his family. More important, all those generations of vinegar are still literally there, still being blended with new mosto cotto to become aceto balsamico.

The plant is really a living museum—with ancient clay vinegar storage vessels that could truly be in a museum. They still make vinegar in the black keg that was shown around European exhibitions at the beginning of the twentieth century, winning fourteen gold medals. And they have barrels that are four hundred years old containing thick, thick vinegars they still sell at auctions or bottle as a special reserve. As the vinegar seeps into the wood the barrels develop a dark patina, as if they sailed on an old pirate ship. Some are banded with metal to keep them intact, others have new barrels built around the old ones, and in a few perhaps it's the vinegar itself holding things together. Some that were beyond repair were opened to find petrified balsamic vinegar that might have been three hundred years old, which looked like coal, but is actually as valuable as diamonds.

I gave Max one of the rarest bottles of Giuseppe Giusti that I had. And a few months later, when he was feeling better, he called me up and invited me over to taste it. "I want to open up this bottle of vinegar," he said, "surrounded by you and my family."

I brought Max a sterling silver demitasse spoon made in 1865 that I'd found at an estate sale in SoHo. I collect these little spoons, so that when I give the vinegar to friends, they have a special implement for tasting it. Max's father asked everyone to make a toast before we all tasted it. And when it came to my turn, I wanted to make sure Max knew the real significance of my gift.

The ancient Romans, I told Max and his family, believed that aceto balsamico was a cure-all. They drank vinegar like wine: if vinegar preserved vegetables from rotting, drinking vinegar would help preserve their bodies too. Balsamic vinegar was even more special: *balsamico* means "a curing." The story I've heard is that balsamic was named by Lucrezia Borgia, who had had a very difficult pregnancy, and would take a little of this special, thick sweet vinegar as a cure. Thus the curing vinegar eventually became *aceto balsamico*. This black essence was so very thick and sweet, I said to Max, that the Italians thought it must be the cure of all cures. Although it could really cure only a little indigestion—it is wonderful as a *digestivo*—maybe the hopes and wishes of the Romans, I finished, could be passed on to us, to cure any of our ailments.

Max lived until he was twenty-nine, remarkable given his condition. But this young man had such passion for life that he lived more in his short three decades than most people live in ten. He was interested in all kinds of things beyond Italian food, too—Japanese tea, photography. I was asked to speak at his memorial where I told the story of the special qualities of the bottle I had given him and how important it was to me that I gave it to him. If anyone truly deserved a bottle of something so special, so layered with history and patience and care—it was surely my friend Max.

BUYING BALSAMIC VINEGAR

TRUE ACETO BALSAMICO TRADIZIONALE DOP IS A VERY SPECIAL INGREDIENT TO be used sparingly, like saffron or truffles. While there is a considerable range in price between vecchio and extra-vecchio, both are expensive, so they are best bought with the idea that they'll be used for special dinners or with other good food: a bottle should last you a good while. The very expensive DOPs, the extra-vecchios, those you should use even more sparingly for very special toasts.

An Aceto Balsamico di Modena IGP is the all-purpose, regular balsamic vinegar, the one to use for vinaigrettes or other recipes, for drizzling over vegetables after they come off the grill. Even here there is a range in quality, price, and flavor. You might want a more expensive, thicker one to use over fresh mozzarella and prosciutto, or a more acidic, less concentrated version for your vinaigrettes or for marinating vegetables. Most companies make various versions at various price points, so before you buy, it's worth asking to taste them or for advice on where this vinegar falls on the scale of sweetness, acidity, and thickness.

You shouldn't buy balsamic vinegar that isn't a DOP or IGP unless you've tasted it. If your bottle says DOP or IGP, then you know that what you're buying was made according to certain rules and with certain ingredients. With DOP bottles, you also know that the vinegar inside has been tested by a panel of professional tasters.

My first suggestion—before you spend even $30 on a bottle of IGP—is always to taste it if you can. I keep at least one bottle of each kind open for tasting, but that's expensive—not every store can offer that. If not, you have to trust the shopkeeper's expertise, which is why you should ask where it was made, what kind of barrels, how old it is. If you are spending $80 to $100 or more on DOP, you're making a real investment.

To taste vinegars of different ages to compare them, I recommend tasting the oldest one first: it's the most complex. Many stores let you taste the least expensive, younger ones first and move you up, but those are harsher and they really ruin your palate for the top of the line. Remember that all good balsamic vinegar should be sweet but also complex—a proper balance of both agro and dolce.

STORING BALSAMIC VINEGAR

NOTHING LASTS FOREVER, BUT IF THERE IS SOMETHING THAT CAN STAND THE TEST of time, it is real balsamic vinegar. Heat, light, and cold don't affect it—it may get thicker, and it won't get any more complex out of the barrel, but it won't go bad. It already is bad, after all. The main thing is to protect the bottles from fruit flies: wipe the neck clean each time you use it and it will keep for many, many years.

SERVING BALSAMIC VINEGAR

FOR ANY REALLY GOOD BALSAMIC VINEGAR—THE MIDDLE TO HIGHER-END IGPS— I recommend using just a small amount, the same way you'd add high-quality sea salt. Try it on vegetables, steak, veal, or swordfish, or atop ice cream. A few drops of balsamic vinegar is all you need to make the dish really special. The natural pairing for balsamic vinegar is on top of a nice chunk of Grana Padano or Parmigiano-Reggiano— they're made in the same place. Try it for a simple dessert after a summer meal; balsamic works with other aged cheeses as well.

I also love to put a few drops on a sandwich made with soft foccacia, fresh mozzarella, and proscuitto crudo. This is one of my favorite combinations. You really want just a few drops so it doesn't overpower the cheese and meat. No need for salt or pepper either.

The Tradizionale DOP is for special toasts or really special dinners: each person would try a drop or two all by itself. You could also use a more expensive DOP as a digestivo after a meal.

I usually use the younger or less expensive vinegars in salad dressings, not only because they are cheaper, but because I actually want their more acidic bite in my vinaigrette. I also use them when I am marinating meat, when I want a little acid to tenderize along with a little bit of sweetness. One of my favorite things is to saute and caramelize sliced onions, especially little mild Italian *cipolline,* in balsamic vinegar. I serve them over steak, mix them right into the mashed potatoes that go with them: it's kind of a riff on the classic antipasto dish *cipolline* agrodolce, or "onions in sweet-sour sauce"—which is another excellent platform for balsamic vinegar.

When it comes to dressing a simple salad with just oil and vinegar, while the French may disagree, I'd say add the vinegar first before the oil, so that it doesn't just run right off the leaves without penetrating into the salad, because oil and vinegar don't mix. Add the vinegar and oil just before you serve it, so the leaves don't wilt.

THE BEST ANCHOVIES
YOU EVER HAD

My best friend, Mike, is also my fishing buddy. He is a co-owner of Pastosa Ravioli, so when we're out on the boat for a long trip, we talk shop. One day while we were out fishing for tuna, he told me this trick for washing salt-cured anchovies in balsamic vinegar before you serve them in oil and garlic and chili flakes. If your anchovies are cured with chili flakes, you can omit adding more because the anchovies will already be spicy; or you can omit the chilies altogether if you don't like the heat. I promise you they will be the best anchovies you've ever tasted. The only catch is you have to use a very good quality anchovy, like the ones from Scalia.

1 2.8-ounce jar Scalia anchovies in olive oil,
with or without red chili flakes

1 cup lowest quality balsamic vinegar of Modena IGP

1/2 cup extra virgin olive oil

1 garlic clove, minced or thinly sliced

1 teaspoon chili flakes (optional)

1. Drain and discard the oil from the jar of anchovies and place the anchovies in a small bowl.

2. Cover the fish with the balsamic vinegar, and with your fingers gently lift them up and wash the oil off in the vinegar, and remove any extra little bones from the fish. You'll see the fillets start to change color, to get a little silvery, as the vinegar reacts. Let them sit for about five minutes, then remove them with your hands, shaking off the excess vinegar as you do, and put them in another bowl.

3. Cover the anchovies with the extra virgin olive oil and the minced or sliced garlic and the chili flakes, if using, and let sit for about ten to fifteen minutes to let the flavor of the chilies and garlic seep into the oil. Serve on toast or as part of an antipasto platter.

CIPOLLINE AGRODOLCE

(Onions in Sweet-Sour Sauce)

MAKES ABOUT 1 POUND OF ONIONS

Vegetables in agrodolce sauce is a classic antipasto, and you'll see the sauce used on everything from eggplant, zucchini, and peppers to whole cipolline, or small flat Italian onions. (*Cipolla* means "onion" in Italian, and thus *cipolline*—pronounced CHIP-oh-lee-nay—is literally "small onion.") Most people use red wine vinegar for their agrodolce and add sugar, but I prefer the complexity of balsamic vinegar with the onions. I think that this dish is better with a good quality IGP vinegar, but you could also buy the lowest quality version and simply reduce it by about half to get the thickness and sweetness you need. You'll often see a platter of these on the counter of antipasto set out at restaurants, and that's how you could serve them too. Or you could slice the onions before you glaze them and add them to your mashed potatoes, as I do.

1 pound small cipolline onions, red or white

2 tablespoons extra virgin olive oil

4 tablespoons good quality balsamic vinegar
   of Modena IGP

Sea salt to taste

1. Boil onions unpeeled until you can pierce them with a knife, about 7 to 10 minutes, then let cool.

2. Heat the olive oil over medium heat in a large saute pan. Peel the onions, add them to the pan, and saute until they just begin to brown and sizzle. Add the vinegar and simmer until the sauce glazes the onions, just a few minutes. Serve warm or at room temperature as part of an assortment of antipasto.

Everyone who comes into my store leaves with at least a little prosciutto—everybody loves it and I understand why. I like to call prosciutto "God's gift," because it is the most delicate and the most elegant of all Italian cured meats. It is one of the world's most respected foods, yet it consists of only four ingredients: pork, salt, air, and time. For most of Di Palo's long history, we didn't sell it. For many years prosciutto wasn't even imported into the United States; instead, we sold cured hams made in the Midwest by companies like Hormel. While it was technically prosciutto—a salt-cured and air-dried hind leg of a pig—it was an American-style prosciutto, a dry, salty ham covered with a thick coating of crushed black pepper. In the 1960s, my father actually did sell real prosciutto San Daniele pre-sliced in a 100-gram can for $1.25, but I never tasted it, and neither did most Italian-Americans.

I do, however, vividly remember the first time I tasted real prosciutto, on my honeymoon in 1973, my very first trip to Italy. Connie and I were eating dinner in an outdoor garden at a restaurant in Calabria, near the southern tip of the Italian mainland. A waiter over at the next table was pushing a cart with a whole leg of beautiful cured ham, the fat as pink as the meat. He was carefully, attentively slicing it with an old red Berkel hand-crank slicer, the Mercedes of slicing machines. He made a perfect plate, cutting each rosy slice so thin it was almost transparent—if you put it down on a newspaper you could read it. "Connie," I said, "we've got to get some of that!"

When the waiter finally placed a plate in front of us, I started reaching out for it with my fork, but he wagged his finger at me. He took a slice, and he held it across his face, breathing in deeply to take in its aroma, and then he ate it, right from his fingertips. And so I took his advice—the aroma was unbelievable, like no cured meat I'd ever had—and it literally melted in my mouth, it was so thin, so sweet and moist. To this day whenever I eat a slice of really good prosciutto, I think of that moment. I just flipped over the sensation; I had to know more about it, I wanted it for our store. When I got back to America, the first thing I told my father was that we had to go back and get some.

What I had eaten was *Prosciutto di Parma,* so named because it is made in the province of Parma in north central Italy, in the region of Emilia-Romagna. Parma is in the foothills of the massive Apennine mountain range that runs right down Italy's spine, its countryside is famously fertile, and home to the original Parmigiano. I now know that every Italian village has its own way of curing pork—there are well-known regional prosciuttos made with whatever local herbs grow wild, those seasoned with truffles up north, or those covered with hot red pepper in the south, especially in Calabria, which is famous for pepperoni, the red chilies that eventually gave their name to what Americans put on pizza. Yet most people believe the best prosciutto is made in just two northern Italian cities, Parma and San Daniele del Friuli, in the northeastern province of Friuli-Venezia Giulia. To understand why, you must understand how prosciutto was traditionally made.

Like many foods in Italy, there's an old fable associated with the "invention" of prosciutto. The story goes that long ago small Italian farmers, the *contadini,* always treated their animals like family—but then the day finally came when the animal had to give itself to the family as food. It was especially hard to slaughter the pigs—by the end of the year, they were like pets. So there was one man in each village who would go around and do the *macello,* the slaughtering. There was no money to give him, so the farmers used to pay with a hind leg of the pig—the meaty ham, the most valuable part.

Now if the *macellaio* did this for only ten families, he had ten hind legs. So he developed a way to preserve them: He'd cover the legs with salt, which would draw out their moisture, then the legs would be hung in the breezes to air-dry. In a little more than a year, the meat itself would be totally preserved, and also very tasty. Some people say this happened in Italy, some people say it was in Croatia, just around the curve of the Adriatic from San Daniele del Friuli. It's a nice tale, but I can assure you people have been curing pork in this part of the world a lot longer than they've been telling that story.

In the centuries before refrigeration, you could either eat your pork right away, or you could preserve it. The trick to preserving meat is to get rid of the moisture where bacteria multiply. By slowly drawing out the water before the meat rots, you preserve it. In colder regions they draw it out with heat and smoke, but in the warmer regions, like most of Italy, they would salt the meat first, to draw moisture to the surface, and then air-dry it. Animals were always slaughtered in the late fall or winter, when it was cold. Not only would this prevent the meat from spoiling immediately after it was butchered, but by the time weather warmed in spring, your leg was already on its way to being cured and ready to eat.

This practice goes back before the Romans, before the Etruscans who came before them, and likely all the way back to the ancient Phoenicians, who first collected salt from the sea. Much of the Mediterranean now makes some form of cured meat in this fashion, but some places are naturally better for it than others. The hotter the climate, the faster you have to extrude the water from the pork, using more salt or by gently pressing the meats. That's why Spanish hams—*jamon*—are flatter, drier, and a little more salty than Italian hams.

But the key factor for prosciutto greatness is the breezes. In the beginning, before there were temperature- and humidity-controlled drying rooms, prosciutto makers had to rely on natural continuous air flow to properly cure pork. Just outside the city of Parma, in a suburb called Langhirano, breezes flow through the rolling hills and low mountains. Today around 160 prosciutto factories dot those hills, catching the breezes. San Daniele, meanwhile, is way up in northeast Italy, almost exactly halfway between the Alpine border with Austria and the Adriatic, where the Alps meet the sea. San Daniele is bathed with cold breezes from the Alps, and warm humid air from the sea.

Today there are just twenty-eight companies producing prosciutto in San Daniele— all that will fit in the area—and by law you're not allowed to build anything that will block any existing factory from the breeze. Even as late as the 1960s, prosciutto factories still hung the drying hams outside for the winter. At the Negroni prosciutto factory in San Daniele, a photograph in the lobby shows the whole side of the building covered with hams attached to a wooden trellis, and down below men painting the exposed ends with lard to protect them from the elements. Today, as at Negroni, even the most modern factories still have windows in the rooms where the hams age, and on nice sunny days in spring and fall, when the weather is crisp and cool, they're opened for three to four hours at a time.

A QUICK GLOSSARY OF ITALIAN SALUMI

PROSCIUTTO IS ACTUALLY JUST ONE OF THE MYRIAD TYPES OF CURED meats made in Italy, which are collectively known as *salumi*. Every region has at least one specialty, and these are some of the most common.

BRESAOLA: This air-dried, salt-cured dried beef—Italians pronounce it brezh-OW-la—is traditionally made in Valtellina in northern Lombardia, right on the Swiss border. While I like to pair many types of salumi together as part of an antipasto platter, I prefer to serve bresaola alone because it is beef, which is leaner, more delicate than pork, and can easily be overpowered. The traditional way to serve it is on a bed of arugula with shaved Grana Padano cheese and a drizzle of delicate olive oil.

COPPA: Also known as *cappicola* in Southern Italy, the most famous coppa comes from Piacenza. It is cured pork shoulder, or *di spalla*. The southern version is usually spiced with a lot of hot chili pepper, while the northern version is milder and more delicate.

CULATELLO: Like proscuitto, culatello is made from the whole hind leg of a pig, though here it is boned, skinned, and tightly tied by hand with butcher's twine into a basketlike form. Typically produced in Parma, the most famous version is from a town in Emilia-Romagna called Zibello, which was once known for its flavorful black-skinned pigs.

GUANCIALE: Guanciale—pronounced gwan-CHA-la—is made from pig jowls cured with black or red pepper, and is similar to an unsmoked bacon, though with a spicier profile and a finer, more delicate texture. You often find it rolled and tied into a tube. It's used for certain classic dishes such as pasta carbonara, or amatriciana.

LARDO: This is spiced and cured fatback, made only from the very best fat on the pig. The most famous versions are typically made in marble basins in the Tuscan town of Colonnata, near the Carrara marble quarries. In the United States, we can only sell domestically made lardo. It can be served alone, but it is often thinly sliced on warm bread so it literally melts.

MORTADELLA: Similar to German bolognas, mortadella is emuslified ground pork blended with spices and cubed pieces of fatback, which give it a unique texture and flavor. You'll often see it made with pistachios too. It gets its name from the Italian words "from the mortar," because the meat is so finely ground.

PANCETTA: Pancetta is cured pork belly, or Italian bacon, though it's often sold unsmoked and rolled into a round with the fat on one side.

PORCHETTA: Technically porchetta is not salumi because it is roast pork, not cured, but I like to serve it cold and thinly sliced, or cubed as part of a salumi platter. There are several variations of porchetta—pronounced with a hard "k" sound—which is traditionally from Rome, Tuscany, and Umbria and is essentially a pork roast typically seasoned with fennel and rosemary. You can roast a whole pig or a pork belly wrapped around a loin, which gives you a crunchy, crackly skin, and which my brother, Sal, makes at Di Palo's. There is also a deli-style version of porchetta, which is steam-roasted so that the skin stays soft. Sal's porchetta is famous in New York City, but we owe the recipe—pork belly and loin, salted and rolled around in chopped fennel and fresh rosemary—to our good friend Santina in the Umbrian town of Spoleto, where we have a tiny studio apartment around the corner from her restaurant Osteria del Matto, or "the restaurant of the crazy." Santina runs the place with her daughter Alessia and her son Felippo, who some people joke is the *matto,* because he's an artist and has always got some new thing he's excited about. When Santina came to Manhattan to visit, instead of sightseeing she insisted on spending the entire time in our kitchen, showing us how to make a few of her special dishes.

PROSCIUTTO CRUDO: When most Americans say prosciutto, they're referring to cured meat. But to an Italian, prosciutto is just a ham—meaning the hind leg of the pig, or *maiale.* (The front leg is a shoulder, or *spalla di maiale.*) In Italy prosciutto can be *cotto* (cooked), *rosticche* (roasted), *bollito* (boiled), or *fumigato* (smoked). *Proscuitto crudo* means "raw ham," which is how Italians refer to cured meats like di Parma or San Daniele or the countless other varieties of cured raw pork leg that exist in their country.

SALAME: In Italy salame is basically air-dried pork sausage, and there are dozens of styles and textures throughout the country. *Finocchiona,* for example, is a soft Tuscan salame that is coarsely ground and made with fennel seed. *Cacciatore* is another Tuscan sausage with a thinner casing. *Cacciatore* means "hunter," and so this is hunter's sausage, originally made from wild boar or venison. In the United States, it is made out of pork with wine, spices, and garlic. *Sopressata,* meanwhile, is a coarsely ground salame mainly made in Southern Italy. Neapolitans make it with black pepper, while Calabria is known for a spicy version made with the red chilies called *peperoncini*. Pepperoni as we know it was actually invented in the United States decades ago by a German meat company that made products for the country's growing number of Southern Italians. Genoa salame, meanwhile, was invented to capture the Northern Italian market, as it's similar to Milanese-style salame, which is mild with a bit of garlic. Note that the coarsely ground sausages should be cut against the grain, so that you have the proper balance between the large chunks of meat and fat.

SPECK: A fusion food from the region known as Alto Adige, where Italy used to be Austria, speck is smoked, salt-cured, deboned ham laced with juniper and other spices, and is described on page 195.

———

It took almost a decade after my honeymoon trip to import real Italian prosciutto. I quickly learned there had been an embargo on all pork coming in from Italy since 1968, because of concerns with diseases in European livestock. There are still a lot of restrictions on importing meats. Today we can legally import a fraction of Italian cured products because every company and slaughterhouse must be approved by the USDA, and there are still some worries over diseases. Every few years we add another product as factories or their products get the green light. For prosciutto, it wasn't until the early 1980s when the embargo was finally lifted—but only for Prosciutto di Parma. We immediately ordered hams from one of the first companies that was importing it. It was a wonderful success—we sold a ton of it—but it was produced on a large scale, and it wasn't as flavorful as the proscuitto I'd tasted on that Calabrian patio. I needed to go back to Italy to find something similar.

At that time I often traveled to Italy with Cesare Gallo. Early on in my discovery of what made one prosciutto taste so much better than another, Cesare said: "It starts with the pig, Lou." In America at that time, pigs were bred to be lean, and were usually cooped up in giant pens eating cheap grain-based feed with thousands of other animals—a very stressful situation. But for great prosciutto, you need fat, happy animals—and of course what the animals eat also affects the end product. It just so happens that at several of the places where we buy our grana cheeses, the pigs are right next to the cheese factory, because Parma and San Daniele are made in the same part of the country as Parmigiano-Reggiano and Grana Padano.

The pigs were there because of the whey—the by-product of cheese-making. There's an abundance of it in factories making eighty-pound wheels of cheese. At that time, most big cheese makers I visited would be on one side of a large courtyard, and big pipes would lead across the factory, funneling the whey to the pigpens. Many cheese factories still do it, and they follow much the same method at small family farms too. It's a win-win situation: not only is there a lot of whey to dispose of in cheese-making—on a large scale, this can be expensive to do—but whey is filled with lactose, or milk sugars, and pigs that eat a lot of whey have moist and sweet meat. Big prosciutto makers and big cheese factories started working together long ago, and they still do.

On my next trip to Italy I asked my contact at the *caseificio,* the cheese factory, if I could check out the pigs. He introduced us to their caretaker, who led us into a big *stalla*—a barn—very clean, airy, and fresh smelling, with pens on either side of the aisle. The stalla was calm, shady with a little bit of sunlight and some soft opera music in the background. Each roomy pen held four or five adult pigs. All of a sudden I turned around and saw these two enormous pigs running down the aisle. Pigs for prosciutto are big—about 330 pounds. (For a ham to be DOP San Daniele, for example, it needs a minimum weight of about 12 kilos, or 26 pounds when fresh.) *"Tranquillo,"* the farmer said to me: "Be calm." All they wanted, he knew, was some attention, a greeting, just like a cat or dog. Those pigs may not have lived on a true farm in the countryside, but they lived happily, without stress. That and their diet—the sweet whey from some of Italy's best cow's milk—is what made the prosciutto so good.

In those early days, Cesare and I visited many *prosciuttificio,* meeting the producers and seeing how they made their legs. Of the 160 companies that make Parma ham, less than a third export to America, and so those were the ones we visited. It's the same with San Daniele, only a handful are certified to export their meat to the States. (That's why if you do visit the area, you should make a point to visit a *degustazione di prosciutto,* or a little shop that sells multiple kinds for you to taste. Sometimes you can also go from factory to factory by bus, like a wine tour.)

While factories vary in size and shape—the really big ones can produce 130,000 hams a year—most of them make prosciutto today in an almost identical manner. As the dressed legs come in from an approved slaughterhouse, they're inspected by hand, one by one, and stamped with a seal that includes a code for the farm, for the factory, and for the slaughterhouse, which has to be USDA-approved, if it's headed to the States. In Italy, hams are usually sold whole, skin-on, hoof and all; if they are American-bound, the hoof or trotter is removed, and the resulting ham takes on a slightly different shape, because the rope is tied through a hole punctured in the shank rather than around the hoof.

Before the hams are salted, the legs are massaged, to relax the tissues and to get rid of any remaining blood. In the old days women were hired to knead the legs with their hands, but now factories use a machine whose metal mallets imitate their thumbs—I call it "the massager." Then the hams are carefully covered with Italian sea salt and left to sit for about a month in a refrigerated room. The salt doesn't add flavor, but instead draws the water from the meat: good prosciutto shouldn't taste salty, but sweet.

At this stage whole rooms are filled with dripping trays of massaged hams with little snowcaps of fluffy sea salt. Then the legs are washed, and the area around the socket bone of the hip—where the leg was cut away—is trimmed of the salt-exposed meat. After that they are air-dried in dark, cool rooms, monitored for temperature and humidity, and checked for mold and defects for at least thirteen months. After four months the temperature goes up about twenty degrees, just as it would in nature. Traditionally pigs were slaughtered in late fall, when it was cooler. After four or five months, warmer weather would arrive with spring.

By the time they are only a hundred days old or so, the hanging hams have already started to develop into prosciutto crudo. They darken in color, become longer and leaner, and the aroma in the rooms intensifies. They look almost like a rustic guitar from the Middle Ages: the thigh is the big round at the bottom, the leg is the skinny neck up top. The clean socket bone of the hip is beginning to protrude, and eventually the meat there is hand-painted with a mixture of flour, salt, pepper, and *sugna*, or lard, to protect the exposed area, but still let it breathe. The key to this process is mimicking nature—a slow evaporation of water over time, a dark, cool room with a consistent temperature like the cellar where the small farmer would have hung his own meat, then finally those top-floor drying rooms, where the hams hang in the breeze just as they did on the building in the spring and fall. Centuries later, it still takes a whole year to make this masterpiece.

Both San Daniele and Parma hams are today DOP, or "Protected Designation of Origin," which means there are consortiums that both inspect product and set rules not just for where the pork is aged, but for where the pork comes from, what it can eat, how much sea salt is used, how long the legs are aged, and so on, and the rules are very similar. Both can be cured only with salt, and both have to rely on the two slaughter-houses that are approved by the USDA. Perhaps because of modernization and consistency in processing and in the pigs, I think Parma and San Daniele taste very similar today. It's hard to distinguish them side by side. San Daniele traditionally is a little smaller and has a more intense, earthy, nutty aroma and flavor, while Parma tends to be more buttery, and it's softer in texture. Many people like to say it is sweeter, though I find both to be pleasingly sweet. Today San Daniele seems to taste more and more like Parma ham, and producers whose hams have that older, rustic flavor are harder to find—I think Prosciuttificio DOK Dall'Ava, which has been curing hams since at least 1955, often does, for example.

With either type, if you ask what makes the difference between one San Daniele or Parma ham and another, the company will usually tell you their secret ingredient is the salt, either from the Adriatic or Trapani. But what really makes the difference is the *maestro,* the master in charge of the tiny details that affect quality: selecting the meat, maintaining the right temperature in the rooms, trimming the ham carefully, watching for spoilage, mold, or bacteria, and on and on until hams are packaged for sale. With prosciutto vigilance really matters—a one-degree change in temperature can make a huge difference in flavor if the meat cures too quickly or too slowly. Fresh legs that have been bruised or compromised should not slip through the first inspection. And over the weeks and months, every single leg must be constantly checked to make sure the salt cure is good, and that there is no mold or other defects.

Once the prosciutto is ready, it's then inspected by the consortium with a long, skinny sliver of smooth horse bone, pointed at one end like a thin dagger. It's inserted into five points of the leg, near the bone, in the muscle mass, and then the inspectors give the bone a sniff. Horse bone doesn't absorb flavors, so for each ham, you can get a true picture of what's happening inside by smell. It may need to be aged a little longer, it may have gone bad, but if the prosciutto passes, it's branded with the seal of the consortium. (If it is still good but doesn't meet the consortium's standards, it can be sold as plain prosciutto crudo. And if it smells especially sweet and fragrant, the inspectors smile—that means they've got a really good leg.) That's part of what's exciting. There is still plenty of variation based on how high up it is in the aging room, how large the pig is, whether the leg is the left or right side, what the ratio of fat to lean meat is. These details mean that each prosciutto can be slightly different from the rest, and there is always the chance that this prosciutto will be the most delicious one you've ever tasted.

I remember one of the first times I visited a prosciuttificio with Cesare, and we saw this whole long process, the hams hanging at every stage, getting smaller and shapelier and ever more aromatic, graduating from fresh pork to cured meat. We finally got up to the windowed curing room, where the legs were exposed to those all-important country breezes. These are huge, open airy rooms on the top floor of the factory, with high ceilings and rows of wooden lattices that climb up to the ceiling. There is natural light up here, and thousands of legs of prosciutto hang in the sun—one large room I've visited held 30,000 hams. It's like a grape arbor, except instead of bunches of fruit, it's hams—it's a field of prosciutto, and the room is rich with their perfume.

And all along either side were rows of small windows open to the breeze, as the weather was just right on the day we visited. The country breezes mingled with the curing meat, and it smelled sweet, a little nutty, totally intoxicating. And Cesare threw open his arms, spun around, and said to me, "Lou! I want to put my bed right here, and sleep among the prosciutto."

No matter the size and scale of the prosciuttificio, that fragrant room of almost-finished hams on their scaffolding is always magnificent, always inspiring. But I didn't find the Prosciutto di Parma I was looking for until I came across the Galloni family—and notice I said *family*. That's always important to me: families tend to care about their businesses in ways most employees don't. When I met the Gallonis in Langhirano, they were a third-generation prosciuttificio, and now they've become a fourth. They pay attention to every detail, the place is clean, pristine, fragrant.

Yet what struck me most about the Galloni factory was that when I entered that final aging room, the lights were dim and there was music, just like the opera at the pig farm. Even when nobody is around they're still playing music, they're still relaxing those pigs. And it's little touches like that that make a difference.

It was right there, when I was standing among the Galloni prosciutto with the breezes gently blowing and the music echoing from the rafters that I finally connected to the memory of my first prosciutto. It was the same aroma I first experienced in that restaurant with Connie on our very first trip to Italy some twenty years before. It came full circle to me then, and I remembered what I had learned then from the waiter. That you take your time with prosciutto, you breathe it in, you enjoy it, and you cherish it as a great gift.

BUYING PROSCIUTTO

THE FIRST THING I TELL PEOPLE WHEN THEY ASK FOR GOOD PROSCIUTTO—AND good prosciutto means sliced and sold by the pound, not prepackaged—is to taste it. While it's expensive, a good shopkeeper should accommodate that request. There are several reasons, and the first is that the flavor and quality of prosciutto, whether you are getting Parma or San Daniele, can vary dramatically, beyond whether you prefer one over the other.

For starters, prosciutto has to be aged a minimum of thirteen months for San Daniele and four hundred days for Parma, or about thirteen months. (The law used to be fourteen months, but like American pigs, Italian hogs are getting leaner, so they cure a little faster.) But you can age prosciutto much longer. The older it gets, the more concentrated, the more intense the flavor, and I prefer the drier texture then. The younger it is, the weaker the flavor, and to me thirteen months is just not enough for full flavor and aroma. I think it is at its best aged between eighteen and twenty months, with a minimum of sixteen, so I buy those that are aged a little longer, or I age them myself. Beyond twenty months you start to get bigger solidified amino acids, the *tirosina,* or little white specks. Some see that as a positive—I like to see it in Parmigiano, but not in my prosciutto, because it can be gritty.

You can age bone-in prosciutto yourself at the right temperature and humidity, and I have both a place in my warehouse and special windows in my store for exactly that purpose. Bone-in legs are the very best quality, in my opinion. But you must either slice them very thinly by hand with a knife using an old stand called a *morsa*—we only use it for special events—or you have to bone them out before you can use a mechanical slicer. I've boned-out thousands of prosciuttos in my time, in fact, back when we sold only American prosciutto and they all had bones.

Prosciutto that comes deboned, on the other hand, can't age anymore. The key to a good-tasting boned prosciutto is to sell it as soon as you can after the bone is removed, before the flavor starts to go. Today in Italy there are authorized boning facilities licensed by the government that remove the bone from a cured ham just before it is packed for shipment. Some makers use a machine to press the ham back into shape and band it together. (Most of the problems our government has with prosciutto processing is at this step, because of cross-contamination of hams from the boning knife.) Once the bone is out, most companies put the leg in a cold press, which fuses the cavity back together. I think that causes stress and dryness, so I choose the companies that put the boned legs into a *banda,* a kind of stitched band. They have a slightly different shape that most companies sell as the *adobo* or the *rotondo*—you'll see that on labels if you look.

Di Palo's sells both bone-in and deboned prosciutto. We are constantly sourcing from various producers, looking for the best based on what's available—sometimes the best has a bone, sometimes it doesn't. We select legs based on freshness and quality, and we try to buy direct from Italy because we want them as fresh from the prosciuttificio as possible, rather than sitting around uncared for in a stateside warehouse. I buy prosciutto from American distributors when supply is low, but I'll go without if they have had the legs in storage for too long. I usually take only fifty to a hundred cases of legs at a time, so they're not sitting around in my warehouse either. We're very careful not to overstock prosciutto—if it sits in that Cryovac bag too long, it gets a funny taste around the edges, which we discard.

Today, even with advances in how prosciutto is shipped and stored, defects are still common, and I have to throw out or return many legs as soon as I get them. They spoil or grow mold, or have bruises or other defects that should have been caught at some point in the process. Truthfully, 2 to 3 percent of all prosciutto is not fit to sell, and that percentage used to be much higher. It's understandably hard to keep prosciutto from spoiling, because it's such a natural product. These are all problems that I have to deal with as a buyer, all reasons that you should ask for a taste before you spend your money.

You also want to ask for a taste so you can see how it is sliced. You can ruin an excellent prosciutto if you slice it too thick, or use a machine that heats it up or is used to slice other things, or even if you don't start off slicing it at the right angle. My brother, Sal, and I both know how to start a leg so that gives you perfect slices up to the end. Italians use a straight-sided slicer, but I am accustomed to the American version, with the blade at an angle. More important than the angle is that the slicer be belt-driven or even manual. Prosciutto is raw, remember—an ordinary meat slicer spins around really fast and creates heat, and that can cook a really thin slice. We have several slicers at our store, with one machine reserved just for the delicate cured meats.

Another reason to taste prosciutto is that it is one whole leg—*una gamba*—of a pig. Each section gives you different textures, flavors, aromas, and degrees of saltiness. The meat closer to the outside is saltier and drier overall. Closer to the hip, it is drier, more intense, and also slightly saltier. The very beginning of prosciutto is so dry and salty we don't sell it. It's deeper red, and we slice it thick and take it off quickly. It's too intense: I sometimes eat it, or use in pasta, soups, or vegetable dishes—it gives a great salty, porky flavor. As you work your way into the middle of the leg, you'll get a slightly sweeter flavor and rosy color; it's so delicate you don't have to chew it. But the sweetest, softest texture and aroma is all the way up the leg around the knee and just above the trotter, what Italians call the *gambetto*—or "the shank." They consider it the best part, but it is also the toughest to slice because of the tendons, which can be stringy or chewy. We work around them, but the rest of the meat has great flavor.

A customer once complained that his prosciutto wasn't as moist as usual. It was from the beginning of a leg, and he didn't like it! That's why I always give customers a taste. I think all parts can be appreciated and enjoyed. To me the part of the leg is actually much more important than whether it is Parma or San Daniele: they are often almost the same these days. Lately I've been encouraging customers to ask for which cut they like rather than which type of ham.

People still have their favorites: Parma outsells San Daniele, probably because it's said to be sweeter. Some people use the word "musty," to describe the intensity in San Daniele, but I don't like that word. In my opinion, after tasting thousands of prosciuttos, they are very similar, and it often depends on which part of the leg you're getting, the tastes of the shop where you've bought it, even where it hung in the curing room. While I always know the name of the producer who makes my prosciuttos, my customers don't ask for brands by name—we are constantly looking for the best supply, so in reality the brand changes often. As my brother often likes to joke, even two legs of the same pig will taste a little different depending on which side the pig liked to sleep on.

Here and in Italy, you can, of course, find many other kinds of artisan, well-made prosciutto crudo beyond the famous San Daniele and Parma, and many of them, like Volpi in Missouri, La Quercia in Iowa, and Olli in Virginia, are excellent, if a little different. Before you could get Italian products, a few American producers made their own versions, and those companies still distribute around the country on a large scale. In 1973 Citterio built a plant to make a Parma-like ham in the Poconos, where the mountain breezes are similar to Parma's. And a company called Daniele makes a San Daniele–inspired product in Rhode Island, a state so small it gets breezes both from the sea and the mountains nearby. Their prosciuttos are not bad, but the hogs are very lean and I find the products are a little saltier as a result.

In Italy there are also many regional variations of prosciutto, made with other animals or with additional flavorings. There is prosciutto d'anatra, which is air-dried, cured duck breast. Valtallina near Switzerland north of Milan, makes *violino di capra*—a goat leg. There is *Carpena* in Marche, and in Umbria a fennel ham called *Norcia*. (Long ago, in Roman times, another famous place for cured meats was the town called Norcia in the green mountains of Umbria. To this day a person who cures pork products is called a *norcino,* no matter where he or she is from in Italy.) You also have *prosciutto di cinghiale* in Tuscany, made with wild boar. You can't get most of these in the United States, but over time more and more will be imported. The USDA recently approved one maker of Tuscan prosciutto, Salumeria Rosi. Tuscan prosciutto is spiced—unlike Parma or San Daniele, it is cured with a blend of Tuscan spices like pepper, garlic, rosemary, and juniper.

STORING PROSCIUTTO

YOU SHOULD TRY TO USE SLICED PROSCIUTTO WITHIN THREE DAYS, AND IF YOU don't eat it right away, store it in a resealable plastic bag in the refrigerator. Once you slice prosciutto, it immediately starts to oxidize, and to lose aroma and flavor. It will also begin to dry. We layer our sliced meats on cellophane, and then we wrap it in parchment paper. But even with all that, after a few days it'll start to dry out and the salt will come to the surface of the slices. But unless you see a little mold, which happens rarely or after a really long time, it's not going to be bad—just drier and a little less flavorful. Unlike regular cooked hams, as long as it's not moldy, don't waste it: throw it in a sauce, a soup, or in a skillet with some vegetables. As it cooks it comes back to life; and also provides flavor to whatever you're cooking.

SERVING PROSCIUTTO

IN ITALY PROSCIUTTO IS TRADITIONALLY SERVED AT ROOM TEMPERATURE—FOR MAXimum flavor and aroma—as part of the first course, before the fritters and salads and other starters. You could serve prosciutto alone as antipasto, perhaps as Northern Italians do with some *grissini,* or long thin breadsticks often made without salt; you wrap a slice of prosciutto around each one and eat it like a prosciutto lollipop. You can also wrap the prosciutto around dates, melon rounds, or the small balls of fresh mozzarella called *bocconcini.* In my opinion prosciutto is really outstanding as part of a composed platter with other types of salumi. The classic Italian salumi platter should be a mix of cured or cooked meats with different flavors and textures, and I recommend setting out at least four different styles, with at least one spicy salumi and either porchetta or mortadella cut into large cubes in the center. Each of the meats should have a different flavor, appearance, and mouthfeel, so that the plate is appealing to the eye and the palate.

My ideal salumi plate starts clockwise at the top with paper-thin slices of prosciutto. To the right I add a mild salami sliced slightly thicker. Next, some thin slices of spicy *sopressata,* which is a coarsely ground sausage. You cut it against the grain to provide yet another texture, and ensures the pieces of fat and meat are at the right balance. Next are thicker slices of steam-roasted porchetta, maybe about an eighth of an inch thick. Then in the middle of the plate, some *cubetti,* or cubed pieces of mortadella or lardo. Italians sometimes send out a few toasts or crackers or *grissini* as an accompaniment, and I like to do that too. One of my favorite pairings is *taralli,* wonderfully rich olive oil breadsticks shaped into rounds from Southern Italy.

Italians also add prosciutto to sandwiches, and we make an excellent *panini* using very soft *focaccia* from our friends at Sullivan Street Bakery in Manhattan, prosciutto, fresh mozzarella, and perhaps mortadella too, which melt together in this soft bread. While I believe high-quality prosciutto should not be cooked but eaten raw, American and Italian chefs now drape it on pizza or add it to scrambled eggs—the heat from the dish is usually all you need to melt the prosciutto. You can crisp it in a skillet and toss it with pastas or mix it into salads, especially those with fruits like figs, thinly sliced pears or apples, or add it to any dish where you would use bacon or ham. Crisped, it breaks into shards, and flavors every bite.

At Di Palo's we sell cheaper ends and trimmings of prosciutto just for cooking, which add great pork flavor and a little saltiness. You can toss an end or a slice that's a little too dry to eat straight into sauce, soup, pasta, or a vegetable dish to add meaty flavor, or chop it up and use it in the filling for ravioli, lasagne, frittatas, or tortas, the Italian version of quiche. At home we sometimes put a dried-out piece in the pot when we're steaming vegetables.

VIOLA DI PALO'S LENTIL SOUP
WITH PROSCIUTTO

SERVES 6 TO 8

This is my mother's recipe for lentil soup, which she makes all the time for supper. It is fast and easy yet full of flavor thanks to the prosciutto. It is also fairly inexpensive to make if you use prosciutto ends, sold by most specialty food stores. If you are lucky enough to have a market that will sell you the neck of the prosciutto, or what's left at the top after most of it has been sliced away, you can use one to make stock to use instead of the water described here. Just be sure to trim off the yellowed, oxidized fat on its exterior beforehand.

Extra virgin olive oil
1 cup diced carrots
1 cup diced celery
1 cup diced yellow onion
1 large tomato, diced
1/2 cup of diced prosciutto
1 pound of good quality green lentils
Kosher salt and freshly ground black pepper
Freshly grated Parmigiano-Reggiano for garnish

1. Heat about 1/4 inch of olive oil in a large soup pot over medium-low heat. Add the carrots, celery, yellow onion, tomato, and prosciutto, and saute until softened, about 6 to 10 minutes or until tender.

2. Add the lentils and 8 cups of water. Turn the heat to medium high and bring to a simmer, then reduce heat and let the soup slowly simmer until the lentils are tender, usually 35 to 45 minutes, depending on your lentils.

3. Once the lentils are done, stir in 4 tablespoons of extra virgin olive oil, letting the soup simmer just a second or two more so the oil is incorporated. Add salt and freshly ground black pepper to taste, then serve in deep bowls drizzled with more extra virgin olive oil and topped with plenty of Parmigiano-Reggiano.

PASTA

My friend Vincenzo Spinosi produces some of the best pasta in the world in Marche, on Italy's eastern coast. He is also one of the world's most colorful characters, with this huge, ear-to-ear smile. He is always so happy, so upbeat, truly loving life. His voice is booming and deep, like a television announcer's or an opera singer's. "LUIGI!" he will say. *"BUONGIORNO!"* He favors brightly colored ties in crazy patterns, plaids and prints, red and yellow pants, and silly baseball hats. When he drives around town in his old silver Jaguar listening to jazz, he gesticulates and talks and breaks into snippets of song with that impressive voice. No matter where you are, he is always the center of attention—not in a bad way, but in that he takes control of the room and wants to make sure everyone is having a good time. You can't help but pay attention to him with that voice: if Vincenzo Spinosi is around, everybody knows it.

Vincenzo's father, Nello, started their *pastaficio* in 1933 in Campofilone, a very small town in the rugged hills of the *marchegiano* province of Fermo. It's in the hills not far from the sea—the coastal plain is narrow in Marche, where small mountains descend sharply to the water. They are covered with olive trees and rhododendrons and scrubby brush. Today Vincenzo lives just two doors up from his shop. He walks to work down a little curving path—past his pet turtles—down the hill, under a date tree, and into the driveway in front of his shop, which is painted electric blue and has blooming window boxes even in wintertime.

Originally Nello made all the pasta by hand from a tiny storefront downtown, using local flour and the rich, deep yellow-yolked local eggs—you could buy it there and in just one restaurant in Rome. Italians care about pasta production, and they have several rules. One of them is that egg pastas must contain four eggs per kilo of flour, but Vincenzo makes his with ten eggs per kilo, making it especially supple and flavorful. Because of that it cooks quickly—in just a few minutes.

Today Spinosi pasta is used in good restaurants all over the world. Vincenzo is proud: he likes to put pictures of himself and his family on the boxes, and he hates it when you refer to his products as pasta. To him it's always Spinosi, never pasta. On his original boxes of Spinosini 2000—his version of spaghettini—he was shown all the way down the side wearing a big smile and his trademark crazy yellow apron. He also makes really good biscotti and cookies, too—laced with candied lemon zest or pistachios, they are excellent. But he calls them *Spiritozzi, Spiritosini,* and *Spiritosine,* of course, and on those packages he's put a drawing of himself on a big-wheeled delivery bicycle, a long, multicolored tie waving behind him in the air, and he has a giant, toothy smile that's wider than his head—just the way a Central Park street artist would draw a tourist. You think, *This must be a total caricature, a complete cartoon.* But then you meet Vincenzo, and that's exactly what he's like.

The first time I met him was in the 1990s, when he visited our shop in Little Italy. "Luigi," he said when he arrived, "we go to a restaurant and we eat!" So he grabs four boxes of Spinosini 2000. He puts them under his arm: *"ANDIAMO,"* he says: "Let's go!"

"Vincenzo," I asked him, "what's up with the boxes? Where are you taking them?"

"We're bringing them to the restaurant," he said. "I'm gonna cook."

But what restaurant owner would let this guy into the kitchen? There's only one person: my friend Salvatore, who's the owner of Benito Two around the corner on Mulberry Street. He's originally from Campania in the province of Naples, and he absolutely loves my family. He was the only one I could honestly imagine letting this crazy *marchegiano* pasta maker with this great product and greater personality into his kitchen. "Ahh, Luigi," Salvatore said when I walked around the corner to ask him. "Anything you want. Go, go!" he said, with a wave of his hands toward his kitchen.

So Vincenzo put his yellow apron over one of his wild ties, and he marched into the kitchen at Benito Two, pushing the chef aside during the middle of service, and with Salvatore's blessing, took over. He started making his signature dish, which is pasta with fresh lemon zest, fried prosciutto crudo, and Parmigiano-Reggiano. You fry the ham in a little oil, then add the cooked pasta and a ladle of its cooking water, which helps to make a rich sauce. You cook the pasta in the sauce for a minute more, then mix in the cheese, the lemon, and a little parsley. It is a simple but excellent dish, and you can have it ready in the time it takes your pasta to cook.

Luckily, Spinosi pasta cooks fast, so Vincenzo didn't stay long in the kitchen. But then, he started bringing plates of his pasta to every table in the restaurant! *Oh my God,* I thought, *this man is crazy.* This was Salvatore's business. We couldn't give them free pasta; they were there to spend money. At this point I broke into a sweat. Here's a guy I barely knew who had literally taken over my friend's restaurant, used his expensive ingredients, then fed his customers for free. But Salvatore couldn't have cared less.

After we ate, when I tried to pay the bill, Salvatore wouldn't let me. "I had a good time," he said with another wave of his hand. "No problem, no charge!" The next day, of course, I sent over several cases of Vincenzo's pasta with my compliments. Salvatore was so proud to have them, he put the boxes on display in the restaurant.

There are many restaurants in Italy that would gladly do the same thing. Contrary to what many Americans think, Italians mainly eat dried pasta from a box—*pasta secco*—rather than fresh pasta. Vincenzo still sells fresh pasta in his little retail shop in Campofilone, but what we sell—and what he is famous for—is his boxed and dried pasta. Of course, shops like the original Spinosi do make and sell fresh, local versions of *tagliatelle, vermicelli, tortellini,* and *ravioli* to take home and cook for dinner—this is called *pasta fatta in casa,* or pasta made in house. In New York City, we also have our own fresh ravioli made by cousin Michael and sell several kinds of gnocchi and other fresh pastas flown in from Italy. But the majority of the best quality Italian pastas are *secco*.

Of course the quality of dried pastas varies. While Barilla is a great commercial product—and still the most popular pasta in Italy—I prefer to sell artisan, regional products, often made from recipes passed down from generation to generation by families like Vincenzo Spinosi's. They are very different from American-made spaghetti.

Most traditional Italian dried pasta is made from semolina flour, a high-protein, durum-wheat flour—it's *semola di grano duro* in Italian. It's yellow, made by milling durum wheat berries cleaned of their outer husks. There are many kinds of wheat, and durum is high protein, tough enough for industrial pasta making, unlike softer bread flour made from other kinds of wheat. Durum flour also doesn't absorb water as fast as other flours, meaning you can get that nice *al dente* texture. The Latin root of durum is "hard." Durum flour is low in gluten, though, so it doesn't yield soft breads—one of the few places where semolina is added to bread flour is Sicily, where they grow a lot of it.

The best artisanal producers make pasta the old-fashioned way, usually by extruding the dough through forged bronze dies—round discs with cutouts in the shape of the pasta—instead of through more polished modern metals. In Abruzzo, the region just south of Marche, traditional *pasta alla chitarra* is made by cutting sheets of pasta into strands with an adjustable wire cutter. This lends pasta a rough-textured surface—if you looked at the pasta through a microscope, that is—which adds a subtle texture and helps sauce cling to its sides. The extrusion machines are now modernized; they often churn the rough mix of flour and water as they extrude the pasta onto conveyor belts. But the factories are often still very small. At Pasta di Stigliano in the region of Basilicata, for example, their excellent organic pasta is made with local wheat flour in one room about the size of a large bedroom. Even Vincenzo, who exports around the world, makes Spinosi pasta in a small space—he almost needs as much storage space for his eggs.

Vincenzo's town of Campofilone is famous for *pasta con uovo,* or egg-based pasta. At Spinosi they still carefully hand-crack the eggs bought from local farmers—the hens are fed grain and sunflower seeds rich in nutrients and omega-3 fatty acids, which give the yolks a brilliant yellow-orange color. Vincenzo doesn't use water—so you're tasting just the Marche flour and those eggs. There is also the quality of that semolina flour itself. The town of Campofilone is also known for its wheat fields, which benefit from the mild climate and salt air from the Adriatic. Food historians usually trace the origins of durum wheat to the Middle East, where it spread north to Italy via Sicily.

In the north of Italy, as in Marche, pasta dough is often made with eggs, or eggs and water, while in some regions farther south, pasta is made with only flour and water. In fact, many people claim Naples makes great pasta because of its water. The mountain town of Gragnano, between the Amalfi Coast and Naples, is known for pasta because makers would hang the strands outside, to be blown dry by the sea breezes. Pastas made in those regions from local water are so respected they're given IGP status, though few makers are letting their pasta air-dry today.

Yet they do take the time to do it just as slowly. Instead of being baked with a blast of heat over 140 degrees Fahrenheit, as they do in large pasta plants, the best pastas, like Vincenzo's, are fully dried very slowly at low temperatures for up to three days, often in darkened, temperature-controlled drying rooms that look like walk-in refrigerators. It takes more time and space, but helps the pasta retain more flavor, nutrients, and aroma from the wheat.

Like olive oil, cheese, and wine, pasta today is an essential part of life to all Italians. Ancient implements and artifacts of pasta-making date back beyond Rome to ancient Greek and Etruscan cultures. Today every province and region still makes its own fresh, dried, and filled pasta—changing the name, the sauce, and the shape to fit their local environment or their stories or customs. Even in Northern Italy—in Lombardia, where they grow rice for risotto, or in Friuli, the home of polenta—they still eat some kind of pasta. In most cases sauce and pasta grew up together: twisted, slender little *trofie* (pronounced tro-FEE-yeh) and basil pesto in Liguria, for example, or in Puglia traditionally handmade *orecchiette,* the "little ears," are served with sausage and broccoli rabe. The pesto clings to the trofie, the orecchiette cup the meat.

Throughout Southern Italy where tomatoes grow everywhere, many pasta dishes are served with some kind of tomato-based sauce. Americans grew up eating that because so many Southern Italians immigrated into the United States. But there are sauces of all kinds, and even in Southern Italy, a lot of pasta is actually eaten plain or with very simple dressings of cheese and oil or breadcrumbs and sardines out of necessity for poor peasants. The rich, wheat flavor of pasta was enough to satisfy, and in fact good pasta can be treated like cheese or olive oil: as an ingredient.

While tortellini are known everywhere, many pasta shapes are unique to their region of Italy. They may be similar to something you know—strands, tubes, filled pockets—but they have a slightly different shape, or a slightly different name based on regional dialects, or a different famous filling of seasonal or regional ingredients. In Umbria, a very long spaghetti called *strangozzi,* or *stringozzi* is popular. In Rome, *fettuccine* is *tagliatelle.* In Piemonte, tagliatelle is *tajarin,* and tiny little ravioli filled with meat and then pinched into little pockets are called *agnolotti del plin—plin* means "pinched." In Trentino–Alto Adige, half-moon-shaped ravioli are *casunziei,* often served stuffed with beets, mushrooms, or pumpkin in fall. In Tuscany thick, hand-rolled pasta strands are called *pici,* while up in Lombardia, a buckwheat tagliatelle is cut into short pieces—it is not as supple as durum wheat pasta—and called pizzoccheri.

Stuffed *cannelloni,* which means "large reeds," were supposedly invented in Sorrento by a twentieth-century chef. In western Sicily, coiled strands called *busiate* are often served with the Sicilian version of pesto, made with almonds and tomatoes. Sardinians make small dumplings that are a cross between cavatelli and gnocchi called *malloreddus,* and tiny slow-toasted rounds called *fregola,* which look like big couscous and are often served with fish stock.

Romans eat *bucatini,* which are hollowed-out spaghetti: *buco* means "hole." Venetians eat *bigoli,* a dense, whole-wheat spaghetti. In Naples the famous pasta shape is *paccheri,* a big tube without ridges and with the edges folded in. In Liguria *croxetti* are flat "coins" usually embellished with a seal or other design that is stamped into the dough with a wooden mold or press. Long ago croxetti stamped with family crests were traditionally made for a noble wedding, so I refer to it as the "pasta of the nobles." It is usually served with a simple fresh tomato and basil sauce. And then there are the different sizes of pasta shapes already more familiar to us: *fettuce, fettuccine,* and *fettucelle* are all similar, just slightly wider or narrower in width. The same is true for spaghetti or *linguine,* which means "little tongues."

This is just a small sampling of pasta names. We probably sell at least a hundred different kinds from regions all over Italy, and I am barely scratching the surface. When you visit Italy, you should be sure to seek out the special pasta of the place you're visiting: it's one of the best gifts to bring home, because you may not find it anywhere else.

BUYING PASTA

GOOD PASTA IS EXPENSIVE—IT MAY SEEM TOO EXPENSIVE COMPARED TO SUPERmarket spaghetti that costs around a dollar a pound. Think of it like buying any other important component of a meal: it is not just a blank slate for sauce. It's an ingredient whose flavor is meant to be appreciated, not covered up.

By law, Italian pastas will use semola di grano duro, though just as in the United States, there are now Italian pastas made with many other flours—buckwheat, farro, emmer wheat, gluten-free, and so on. Other than flour, good pasta—even fresh or frozen pasta—shouldn't have preservatives or additives other than flour, eggs, water, salt, or any other ingredient used for flavor. Fresh pasta should be made as recently as possible, and imported fresh pastas should have an expiration date. It shouldn't look mushy or feel gummy or sticky. With dried pasta, you should be able to see that the pasta's surface is not totally smooth—that it has a rougher texture from the bronze dies used to cut it. It should also not typically have that dark yellow-brown color of commercially made box pasta that comes when pasta is dried at high temperatures.

You may also see symbols such as DOP, IGP, or other qualifications on the bag, which show that pasta product is typical of a region in Italy, or made of organic flour. They are usually a sign of good quality. You'll also usually see the word *artigianale*— artisanally made. And you'll see *pasta alla chitarra*—that is, sheets of pasta that have been cut into strands using an adjustable wire cutter. That method of making pasta, originated in Abruzzo, makes pasta with enough texture to hold on to the sauce.

STORING PASTA

WITH OR WITHOUT EGGS, DRIED PASTA USUALLY HAS AN EXPIRATION DATE OF about a year, and you should use it well before then. (Like all grain-based products, pasta may carry microscopic weevil eggs that will develop into tiny insects if you keep them for too long.) Unopened, keep the packages away from light and heat. Keep opened pasta in an airtight container away from moisture.

SERVING PASTA

ITALIANS EAT MORE PASTA THAN AMERICANS, THOUGH THEY'LL USUALLY CONSUME less of it at a time. A typical Italian pasta serving was traditionally just a few ounces, served as a *primi*—or first course as part of a long meal, or maybe for lunch.

You should follow two guidelines when cooking pasta: First, dried pasta will absorb more water and will give you more yield than an equal amount of fresh pasta. In other words, half a pound of dried pasta when cooked yields about as much as a pound of fresh pasta—so be careful when you're substituting one for the other. The second guideline is, follow the Italian approach to saucing. Treat pasta the same way you treat good cheese or good olive oil: like an ingredient whose flavor should be savored. Pasta is not meant to be a vehicle for sauce, but a partner with it—they should complement each other. Many of the best-known Italian pasta dishes include just a handful of ingredients that cling to the pasta and dress it the way vinaigrette dresses leaves of lettuce in a salad.

To choose the right sauce, I like to think regionally or traditionally. There are at least a few pasta sauces for every region based on the ingredients found there. Most pasta shapes are associated with specific sauces and have proven over time to work well together: tagliatelle with ragu Bolognese, spaghetti with clams or carbonara, *gnocchi di patate* with butter and cheese, tiny *ditalini* pasta in *brodo* or soups, *orecchiette,* or "little ears," with sausage and broccoli rabe. So if you need inspiration, my advice is always to look to the part of Italy where the pasta shape originated, and discern what other ingredients the region is known for.

Strand pastas or pastas with ridges need a sauce that clings, while chunkier toppings tend to work well with smaller pastas with curvy shapes to cup them. Filled pastas, like ravioli or tortellini, are often best with simple butter and cheese, meat sauces, or in broth. Ridges also hold sauce, so I tend to use pasta shapes like *ziti* without ridges for baked dishes with vegetables or bechamel or marinara—the sauce evenly infuses into the pasta. Egg pastas have a unique flavor, and require even simpler sauces because you want to taste the richness of the pasta. Not only do they cook very quickly because they are less dry, but they tend to give you more yield—they expand a little more.

To prepare most pasta dishes, start with well-salted water, which helps add flavor to the pasta and the pasta water, which Italians often use to help thicken and emulsify many sauces. You should use a tall spaghetti or soup pot to cook a whole pound of pasta—your pasta should not be overcrowded as it boils, especially filled pastas—and at least a teaspoon or two of sea salt. Generally you want the water to taste salty. I use sea salt for everything; in bulk, it's not that expensive and the flavor is better. The pasta should usually be cooked until it is *al dente,* or "to the tooth," so that when you bite into a strand or piece, there is a tiny band of white in the middle. The best way to know when it is ready is to taste it. Some pastas with complicated shapes won't be totally al dente all the way through; farfalle—or "bow ties"—is unique, for example, because it has two textures. The wings will always be more cooked than the middle.

When you drain the pasta, save a little of the water to incorporate into your sauce. Many people also cook smaller pasta directly in broth or soup, or add the pasta to the pan with the sauce to let it finish cooking for the final minute. If you choose the latter route, drain the pasta just before it's truly al dente.

When you sauce your pasta, you should follow Vincenzo's lead. He mixes everything together as he prepares it. Americans tend to serve plain pasta with a big ladle of sauce on top, but in most good Italian restaurants, the sauce and pasta are well integrated or even cooked together for the final few minutes, so that the pasta absorbs the flavor of the sauce while it is still very hot. Then grate a little hard cheese on top for more flavor, or add a little chopped parsley for brightness and color, and serve it immediately.

VINCENZO'S SPINOSINI
AL PROSCIUTTO E LIMONE

(Spaghettini with Prosciutto and Lemon)

SERVES 4 AS A FIRST COURSE, 2 AS A MEAL

Because of the number of eggs Vincenzo uses in his pasta, Spinosi products are more like fresh pasta: they cook in just a few minutes, and you only need half the quantity of pasta as you'd normally use with dried. Because Spinosi pasta is made with so many eggs, it expands much more than most dried pasta, and its flavor and texture is also more like a fresh pasta. That's why if you can't find Spinosi, I'd recommend using twice the amount of fresh pasta for this recipe instead—just look for the thinnest noodle you can find. Vincenzo has made this almost every time I've seen him, which is how I learned his secret method to cutting prosciutto evenly, which can be difficult. He sprinkles on a few breadcrumbs, so the ham doesn't stick to the knife. You could also use a pair of kitchen shears.

1/2 pound of Spinosini 2000, or 1 pound of thin fresh egg pasta

1/4 cup extra virgin olive oil

3 slices prosciutto crudo, cut or torn into thin strips

Zest from 1 large lemon

1/4 cup grated Parmigiano-Reggiano

1/4 cup chopped fresh parsley

1. Bring a pot of salted water to boil then cook the pasta until al dente, usually just a few minutes for fresh pasta. Drain, reserving the pasta cooking water.

2. Meanwhile in a large skillet or saute pan, cook the prosciutto in the olive oil over medium heat for a minute or two, until it begins to color and crisp.

3. Add 1/3 cup pasta water to the pan with the prosciutto and bring to a simmer. Turn off the heat and add the pasta, tossing it with the sauce. Add the lemon zest and cheese, toss to mix well, and serve immediately topped with a little chopped fresh parsley.

DI PALO'S PASTA RICOTTA

SERVES 4 AS A FIRST COURSE, 2–3 AS A MEAL

When Vincenzo Spinosi printed a cookbook of recipes using his pasta from kitchens around the globe, I was the only non-chef included, and this was the recipe I gave to him. The dish, which my grandmother Concetta made often, is an excellent way to use up a little leftover ricotta. It's not fancy, but is more meant to be an easy meal at home, a little bit of quick comfort after a long day. The real trick is you have to work fast and eat it immediately, or the ricotta sauce will dry out. While it is excellent with Spinosi pasta, my grandmother of course made it with whatever good dried pasta she had on hand.

1 pound of dried strand pasta, or 1/2 pound Spinosini 2000
1 cup good quality fresh whole milk ricotta
Extra virgin olive oil
1/4 cup grated Pecorino Romano
1 tablespoon finely chopped chives
Freshly ground black pepper and sea salt to taste

1. Put the ricotta in a large saute pan and mash it with a fork. Add 1/4 cup of extra virgin olive oil and blend it with the ricotta until the mixture is very smooth.

2. Bring a large pot of salted water to boil. Cook the pasta until al dente, usually just a few minutes for fresh pasta. Drain, reserving the pasta cooking water.

3. Stir in 1/2 cup of the pasta cooking water to the ricotta mixture, taste for salt, and turn the heat to low.

4. Add the pasta to the pan and, working as quickly as possible, toss the pasta aggressively with ricotta mixture for about a minute, sprinkling on the grated Pecorino as you do. Add more pasta water as needed—the ricotta-oil mixture should coat the pasta but be loose and creamy. Turn off the heat, mix in the chives, then serve immediately garnished with ground black pepper and more extra virgin olive oil.

PIAVE AND OTHER MOUNTAIN CHEESES

Many years ago Cesare Gallo brought me a cheese I'd never seen before. "Lou," he said, "you've got to taste this!" It was *Piave*, a hard cow's milk cheese named after the river that flows from the Italian Alps down through the province of Belluno in the region of Veneto, where this cheese was made. The Piave River skirts one of the country's biggest national parks in the Dolomite mountains: it's wide, fast, and clean, its slopes are lush and green, and it is tremendously important in the history of Italy. In 1918 a battle took place by its banks, in which the Italians finally pushed the invading Austrians back north to their borders. So many men were killed, the stories go, that the river turned red with blood. Where this cheese was made was there at the point of retreat: to Italians, the Piave River is known as the turning point of World War I.

But I didn't need the river or its history to convince me to sell Piave. Cesare was right—this cheese was fantastic. It was unbelievably good on every level, deep and rich, with the nutty flavor of hazelnuts. It was firm in texture and had a long-lasting, satisfying finish. The quality was always consistently good, too. For several years I sold tons of it without having even met any of the makers, buying it through Cesare—who got it from another distribution company near the Dolomites. A few years later we got word that Piave was going to make its "debut" in America: Nisio Paganin, who runs a big cheese distribution company in Northern Italy called Agriform, was to be the sole person to export Piave. The cheesemakers didn't even know Cesare and I had already been selling it in the States! But then again, I didn't know much about Piave, either—I could barely explain it to people other than how good it tasted. So on one of my next trips to Italy I made a point to meet the cheesemaker. I made arrangements to drive up with Nisio, whose company was south of the city of Feltre, where the cheese was produced.

Feltre was only about eighty miles away, but it takes forever to get there because you have to drive through some serious mountains. You know those famous Alpine photos of yellow-flowered valleys surrounded by perfect Christmas trees, white-capped peaks, and pale blue skies filled with puffy clouds? That is what we saw as we drove through Belluno. The Dolomites, whose snowcaps and streams feed the Piave River, are part of the southeastern Alps. They are not one big solid range, but instead a series of peaks separated by green valleys across northeastern Italy—most of the biggest peaks are in Belluno. Millions and millions of years ago, this mountain range had been completely covered with lagoons, but now the remnants of those ancient reefs are these immense limestone peaks, their steep, sharp sides now dotted with old castles and gently sloping into valleys covered with silver spruce, tall firs, and shaggy pines. The Dolomites are famous for their knife-sharp points and twisted forms, sculpted by years of wind and ice. Even in the summer, they seem to be topped with snowcaps—but it isn't snow, it is just bare stone, glinting in sunlight. The tops of those mountains are above the tree line—nothing can grow. Their colors change with the sun, from orange and gold to purple and rose.

The company in Belluno I was visiting was called Lattebusche, a big caseificio and latteria in the valley around Feltre, an ancient Belluno town with both Roman and Etruscan ruins in the city center preserved under glass walkways. Piave became a DOP cheese in 2010, but Lattebusche is still the only dairy that makes it. The company sought to have it made DOP themselves; though it would bring competition, it would also bring more status to their local product. Lattebusche is technically a cooperative of many dairy farmers raising cows and goats in the Dolomite mountains. The farmers send their milk to the factory, which produces yogurt, ricotta, mozzarella, and aged cheeses, and distributes gallons of milk to supermarkets and to other cheesemakers. The farmers—the co-owners—are paid based on the amount and quality of the milk they provide, and the best goes to make Piave. Lattebusche tells me there are two hundred farms for Piave, and two hundred for everything else.

Their plant sits in a valley just above the Piave River. It is a huge white building, with a full-scale cheese shop and cafe called Bar Bianco—the "white bar" where locals stop for a *stracciatella* gelato or a liter of milk or to buy Lattebusche cheese. My plan, when we arrived at the factory side, was to commend the *casaro,* the head cheesemaker, to tell this person how impressed I was with his cheese. We were met by Chiara Brandalise, who then worked at Lattebusche and has since become a good friend and the director of Piave's consortium; over the years she has shown me pastureland all over Belluno. By this point I had already been to many cheese factories all over Italy, from the smallest little caseificios to the big houses making wheels of Parmigiano-Reggiano, and I wanted to tell the maestro di Piave what an excellent job Lattebusche was doing. So we were led into the cheese-making side, and we stopped in front of a massive office, one big bank of computers and graphs and displays. On one side of the room was a window, where you could look down on the huge factory floor to see the cheeses being branded, salted, and put into forms. But there were no people, no maestro di Piave, no cheesemakers at all—just computerized assembly lines, and one guy on hand to stand there and push the button.

When I saw this, my mouth hung open in shock. It was actually the single biggest disappointment I've ever had in this business. But at the same time, it also became the biggest enlightenment. "It's the mountain," Chiara told me when she saw how disappointed I was. "Look around us," she said. "Do you see the pristine quality of the air, and all the different kinds of flowers that are growing, and the green, green grass, how vibrant it is? That is what makes this cheese so good."

For years I'd said the most important thing for making excellent cheese was the cheese maker, responsible for every step in the process. With modern technology Lattebusche had duplicated what a master casaro does—"electric hands," I call it. Yet what made Piave wasn't only the maker, but the milk from those mountain cows. It was at that point that I realized what the mountains—their purity, their semi-isolation, the diversity of their landscape—really meant to Italian cheese-making. I also realized what some of my favorite cheeses—Piave, *Stelvio, Asiago, crucolo,* Bitto, *Taleggio, Montasio, Robiola, Gorgonzola, La Tur,* even my favorite granas—had in common. Some were made from a mix of goat's milk or sheep's milk, some were soft-ripened, some well-aged, some in the west, some in the east—but what they shared was that they were all made amid Italy's highest peaks.

The very best milk in the world comes from places like Belluno—the high Alpine pastures in the mountains where Italy meets Austria, Switzerland, and France. Italians call those pastures *alpeggio.* On certain cheeses in this region, labels say *d'Alpeggio,* to let you know they were made in the mountains. During the wintertime, you can't get to the alpeggios, as there's far too much snow, so the cows stay down in the valleys. But in the short cool summers, by about mid-June, it is warm enough for the cows to make their way up the steep paths to graze, where they feast on a carpet of grasses, herbs, and flowers loaded with dozens of unique aromas and flavors. Even in early October there is deep, lush grass layered with purple blooms of asters, spikey dandelion leaves, prickly wild artichoke, plus yarrow, burdock, clove, and alfalfa.

Some Italian cowboys—the *vaccari*—still march their cows each summer up to those rich, fertile grasses of the alpeggios across the mountains of Northern Italy, though today they have the help of pickups and all-wheel drive. The hotter the weather, the farther up they go, up to where the chairlift lets off skiers in the winter. In the really old days it was too hard for the vaccari to go home, so instead they'd stay in one of many little rustic huts, or *baite,* made for herdsmen in the plateaus between peaks. These areas are called a *malga,* and the farmers would stop and milk the cows and make the cheese right there in the malga. Many of Northern Italy's hard, aged mountain cheeses were traditionally made only in the warm months of summer, because that good alpeggio grass was considered a key part of their flavor. Today many cheeses are made year round, and now that roads and refrigeration enable milk to be trucked down the mountain to places like Lattebusche, true malga cheese is rare. But you'll still find cheeses made the old way. There are cheesemakers way up in the mountains, staying in huts or even pitching tents, and making cheese right where they are. I know one guy whose cows are up so high beyond the reach of most trucks, he sends his milk back down the mountain on the ski lift cable cars.

There is another important virtue of mountain milk. An average farm in the mountains has forty, fifty cows—many herdsmen keep only twenty cows, maybe as few as a dozen. Where they make grana cheeses in Italy's great plains, farms can have hundreds of cows, often kept inside. Mountains are not easy places to maneuver or to build big barns. While there is some modernization, particularly for cheeses produced in large quantity, many farmers free-graze their cows on wild forage, and these are usually old breeds used to walking these mountains—the little dwarf cows called *razza rendena* or the *bruna alpina* and *grigia alpina*—brown and gray cows—you see all over the Alps. They are known not for quantity but for the flavor and richness of their milk. In reality they don't live on farms—the herdsmen simply lead their cows up the mountainside to open grassland.

Many of the farmers are like Nisio's father or Marcello Martini Barzolai, a farmer I met whose family has been keeping cattle high in the Dolomites for 450 years. He has one hundred cows, but only fifty produce milk at any time, and his farm is one of the biggest in the cooperative—all of his milk is of such good quality, it goes into making Piave. Even so, his milking parlor is at the top of a winding mountain road in a lovely small town called Casamazzagno. His beautiful alpina cows graze freely in the hilly fields, their cowbells clanging as they come to greet him; the only thing keeping them from the town is a tiny rail of electrified wire along the road.

Piave wasn't traditionally made in a malga, but is instead one of a family of Italian mountain cheeses called latteria, first made in Friuli-Venezia Giulia at the end of the seventeenth century. Then in the nineteenth century, the mountains were poverty-stricken, and people were leaving to find a better life in the cities. As the population dwindled, dairy farmers pooled their assets to build an infrastructure for milking and cheese-making. A *latteria turnaria* is what they called their commonly owned dairies, where farming families collectively owned the factory and the equipment, but each took turns milking their cows and making milk butter and cheese under their own names. In the local dialects, they also called the place a *casello*, or *kasèl*, similar to what Lattebusche is now. The latteria-style cheeses—Montasio is one of the most common—are usually semi-hard to hard flat wheels with a yellow interior like Piave, and they come in various ages, mild, or *fresco*, to very *stagianato*, or aged.

ITALIAN AFFINEURS

WHEN A CHEESE IS ALLOWED TO REACH ITS FULL POTENTIAL BASED on traditional standards, that's *stagianato*. When a cheese is altered to become something else entirely, that's *affinage*. Unlike France, Italy has not had a long history of affinatores, those who take the cheese from a cheesemaker and apply their own special twist. One of the first to do so in Italy was a man named Antonio Carpenedo, originally a cheesemaker from a Venetian town not too far south of the Piave River called Povegliano.

Until I met Antonio, I had never been a fan of affinage in Italy. To me it seemed like hiding sins, as they say—taking a bad cheese and trying to make it salable. But Antonio won me over. One July when he was with his wife in the mountains selecting cheeses, he found himself stuck behind a slow-moving tractor overflowing with freshly cut grasses, wild herbs, little flowers, pine needles, and Alpine firs. The wind was blowing, and the aromas were just overwhelming—truly the aroma of the summer wind, said Antonio, the *vento d'estate*. He bought a few sacks of hay and packed some of the cheeses he'd selected in it to age. In November he cut open a cheese and found a wonderful herbal, sharp, and spicy flavor, with a hint of menthol from the pine—best yet, the fragrance of that summer breeze was still intact. Today that cheese is sold as *Vento d'Estate*.

Carpenedo is also known for his riffs on a style of cheese called *ubriaco,* which means drowning in wine—Italians use the term when they drink too much. Years ago when Austrian soldiers stole from Northern Italian peasants, the stories go, the peasants hid their cheeses deep in the composting must from wine-making. If Carpenedo is inspired mainly by nature or a riff on an old tradition—one of his early inventions that became widely copied was a truffle cheese aged in ash—my friend Hancie Baumgardener in Alto Adige is even more creative. We can't yet import his cheeses, so I just visit his shop, called Degüst, whenever I'm in the region.

Hancie's cheeses are unique. He might take a soft cheese out of its form, scoop out the center, blend it and pack it back in, or wrap them in seaweed, tea leaves, or gold leaf.

His cheese cave is a huge World War II bunker, used by Mussolini's troops to scope out the mountainside. The rooms, once used to store munitions or hide soldiers during battle, twist and wind up and around various floors kept at different humidities and temperatures, depending on how Hancie wants to alter the cheese. Hancie isn't an old cheesemaker but a young, cutting-edge chef—he left a Michelin-starred restaurant in Alto Adige to do this full-time; that's how strong his passion is.

———

There are many famous mountain cheeses beside Piave, especially the classic Alpine cheeses—those firm, pressed rounds often speckled with little almond-shaped eyes like Gruyère and Emmenthaler made just across the border. The holes in these cheeses—which range from pinholes to the size of cherries—result from the addition of fermented whey from the previous day. The most famous of them is Asiago, which has been made for centuries around the city of the same name. There are two completely different styles of Asiago, the younger, soft and creamy fresco, or fresh version, and the aged *d'Allevo*, which is sharper and drier. Both are DOP, meaning they can be made only in the plateau region around Asiago from the milk of local cows.

Once, Cesare and I stopped at a small caseificio in Trentino just south of Alto Adige. The milk came right from the farmer; we saw him still in his muddy boots bringing the cans into the store. The caseificio made a cheese that was semi-hard, creamy, rich, and full of almond-shaped holes in the Alpine fashion, a little like younger Asiago. The cheesemaker called it *nostrana*, or "our cheese." I laughed. "I know it's your cheese," I said. But what he meant was it was literally his cheese, made his way. It was similar to Asiago, but he was not in the right region to name it that, and in fact it was a little different in flavor. It was delicious and I loved it, but his shop didn't make enough for me to sell at the store.

One day months later, back in Di Palo's, Cesare brought in something very similar to that nostrana, and from the same province. It was crucolo, made by a family with a three-story, family-style restaurant wedged into the side of the mountain above the tiny town of Spera, where they also own a hotel. These Alpine places are called *rifugi*, because they are literally a refuge for hikers, and this particular one is Rifugio Crucolo. Crucolo was originally aged in the cantina, the basement of this place, along with the family's wine and cured meats. They make huge rounds of it, aged for a few months—the small ones are twenty-eight pounds and the really big ones are up to fifteen hundred pounds. We get them somewhere in between, about three or four hundred pounds, and they are a beast to cut; we have to use a wire. This family has a good sense of humor—they also make giant sopressa, or salamis that hang in loops around the cantina ceiling, and smoke whole pigs into the spiced Italo-Austrian cured meat called *speck*, and stand them up in the hay as if they were still alive, with little signs that introduce the pig as "Tino from Trentino." They now have a bigger facility, but they still age and store some of the cheese in the cantina. If you're lucky, you can go down, and they'll pour you a glass of wine and slice you off a sliver of their meats. On the walls you can see the names of hundreds of visitors over the past century, who've scribbled their names next to racks of wine and hanging salumi.

Upstairs at the rifugio, visitors are treated like hikers even if they're not. You don't have to order—course after course arrives. Thinly sliced cured meats from the basement, skewers of fire-roasted beef and pork, rabbit ragu, fat *cotechino* sausages and cabbage, gnocchi with spinach, little Trentino *knodel*, or bread dumplings, in tomato broth, big boards of polenta served with *fuso di crucolo,* melted pots of their house cheese blended with a little milk. You eat and you eat, and your meal always ends with a few kinds of powdered sugar–topped pie and a housemade coffee liqueur called *Parampa'mpoli*. At dinner, there's music and dancing. One night Cesare and I drank so much Parampa'mpoli, he started dancing around with a coatrack, spinning it around as if it were his date.

At Di Palo's we carry many other subtly different Alpine cheeses. The nutty-flavored, ruddy-colored Stelvio—or Stilfser as it was originally called in German when the Austrians still owned that part of Italy—is made in and named after the highest pass in the eastern Alps, just below Switzerland on the western edge of Alto Adige. Bitto is another fascinating old Alpine cheese made the same way for at least two thousand years in northern Lombardia in an area known as Valtallina. Bitto, the first cousin to Swiss Sbrinz on the other side of the Alps, is only made in the summer from milk of free-grazing cows. Cows and goats are still milked by hand, and the cheese is made right in the malga in old copper kettles and handmade wooden molds. No two forms of Bitto are ever the same.

Farther west along the Italian Alps, toward France and into the regions of Valle d'Aosta and Piemonte, the best mountain cheeses are totally different—soft and fresh, more like the cheeses we associate with the French. There is the true *Fontina,* one of the great mountain cheeses of Italy, originally made in Valle d'Aosta, where both Italian and French is spoken. Fontina is pressed and has holes, but it is softer and extremely aromatic, with an orange, natural rind formed from washing it with a saltwater brine. It is copied all over the world, but it is the best when it's made in the alpeggios of Valle d'Aosta. This Fontina—it will be labeled Fontina d'Aosta DOP—is pungent and earthy, much more flavorful than Fontina-type cheese made here in the United States or in other parts of Europe.

Across Lombardia, Piemonte, and the Veneto, mountain milk is also used to make a family of cheeses called *crescenza,* or *stracchino.* Stracco is Lombardian dialect for the word "tired," because the milk for these cheeses came from tired cows: it's made in the fall, once the cows are returning from the alpeggio. The milk is high in fat but also very "active," as cheesemakers say, full of enzymes and bacteria because the cows are stressed. Its most basic form is stracchino, which is a fresh cheese, soft, tart, typically square, and eaten after the cheese is ripened for just a few days. It is traditionally made from raw milk, which we can't import into the States—U.S. rules require that cheeses must be aged for at least sixty days or be made with pasteurized milk—but raw milk stracchino is not very common anymore in Italy either.

They make two more famous types of stracchino in western Lombardia: Taleggio is the famously pungent pale orange square of cheese with a natural rind that turns orange like Fontina, because it is washed with a brine as the cheese ages. Taleggio, now produced in great quantities, was originally made in Val Taleggio in the Lombardian province of Bergamo and Valssasina near Lake Como. The legend about its square shape is that in the old days makers would sneak the cheeses through a rugged mountain pass to avoid paying the taxes to bring Taleggio to market. If the cheeses were square, they could fit more of them in the saddlebags of their donkeys.

According to the old tales, Gorgonzola started out as a stracchino too. One day a cheesemaker made it with a blend of drier curds from the evening and fresher curds from the morning. The two curds didn't come together uniformly—there were cracks and holes. Left to age, this cheese would be infiltrated with microflora—seven different molds would start to form, and they'd cause the blue veining and sharp, *piccante* flavors striped among the creamy stracchino. Maybe a thousand years ago some farmer tasted it, liked it, and he brought it down to a market in a town called Gorgonzola, near Milan, and sold it as *azura stracchino*—blue stracchino. It was the birth of Gorgonzola, which today is made with the addition of pencillin spores to the milk instead of natural molds. It wasn't called Gorgonzola until it received its DOP status in the twentieth century.

One of my favorite makers of Taleggio is a man named Locatelli, like the famous Pecorino Romano makers, though he's not related. Many families in Val Taleggio have the name Locatelli, and this one makes their Taleggio by hand. The rinds are washed with a little salt and water each day, with the grigia and bruna alpina cows in the barn just yards away. One of Locatelli's cheeses is a little round called *strachitunt*: *rotunt* for "round." This is the original blue-veined cheese—predecessor to today's mountain Gorgonzola—made with a dried calf's stomach, following the old tradition.

In the hilly Alta Langhe area of Piemonte—high above the region's famous vineyards, almost in France—a company called Caseificio dell'Alta Langa also makes some of my favorite soft-ripened cheeses using a mix of sheep's, cow's, and especially goat's milk—sourcing much of his milk from animals that live high up in those wonderful Piemontese hills. They make special versions of *Robiola,* a soft-ripened cheese made with various blends of milk, and also *toma* cheeses. Toma are based on an old French style called *tomme,* a small round of cheese. The story is that two brothers used to make this incredible cheese together, and their caseificio had grown so large and respected they eventually sold it off. But then one brother died, and the other wanted to set his nephews up in business, so he taught them to make cheese and started Caseificio dell'Alta Langa, which quickly grew its own reputation. Their labels look like Renaissance paintings and have French names: Brunet is made from milk of goats with long brownish wool; La Tur from a mix of cow, sheep, and goat milk—both are mold-ripened and creamy, with thin rinds and a layer of custard between the soft paste inside.

These cheeses are now famous—La Tur is considered one of the world's most decadent, as soft as a cloud—and Di Palo's was one of the first shops to sell them in the United States. It was really at the urging of my friend Margaret Cicogna that Caseificio dell'Alta Langa was even imported into the States. Margaret works for a food importer and distributor, and at first the uncle, the *zio,* didn't want to export any cheese outside of Europe. So she drove me all the way up to their remote factory to convince this zio how seriously I took cheese. Surrounded by all these soft, runny, creamy cheeses, it was there I realized that there was such a strong French influence in this part of northwestern Italy.

What I also noticed was the pristine quality of the pasture, the place. This part of Piemonte, the hills to the south and east of the Tanaro River in the province of Cuneo, is famous for cheese, wine, and truffles—there you'll find the famous truffle town of Alba, where DOP mountain cheeses like *Castelmagno, Bra Tenero, Bra Duro,* and *Toma Piemontese* are made. It is divided into ranges: the Basso Langa and the Alta Langa, *basso* is "low," or bass, and *alta* is "high." Caseificio dell'Alta Langa occupies a beautiful, pristine spot hilltop, surrounded as far as you could see by hazelnut groves, the other famous crop of Piemonte.

Carlo Piccoli at Latteria Perezin near Treviso—who makes fantastic Montasio—also makes fresh and aged mountain goat cheeses and gets his milk from organic goat farms in the Dolomites where Piave milk comes from. Many years ago, Carlo took me up this long dirt road to a small farm where there was just one farmer, her two children and an entire herd of goats running around freely. There were absolutely no obstructions—we were completely surrounded by beautiful mountain ranges, with those jagged white peaks and green valleys. *You can't get more organic than this,* I thought. Those mountains filtered everything out—they protected the air and the rivers and the grass. I envied these goats for living in the most beautiful place I'd ever seen—they had the best mountain view of anybody in Italy!

Those pasturelands—and those of all mountain cheeses—are literally in the clouds. Down the mountainside, you spy little villages dotted with church spires and Alpine cottages, green valleys striped with marks of tractors readying hay, vineyards far below, and the occasional castle ruin. Look up, and you almost always see snow. There is such a sense of serenity and beauty in this part of Italy—you hear the sound of the water rushing down the road from the melting snowcaps on higher peaks, the cowbells always clanging in the distance. Once I visited with a vaccaro in the mountains of Trentino who had a herd of tiny razza rendena, also known as *la vaca nana,* or the dwarf cow. Their milk went to make *Trentingrana.* He gave me one of those bells from his lead cow as a gift—a big, beaten-up metal cowbell with a leather strap that could have been a hundred years old. Today it's in the window of our store in Little Italy. Like the realization that it is the mountains that make the cheese, it was one of the best gifts I'd ever gotten.

GIULIO'S MOUNTAIN
CASTLE

WHEN I WENT TO CASEIFICIO DELL'ALTA LANGA IN PIEMONTE FOR the first time it was during Slow Cheese, an artisanal cheese conference that Slow Food, the nonprofit group that aims to preserve our foodways, hosts every two years near its Piemontese headquarters. I hadn't booked a place to stay, and every hotel in the region was full because of the event. Luckily a friend knew of a man who rented rooms near where the rest of our group was staying in the beautiful little wine town of Monforte d'Alba—in the hills, surrounded by vineyards. This man's family ran a pharmacy. We were going to get there late, so I was supposed to ring the doorbell of the apartment above the pharmacy, but I didn't have an address. Luckily there is only one pharmacy in Monforte d'Alba, located in the town's main square. I rang the bell, an old woman opens up her window to peek below, and within two minutes this big, burly man—her son Giulio—comes barreling down the steep streets of Monforte d'Alba in his jeep.

We follow him up the mountainside to his little hotel called Le Case della Saracca, and when Giulio opened the old wooden door, it was extraordinary, a vision of the past and the future. The hotel was originally a thousand-year-old home built directly into the stone retaining walls of the city. The rooms and passageways were like caves and the walls were stone and rocks, but they were decorated with contemporary art, recessed lighting, and modern metal. It was an experience just to walk into the place.

My son Sam was with me, and he'd already run up the stairs to the second floor to look around. Suddenly he stuck his head over the balcony and said, "Dad! You're even here in Monforte d'Alba." This town was full of major wine producers who grew the fine *nebbiolo* grape of the region. In this hotel's common room, there were copies of magazines like *Wine Spectator*, including their New York City edition, which featured our store. Not only did we get a room, when we went downtown with Giulio later for a glass of wine from the local enoteca (across the street from his pharmacy, of course), he pointed us out in the magazine to everyone he met.

Over the years I've come to realize that Giulio is a creative genius. The first time I visited he just had those rooms, but by my next trip Le Case della Saracca also had a wine bar and an enoteca—a little place where you could buy the region's wines that he's been storing for decades, or drink them standing at the counter over a few plates of complimentary antipasti. Later he bought the house next door and added a chef and a restaurant, where he serves typical plates like the local pasta called *tajarin* with truffle or chestnuts or porcini mushrooms. Now he's added a cantina where he's aging and serving salumi and Piemontese cheeses. Many who come from out of town are in the food and wine business—distributors or chefs who've come to buy wine—so it's always an international, interesting crowd around his little bar. Like the rooms above, the enoteca and restaurant are built into the stone, but have modern touches—a metal and glass spiral staircase winds up the rock, with a single table wedged into the earth on each level. At the very top, you dine with a view four stories down! I appreciate his approach— the embracing of old and new, blending tradition and modern technique—very much. In fact in our wine store, you'll see where we've integrated stone, old wood, and dried grape vines into a very modern store. If you visit Piemonte, you should make a point to seek out Le Case della Saracca, and even if you can't spend the night, stop in to see the enoteca or the restaurant. Tell Giulio that Luigi from Di Palo's sent you, and he'll be sure to treat you well.

———

BUYING MOUNTAIN CHEESES

MANY TRADITIONAL ITALIAN MOUNTAIN CHEESES, SUCH AS TALEGGIO, FONTINA, and Asiago, are made on a large scale, and sometimes other regions or countries call their products by these names. To make sure you are getting the real thing, you'll ask to see the label. If it's marked as DOP or says d'Alpeggio or something like *prodotto nella montagna* ("produced in the mountains") those are signs that it is made in the Italian mountains.

There are actually two kinds of Gorgonzola, which can be DOP, and you should be sure you're buying the right one. There is the mild *dolce,* which means sweet; this is a soft, scoopable version we call *molto cremoso,* which means very creamy. And then there is *piccante,* which is an aged mountain style.

The flat, latteria-style cheeses like Montasio and Piave come in various ages, mild and fresco to very stagianato, or aged. As they age, they become sharper, drier, firmer, nuttier, and more like a grating cheese like Parmigiano-Reggiano—and those are typically what we get in the United States. Montasio is a wonderfully sweet and nutty DOP cheese that can now be made in both Friuli-Venezia Giulia and in the Veneto—old documents trace this cheese back four or five hundred years to a skilled monk who may have created them. There are many others, like the slightly bitter rounds called Fagagna and the sweeter Spilimbergo, both made in the Friulian towns with those names. They are similar, but each has a subtly unique flavor based on the type of cows and the microclimate in their mountain region.

Latteria cheeses are typically classified and sold according to their age, so if you don't know what style you want, ask to taste them, if possible. In Italy, both Piave and Montasio are sold as fresco, or aged twenty to sixty days. Here in the United States we get only *mezzano,* or aged up to 181 days (for Piave, it will have a blue label), and vecchio, or aged more than six months. After ten months, Montasio is called stagionato. Piave, on the other hand, is either aged for twelve months and given a red label—and the name *Vecchio Selezione Oro*—or aged for eighteen months and called *Vecchio Riserva.* That gets a black label, and isn't available in the United States.

Asiago also comes in several varieties, so you need to know what the labels mean before you buy one. The fresh, or *fresco,* Asiago is also called *pressato,* and is aged just twenty to thirty days—it's made from pasteurized milk so it can be imported. (U.S. rules currently say cheese must either be made from pasteurized milk or raw milk aged for at least sixty days, so that certain strains of bacteria are no longer active.) The curds are dry-salted in a big pan, then scooped up, placed in a mold, and gently pressed: hence the name *pressato.* It is soft and spongy, with a sweet and creamy taste. Then there is Asiago d'Allevo, which is made of a mix of partially skimmed and whole raw milk and is aged at least six months, and often up to two years. It's denser and drier, with a sharper flavor that intensifies as it ages. Both are dotted with little holes, or eyes, from the addition of fermented whey.

As well known as Asiago is in Italy, it became popular in the United States because of a cheesemaker in Connecticut who had emigrated from that area of Italy. He started making cheese here based on d'Allevo and called it Asiago—but it's really different from Italian Asiago, the same way American Romano and Parmesan just aren't the same as Pecorino Romano or Parmigiano-Reggiano. For many years it didn't matter, because Asiago from Italy was never available. Now I can import it—but I still sell domestic Asiago, too, because so many Americans grew up with it.

The general rule of thumb is to buy cheeses that look and smell good and to not buy more than you think you will consume within a week, especially softer cheeses which continue to ripen and change over time. For softer cheeses, generally the oozier they are in the center, the more ripe they are, so they won't last as long. And with any cheese, even French-style mold-ripened cheeses, you don't want to see mold that is black or green.

STORING MOUNTAIN CHEESES

CHEESES BEGIN TO OXIDIZE AS SOON AS YOU CUT INTO THEM, SO BUY ONLY WHAT you intend to eat or serve within a week or so. Let it sit out for a few minutes before you eat it, and then wrap it in parchment paper and foil when you refrigerate it, and change the wrapping every time you take it out of the refrigerator to avoid condensation forming on the cheese. With *toma*-style cheeses or mold-ripened cheeses, these are often sold in a small plastic container, which protects the cheese in the refrigerator, though you'll probably want to change the wrapping. Softer cheeses will also continue to ripen over time—to soften and liquefy. They won't go bad, per se, but they will change dramatically in flavor and texture and become more pungent and intense, even in the refrigerator.

SERVING MOUNTAIN CHEESES

THOUGH THEY RANGE DRAMATICALLY IN TEXTURE AND FLAVOR, ANY MOUNTAIN cheese is going to make a great table cheese and would be a good part of a composed cheese course or plate. In fact, you could easily prepare one from all mountain cheeses: a soft and fresh stracchino, a washed-rind Taleggio, an aged Piave. Like salumi platters, which I describe on page 148, a classic cheese plate should have not just a range of flavors but of textures, shapes, and colors. I usually recommend using cheeses from different types of milk—cow, goat, sheep, buffalo—and also cheeses of different ages, which will be cut into different shapes.

One of my favorite platters has five cheeses, the majority of them mountain cheeses. Working clockwise, I begin with cow's milk cheese with a soft texture, like Asiago Pressato or crucolo, the rind removed and the cheese cut into large cubes. Next lay a few wedges of a medium-aged pecorino, which will have a little more intensity and a denser texture. Aged pecorinos come in wheels, so I trim the rind, then slice the cheese into triangles about a quarter-inch thick. Next comes ragged hunks of Parmigiano-Reggiano, which have a deeper flavor and a nice granular crunch. And then I have a few large cubes of Gorgonzola piccante, which has an intense salt flavor and wonderfully creamy texture. In the middle goes a whole small round of a mixed milk mountain cheese from Piemonte, such as La Tur or Brunet.

I always recommend serving cheese plates with at least three accompaniments: a mostarda (a spicy-sweet Italian condiment made with mustard seeds), a honey, and a confettura, or preserve, such as grape or fig. To do it right, I recommend serving cheese platters with two to three types of honey, such as an assertive chestnut honey and a more mild acacia.

I also like to serve soft cheeses like La Tur whole. Before serving them, I keep them in the packaging and let them ripen until they are gooey on the edge but still firm in the center—cheese matures faster around the edges. Some people cut the whole thing into wedges, but I prefer to take a knife and scrape or slice off the very top layer. Then I scrape my knife across the whole wheel, so I get a good blend of all of the textures. (It is also excellent for breakfast with a bit of preserves on toast.)

Beyond a cheese plate, well-aged cheeses like Piave, the older Asiago, Montasio, and other latteria cheeses are also excellent for grating atop pasta, salad, or anywhere you'd use Parmigiano-Reggiano. In fact, Montasio, originally from Friuli-Venezia Giulia, is actually the original cheese for the famous dish *frico*—where you grate a little hard cheese and fry it until it is crispy and crunchy; the more aged the Montasio, the less gooey it is. Friulians also make a potato version, in which you mix grated cheese and grated potato and fry them together until it develops a crispy crust. You could really use any hard cheese for these—though today when you see frico it's usually made with Parmigiano-Reggiano.

Like most Alpine cheeses, the younger Asiago is made for melting. Stelvio too—it has a nutty aroma and a buttery mouthfeel. Another of my favorites is crucolo, which is formed into huge rounds with big holes, and made by just one family deep in the mountains in Trentino. They serve it blended with milk in *fuso,* the Trentino version of fondue, or *fonduta* in Italian. You can use them anywhere you'd use Swiss cheese. Taleggio and Fontina are also good melters and you often find them in fancy macaroni and cheese. In Piemonte there is a traditional baked polenta layered with slices of Fontina appropriately called *polenta grassa,* or "fatty" polenta. There is also *Branzi,* made deep in the mountains of Lombardia around the town of Bergamo, and Bitto, made with the addition of a small amount of local goat's milk near the Bitto River in Valtellina near the town of Sondrio.

Lombardian cheeses in particular—Bitto and Branzi—are traditionally grated into polenta, which is as popular in many parts of the region as pasta. They are also melted into *pizzoccheri,* short flat pasta made with buckwheat, which grows better than durum wheat in this region of Italy. In Valtellina it's often served with potatoes, greens, and Bitto or *Valtellina Casera,* another cheese made in the same region. You see these and other mountain cheeses added to risotto, too—Italian rice varieties like *Arborio* and lesser known *Carnaroli* and *Vialone Nano* were also traditionally grown and eaten in Lombardia, the Veneto, and Piemonte.

Plain stracchino, on the other hand, is great for dessert with honey or preserves. At Di Palo's we also make focaccia sandwiches with it—you could add prosciutto or fig jam. In fact, I like to pair soft, creamy cheeses like stracchino and Piemontese La Tur and Brunet—the latter two are almost cakelike—with something sweet like Italian preserves or wild honey. And Gorgonzola piccante is great paired with a sweet *passito* wine, while the dolce is wonderful with a softer red wine, like a Sassella, a lighter version of the Sforzato you'd drink with Bitto.

These rich, fatty cheeses are also great paired with the intense wines of the region, especially a big red Barbera, but on a hot summer day I opt for something a little bit chilled, an Arnese wine from the same region. In Piemonte thinly sliced *carne crudo,* or raw meat, and a black-pepper-spiked raw sausage called *salsicce di Bra,* which is named after a famous town now home to the international offices of Slow Food, are both served with these types of cheeses too.

When it comes to pairing the rest of all the mountain cheeses with wine, well, you can probably guess what I am going to say: choose your wine regionally. If you buy a wine made near where your cheese is made that meets the same level of intensity, it will probably be a perfect fit.

POLENTA CON FORMAGGIO CRUCOLO FUSO

(Polenta with Crucolo Cheese Sauce)

Crucolo is a semisoft cow's-milk cheese, sweet and creamy like a fresh Asiago, that's made by a single producer in a Trentino mountain valley called Valsugana. This is a traditional pairing from that region: polenta with a fonduelike sauce. You can also use this sauce over potatoes, with bread or however you'd serve fondue. This sauce works better with polenta that is firmer. If you can't find crucolo, substitute the similar Asiago fresco.

> 1 pound polenta
> 1 pound crucolo or Asiago fresco, cubed
> 1 cup milk
> Sea salt and freshly cracked black pepper to taste

1. Preheat the broiler. Prepare polenta following instructions on the package. When it is ready, pour it into a sheet pan or lasagne dish and let sit till firm.

2. Cut your polenta into desired shapes about 4 inches wide, such as squares or circles, and toast them on a sheet pan in the broiler.

3. Meanwhile, in a medium-sized heavy-bottomed skillet, add 3/4 cup milk and the cheese and heat over medium low, stirring constantly with a whisk or wooden spoon until the mixture is smooth and the cheese is melted. Do not let it boil. Add more milk until it reaches your desired thickness, then season with salt and pepper to taste. Remove from heat and serve immediately, ladling it over the piece of polenta for each guest. Alternatively, you could reheat the polenta whole in the pan, and pour the sauce over the top or serve it alongside at the table.

SPECK

In the province of Alto Adige in the eastern Alps—Italy's northernmost point—everything is written in two languages: Italian and German. Formaggio is also *käse,* vino is *wein.* The capital city of Bolzano is also known as Bozen, and Alto Adige itself is Südtirol—in fact you usually see it written Alto Adige–Südtirol. In this part of Italy, on the Austrian border, ivy-covered beer halls are just as popular as enotecas, and the farmhouses tucked into the deep woods look as if Hansel and Gretel lived in them. For many who live here, German is their first language—so when they say my name it isn't Luigi but "Lü." That's because until recently, this really *was* Austria—controlled by the Austro-Hungarian Empire, when it was collectively The South Tyrol, or Südtirol to Austrians. But after World War I, the boundaries of Europe changed and this little piece of the Alps, which straddles the Adige River, landed in Italy. Today, to be fair to both cultures, you can't just say Alto Adige (or top of the Adige River, in Italian), or just Südtirol (or the bottom of Tyrol, in German). You really have to say both.

Except for speck. Now if you went to a butcher in Germany and asked for *speck,* you will get something like fatty bacon or Italian lardo, or essentially cured fat. But to Tyroleans—and I still like to refer to the people of this truly autonomous province as Tyroleans—speck is their very special, spiced, cured, smoked, and air-dried pork.

Thousands of years ago there were two basic ways to preserve meat. Where it was warm, you'd salt it, like prosciutto—it's a ham, a pig's hind leg, that's salted and air-dried. The salt draws out the moisture, preventing food-spoiling bacteria, and then natural breezes dry the meat. But in the Germanic countries where it's cold, moisture is removed with heat. Centuries ago, farmers noticed that when they hung their fresh hams in a kitchen corner near the constant wood fire, not only was it preserved, but over the course of a few weeks the flavor changed, too, the meat was sweet, earthy, smoky, and complex.

The Alpine villages of Alto Adige–Südtirol are exactly where these two ancient methods meet: Speck is a taste of this special bilingual province of Italy. (To be fair it's really trilingual; there is an ancient Latin-based language called Ladine spoken in the Dolomites by a small number of Tyroleans. Luckily speck is *speck* in Ladine too.) Before the ham is air-dried with help from the cool, crisp breezes in those high mountain peaks, it's cold-smoked over local wood for thirty-six hours, instead of days or weeks, like German hams. It is then deboned and aged for just five and a half months, unlike the yearlong wait to make a prosciutto crudo. And instead of a simple sea-salt brine, speck is coated with juniper, laurel, thyme, white pepper, and other flavors collected from those deep Alpine mountain forests—if you ask for a recipe, you'll quickly be told it's a family secret. Speck has this delicate balance of smoke, salt, and Alpine spice—a sweet beginning with a mildly smoky finish, slightly drier than prosciutto, each thin slice a blend of lean, deep-red meat marked with an outer ribbon of creamy fat. It's wonderful.

Speck (pronounced by Tyroleans as *schpeck,* with a "shh" sound) is everywhere in Alto Adige–Südtirol, and even the surrounding provinces. Tyroleans have traditionally eaten it stuffed with pickles, Stelvio cheese, and horseradish into black bread for lunch, thinly sliced as antipasto at every formal meal, or shredded into fat *canederli,* the steamed bread dumplings seen at any classic Alto Adigean meal. Every Tyrolean farmer makes their own speck, and every Tyrolean chef typically serves it—from the little gas station counterman to the Michelin-starred chef. Today it also adorns pasta, pizza, and countless other creations.

Speck is now all over menus in the States, too, though it took years to get it here. I went to visit my first speck company in 1999 with Cesare with high hopes that he would be the first to import it and I would be the first to sell it. We drove to a family-run factory in a little town called Chiusa, just thirty minutes south of the Austrian border, my first trip to the province. But I didn't sell it in my store until 2005. In America there are countless rules and regulations for importing cured meat, especially pork products. The factory has to be approved and inspected by the USDA, the pigs have to come from special registered farms and slaughterhouses, the company has to fly to Washington to approve their labels . . . it is a very involved process, and most speck makers didn't produce enough speck to warrant the trouble.

If my friend Franz Mitterutzner, then the director of the Consortium of Speck Alto Adige–Südtirol, hadn't worked so hard to help two companies be approved in 2004 so we could finally get it to Little Italy, it may never have happened. (Even today only three producers export it to the States.) The first company to be approved was Recla, and it was just as big a deal to the company as it was to us. They came to my store and literally handed me a speck, and that was the first one sold anywhere in the States.

Part of Franz Mitterutzner's job was to help get speck into the States, but for him it was also very personal. His last name means "middle of the Rutzner mountain," because his family was from the middle of that mountain in Alto Adige–Südtirol. Tyroleans take their province very seriously—one of two that make up the region known as Trentino–Alto Adige–Südtirol, it is still legally considered almost an autonomous, separate entity. But Franz really loves his home. The food and culture of this region is his passion and his life; his wife runs a traditional coffee roaster and candy shop in the middle of Bolzano, complete with the old blue-painted urns to store the beans. Cesare and I immediately realized we had found a kindred spirit—a person who shared our passion and respect not just for food, but for the food and culture of Italy. In many ways over the past decade, he became our de facto tour guide to the region.

Franz invited me to be the first American at Bolzano's annual Speck Fest, where I ceremoniously cut open a ham to make sure it was properly cured. Franz picked me up at the airport and whisked me straight up into the mountains to an eight-hundred-year-old stone farmhouse about a half hour north of Bolzano in the *Valle Isarco,* or the Eisack Valley at the edge of the Dolomite mountains. Farmhouses are all called *hofs* in this part of Italy—*bauernhof* is German for "farm"—and this one in a small village called Villandres was known as the Johannserhof. Today its owner is an older farmer named

Georg Brüner, who cures his own speck just as his great-great-grandfathers did—all at the top of a winding road so narrow you can barely fit even an Italian car through the curves.

Inside his old house is a tiny four-poster bed, raised up about five feet off the ground. This front room was once an all-purpose space—a living room, dining room, a parlor—and it also had this tall wooden bed. Underneath the bed is a big stone dome that went through the wall to the original kitchen, where the Brüners did some of the cooking. That's what Franz had brought me here to see: in that old kitchen there was an opening into the dome, where the family would build a fire to heat the parlor, but keep it free of flames or smoke. In the old days, if you were elderly or sick or you were just in from the cold, that bed is where you slept—right on top of those stones that stayed warm for hours. In the old kitchen where they built the fire, on the other hand, every inch of the place was black as night—even blacker. The ceiling was charred, and the place reeked of burnt wood and soot—that was the point. "In rooms just like this," Franz told me, "is where speck Alto Adige was created!" In fact, Georg Brüner still slaughters his pigs in his courtyard and smokes his speck hanging up in that kitchen, right inside his house.

He ages them just a few yards from his front door, in a dark room built right into the side of a hill under the old barn. It's more like a cantina, a basement, with a bumpy dirt floor and two little wooden windows at the ground level, which are usually halfway open. The speck hangs from the ceiling, covered with that bluish-white mold, which grows with the help of the breezes from the Dolomite peaks. Georg's specks are still hung with ropes in the old-fashioned manner, one knot on either side. As gravity pulls the ham down, eventually the meat takes on the shape of a heart—narrow on the bottom and a little wider on top. (With most speck today the pig's hind leg is fully deboned and left to cure flat on racks, which results in a square.)

Georg also makes what Tyroleans call *bauernspeck:* one entire side of the pig, the skin and head still on, seasoned, dried, and smoked. In the really old days, you didn't want any part of the pig to go to waste—so you'd make speck with a whole side of the animal. You can try different parts of the pig—the shoulder, the belly, the leg, each with its own texture and slightly different flavor, based on the ratio of fat to lean in the cut.

The first time I visited the Johannserhof, Georg climbed up an old rickety wooden ladder with his big wood-handled knife and carved off two pieces of *bauernspeck* speck for us to taste, one from that year's slaughter, and the other from the year before. Speck must be cured for at least five and a half months, but Georg ages his for much longer: it becomes a little drier, more intense in flavor. As Georg served us dinner at a table next to the bed in that funny living room—with a clay mug of his homemade wine and the hard Tyrolean discs of bread you break apart with a smash of your fist on the dinner table—he showed me how to serve speck the farmhouse way. Typically you use a machine to slice speck into long, almost transparent thin slices, just like prosciutto. But Georg cut his into thick, smaller pieces with his old wooden-handled utility knife, which gave it a rougher texture and deeper flavor—you get a bigger sense of the spice, the smoke, the cure. Whenever I do my seminars on speck today, I slice it with a small knife just that same way.

As you can imagine, speck made in houses like the Brüners' can't be imported into the States, but the modern way of making it is not that far off. Franz Recla, who runs a large speck factory with his brother Gino, is just like me; he runs a third-generation family business. His grandfather was a butcher who ran a tiny shop, his father built the first speck factory, and now his sons and nephews are working there too. The Recla company is on the western side of the Eisack Valley just outside of Merano, a city full of natural spas and springs that are a huge tourist attraction. Pavarotti would go there to the spas to lose weight. There's a small food market in Merano, similar to my own store; Franz Recla took me there years ago to meet my Tyrolean counterpart, an old man in his eighties slicing speck by hand on an old manual slicer. Because he was so busy serving his customers, he had no time to talk to me. "You know what he does?" Franz once whispered to me. "When Pavarotti comes here to lose weight, this old man sneaks him food in the spa. He feeds him my speck every night!" Naturally, Pavarotti never lost a pound.

In recent years the Reclas have turned their company into a truly modern operation at the base of Ortler Mountain, which is twelve thousand feet above sea level, the highest summit in the eastern Alps, formerly the highest peak in all of the Austro-Hungarian empire. It's capped with a real glacier and is a famous place for mountain climbers all over the world—in German it's known as "König Ortler," or King Ortler. Recla happens to be on the warm side of Ortler Mountain, what's romantically referred to as the "sunny balcony." Despite its size, the factory is almost hidden off the roadway, there are rows and rows of carefully tended apple trees just across the blacktop and for miles down the hillside. The humidity and temperature are perfect for those fruit trees—Alto Adige–Südtirol sells its fruit all over the world—which in turn helps make the very best speck. When you drive up to the factory, the air is so pure you can get a whiff of the spices from the factory in the parking lot: a bit of juniper, maybe laurel and pepper. When you step inside, it smells not like you'd think a meat processing plant might—of bleach and blood—but smoky and sweet, with the fresh, clean scent of those mountains.

There, on that dappled sunny balcony, hundreds of specks are now funneled up and down the floors of the plant into big smokers by tall elevators, or moved swinging from room to room on mechanically operated racks. A whole team of butchers trim the raw legs as they come in, weighing them, inspecting them, and deboning them by hand before they run down a conveyor belt to be seasoned.

The legs stay in Recla's salt-spice mixture for two weeks, one week per side. Instead of piled in big tubs as in most factories, they stay stacked on special racks so that the weight of each one presses down on the others naturally, to help remove moisture from the meat. Not only is the cure more consistent from speck to speck, Recla uses less salt. While the amount of salt producers can use is a range set by rule of the consortium, each one can work within those percentages to find perfection. That's what helps make Recla speck just a little bit sweeter. Not surprisingly, when I asked Franz what spices he used, he answered me exactly the same way Georg and everybody else had: "Lü," he said to me in German-accented English with a very big smile, "that's our family secret."

In the chilly air-drying room, the walls are inset with open tubes—like giant polka dots. The first time I visited, Franz made me put my hand up to the holes, so that I could feel a cool breeze coming from each one. But it wasn't from refrigeration: Franz was pointing out a window to the peak off in the distance. "This is the cold air coming from the Ortler Mountain," he told me. "*This* is where we get the best flavor."

That mountain air also comes into play in the last stop for the speck—the darkened halls where thousands of hams age for their last four months. Each piece of pork sprouts a thick coating of poofy bluish-white mold, which is brushed off before it is packaged for sale. Franz proudly calls them "my mushrooms," but it is really his bacteria, a microflora from his region delivered by that cold Ortler air. If you've ever spent any time with me at all in Di Palo's, you know I always talk a lot about microflora—those are what help give meat, cheese, and vinegar their unique flavor. Recla's speck, I think, is a little more intense than the others imported into the States. Maybe part of that is in their spice mix, but I believe much of it is where their factory sits, right at the foot of massive Ortler Mountain.

That is partially why Franz Mitterutzner spent nearly a decade trying to get me to climb up those twelve thousand feet. But I'm no athlete, and for years I'd just put him off. "I've stopped going to the gym," I'd groan. "I'll get in shape, and when I come next fall, we'll go mountain climbing." But then I'd go back the next year and say the same thing. Finally my son, Sam, was traveling with me—it was October, the time of the annual harvest picnic in the mountains, when everybody wears deerskin lederhosen. I thought, *If I don't go up this year, I'm never going.* "Okay, Franz," I conceded, "we climb."

So Franz made plans with a famous mountain climber named Toni Stocker—he's a buff guy with shoulder-length blond hair, shorts, hiking boots, and one of those Alpine hats. "The only thing you have to do is buy mountain climbing shoes," Franz told me. Sam and I went to a sporting goods shop in Bolzano, and not only did we buy mountain shoes, we bought mountain pants, mountain socks, mountain jackets—mountain *everything*, including expensive mirrored mountain sunglasses for Sam. "We're ready to go!" I told Franz. He took one look at us and he said, "You're crazy."

Franz Recla couldn't come with us, but instead he sent Paul Yorg—Recla's export manager, an accomplished climber and the man who handed me my first speck back in my store in Manhattan. There were three big mountains next to Recla: the tallest is Ortler, then Konig Punt, and then finally Suldenspitze. That's the one we had to climb, Toni told us, because they were predicting an avalanche on the other two, which faced a different direction. And as it turned out, they were right: as we traversed the frozen crevasses of Suldenspitze, tied together one-by-one the next day, we watched the face of Ortler fall away.

It takes a day to climb a real mountain. Very early in the morning, we took a cable car to where the ski slopes start their way downhill. That's where we started walking, and I thought, *Oh, this is going to be easy.* But then we're at the edge of a glacier, putting on the clamp-ons for our shoes—before you know it, we're in a meter of snow. It's very difficult to walk through a meter of snow, let me tell you: now we really had to climb *up* the mountain. It's so steep you don't go straight up, you traverse, you go back and forth, back and forth, and remember, you are all tied together. Toni the guide, then me, then my friend Paul, my son, Sam, and at the end, Franz Mitterutzner.

That hike turned out to be one of the hardest but most exhilarating days of my life. When we all finally got to the top and sat down—on a rare crystal clear afternoon, we were told, where the view wasn't only of the clouds—out of Franz Mitterutzner's back-pack miraculously came real wineglasses, a bottle of wine, a round of that hard Tyrolean bread, and of course, speck, which Toni cut into slabs on a wooden board with his pocketknife.

"Lü," Franz told me after he'd poured us each a glass, "in every house in the Südti-rol, we have three things on hand at all times for our guests: speck, wine, and bread. And wherever we go on a journey," he finished, "we always bring speck, wine, and bread." Toni was taking photographs—he'd been taking them on this whole trip—and there's an unbelievable photograph of my son on that peak, standing up at the edge in those expensive mirrored sunglasses. I could see one mountain behind him, and in the reflection of the glasses I could see Ortler, too, just across the way.

I like to say that I come from the south of Italy, where my ancestors were from, and that I own an apartment in the beautiful green hills of Umbria in the middle, but my heart is there in Alto Adige–Südtirol, in those beautiful mountains. Once you climb them, they own you. I now have such a strong connection to that province, to the two Franzes, to the Brüner family, to this wonderful place, and the best part is knowing that it was speck that brought us all together.

BUYING SPECK

IN THE NORTHEASTERN ALPS, YOU'LL FIND SPECK MADE IN HOMES, IN SMALL butcher shops, and by factories. The best of the latter will be certified by the consortium as Alto Adige–Südtirol IGP, which means the product follows the speck consortium's guidelines for making the traditional product of the region, but it's slightly different because the pork headed for the United States is usually from USDA-approved slaughterhouses in Denmark or Holland. A few producers in the United States, like La Quercia in Iowa, now make great American speck, too, but it's not quite the same: They don't have that Alpine air. They also can't call it Speck Alto Adige–Südtirol. La Quercia, for example, calls theirs Speck Americano.

No matter where it's made, good speck is a little drier than prosciutto, but it should still be very moist and deep red in color, with a band of cream-colored fat along the outer edge. Some people think that is too much fat, but that's exactly what you want with speck. When you buy it, you should follow most of the same suggestions for buying prosciutto. The most important is to taste a sample before you buy it, if you can, and for the very best flavor buy it freshly sliced to order from a purveyor you trust to cut and store it properly.

STORING SPECK

HILE BUTCHER SHOPS (AND FARMERS LIKE THE BRÜNERS) KEEP SPECK HANGING until they need a slice, at home it's best to treat it as you would prosciutto. Buy smaller portions and keep them well-wrapped in the refrigerator so that they won't dry out, and consume them quickly, within a day or two. As soon as it is sliced, speck begins to dry, to oxidize, and after a day or two its flavor and moistness will have already started to deteriorate. It won't be bad—and you can always cook with it—but it won't taste as good. If you see mold on thinly sliced pieces, you should throw them out. If you have bought a larger piece you plan on cutting yourself farmhouse-style, it will last longer in the refrigerator, and you could cut off any mold you see on the outside, the same as you would for other salumi.

SERVING SPECK

IKE PROSCIUTTO, SPECK IS TRADITIONALLY SERVED AS ANTIPASTO. IT IS PREPARED one of two ways: sliced very thin, almost transparent, so that it actually melts in your mouth, or farmhouse-style with a knife, into squares about an eighth of an inch thick, like a quarter strip of bacon. In Alto Adige, you'll often get a platter of speck all by itself with a few pickles and some brown bread and mustard, as per its Austrian influence. If you're serving speck as a first course to a traditional Alpine meal, that's a great way to serve it, with a wine from Alto Adige–Südtirol (*Schiava* or *Lagrein,* which are local reds, or *Kerner,* which is a white wine) or even a German-style beer like the Merano-made brand called Forst.

It can also be added to any antipasto platter with any mix of other Italian salumi, or cured meats, and today that's often how you'll see it in other parts of Italy or here in the United States: paired with prosciutto, culatello, spicy salami, or sopressata. In Italy, all cured meats are typically served at the start of a meal by themselves or with other cold antipasti such as marinated vegetables or occasionally some cheese. Like prosciutto, you should really savor each slice—hold it up and smell it deeply before you take the first bite for the fullest experience.

Traditionally, Tyroleans didn't often cook with speck—they might wrap small boiled potatoes with a slice for a snack, or mix potatoes with melted cheese and speck, or dice small scraps and add them to their canederli or soups. There are always end pieces and scraps, and like prosciutto bones, these are great for adding flavor to other dishes. If you buy your speck from a shop that cuts it to order, consider asking them to save you the end piece and sell it to you at a lower cost per pound.

Of course, just as with prosciutto, today modern cooks from Italy to Iowa now incorporate speck into all kinds of recipes. I prefer speck uncooked, when you can really taste its flavor and nuance, but I do enjoy all kinds of dishes made with it. It is sliced thin into almost any kind of pasta, added to omelets and quiches, on top of pizza, served with greens and shavings of cheese drizzled with a little olive oil, or tossed in warm vegetable salads. You could use it as a substitute in any recipe you see with prosciutto, such as the easy pasta supper my mother always makes with tomato, peas, and leftover prosciutto. Just remember the speck will add a bit of sweetness, smoke, and spice.

DITALINI CON PISELLI E SPECK

(Ditalini with Peas and Speck)

SERVES 4 AS A SMALLER COURSE, 2 AS A MEAL

This is another simple but flavorful recipe from my mother, Viola, who likes to make it so often she insisted I include it in the book. You can get a great amount of flavor here with a very small amount of meat. We often make it with leftover proscuitto, and traditionally people would use guanciale or pancetta, which is often smoked.

1/2 pound ditalini

Extra virgin olive oil

1/4 pound speck, cut into thin shreds

1 onion, diced

1 large ripe tomato, diced

2 cups peas, fresh or frozen

4 cups chicken stock or water

1/4 cup fresh basil leaves, optional

Parmigiano-Reggiano or Pecorino Romano,
    for garnishing

1. In a large spaghetti pot, bring salted water to a boil. Add pasta and cook until just al dente, then drain and set aside.

2. Meanwhile coat the bottom of a large pot with olive oil and bring to medium-high heat. Fry the speck in the oil until it begins to crisp, then add the onions and tomato until the onion is soft and the tomato begins to break down, about 10 minutes. Add peas and stock or water and simmer until the peas are soft.

3. Add the drained pasta to the pot with the peas and speck, stir in the basil if using, and heat through. Serve in deep bowls topped with grated cheese and a drizzle of olive oil.

ACKNOWLEDGMENTS

Thank you, Dad, for giving me the opportunity to work with you and for sharing your passion and knowledge of our life's work. You are always in our hearts.

Thank you, Mom, for your dedication to Dad and for your love and continued support to your children.

Thank you, Sal and Marie, for working side by side with me for decades and for giving me the opportunity to write this book.

Thank you to my daughter Allegra for showing me that dreams do come true.

Thank you to my son, Sam, for your contributions in taking Di Palo's to the next level by introducing new products both in food and wine in your travels to Italy from north to south.

Thank you to my daughter Caitlin for putting up with me during our travels to Italy for this book and documenting it with beautiful photographs.

Thank you to my grandsons, Ferdinando and Tommaso, for giving me a special love in my life.

Thank you to Uncle Mike for the special years we worked together.

Thank you to my aunts Anna and Rita.

Thank you to my sisters, Concetta and Yolanda, who worked alongside us while attending school. Although you pursued careers in education and finance, the spirit and passion of Di Palo's has always remained with you.

Thank you to my niece, Jessica, for your dedication and support in representing our fifth generation along with niece Cali and nephews Mikey, Carlos, and Steven.

Thank you to Uncle Al Cali, who as a teen worked with my parents and grandparents and went on to become a successful engineer who helped guide me with the expansion of Di Palo's.

Thank you to my cousins Louis Michael, Lena, John V., Philip, Sally Ann, and John C., who worked with us over the years.

Thank you to Tony Camacho, Joe Ferrantelli, René Alvarado, and the entire staff of Di Palo's past and present.

Thank you to Anthony "Tony" Ajello—my friend and mentor, who throughout the years guided me with his wisdom and many stories of our business—a true visionary.

Thank you to Mike and Susan Ajello for being good friends; Mike, a big thank-you for giving me the opportunity to catch "the giant tuna."

Thank you to Stanley Rosenblum, my lifelong friend, who contributed a very special photograph of myself, my father, my mother, and my aunt.

Thank you to my agent, Jonah Straus, for his persistence; to my editor, Pamela Cannon, for her patience and her vision; to Evan Sung for his fabulous photographs; and to my co-author, Rachel Wharton, for spending two years working on this book with me and my family.

Thank you to Martin Scorsese for his contributions to this book.

Thank you to Kent Jones.

Thank you to my friends who traveled with me in Italy: Cesare and Palma Gallo, Margaret Cicogna, and Larry Saia, aka "Larry Cheese."

Thank you, Santina, Felippo, and Alessia of the restaurant Osteria del Matto in Spoleto, Umbria, for sharing their home, hearts, and recipes with us.

Thank you to all my friends in Italy: Giulio Perin, Giorgio Colutta, Orietta Varnelli, Alberto Gracci, Alessandro Modica, Carlo Piccoli, and Emmanuela Perezin, Nicio Paganin, Chiara Brandalise, Franz Recla, Paul Yorg, Franz Mitterutzner, and Sofie, my interpreter in Alto Adige.

Thank you to my friends who have worked with me in promoting the specialty products of Italy throughout the United States: Vincenza Kelly, Elisabetta Serraiotto, Paolo Grandjacquet, and Gino Colangelo.

Thank you to my suppliers who over the years have provided Di Palo's with the finest products Italy has to offer: Cesare Baldrighi and Oliverio Olivieri of Latteria PLAC; Paul La Pietra of Penta International; Pierre Zriek of Eatalia Imports; Angelo Ronconi of Ranieri Fine Foods; John Bricca and Chris Suplicki of Food Solution; Pierluigi Sini and Michele Buster of Forever Cheese; George and Tom Gellert of Atalanta Corp.; Phil Musco of Musco Food Corp; Sal Pugliese of D. Coluccio & Sons; Frank Angeloni of Liuzzi Angeloni Cheese; Alessandro Sita of Cibo Italia; Luigi Ferrari of Latteria Soresina USA; Mirella and Carlo Galloni and Laura Antorino of Galloni USA; Tiziano Rossi and Fausto Vecchi of Negroni USA; Peter Lifson of Lifson and Rossi and Food Brokers, Inc.; Antonio and Alberto Auricchio of Auricchio Cheese; Giulio and Adrian Sottovia, Remo Tozzi, Frank Muchi, and Rosario Castorina of the Alps Provisions Co.; Michael Martella of Frank Brunckhorst Co.; Giorgio Cravero of G. Cravero S.R.L.; Vincenzo Spinosi of Spinosi S.R.L.; Roberto and Raimondo of Sant'Eustachio Coffee; Luciano and Claudio Stefani of Giuseppe Giusti; Bernie Sezon of Illy Caffè North America; Silvia Musto Beam and Jan Anderson, for sharing with me a memorable lunch with Dr. Ernesto Illy; and Gregory Tredanari of Gregory's Trading. And thank you to my son-in-law, Ludovico del Balzo of Mediterranea Italia, for bringing to America the finest tomato and olive oil products. Thank you to my friends Frank Angelino and Franko.

Thank you to Gianni "di Stigliano" Capalbi and Mimmo Balsano, who helped us rediscover my family's region of Basilicata.

Thank you to Jacob El Hanani, the SoHo artist, who, while patiently waiting to be served in Di Palo's, captured my family over the years through his caricatures.

Thank you to Christine Andreas and Marty Silvestri for the wonderful song you sang and played for my birthday.

Thank you to all our friends, neighbors, and merchants in Little Italy who, like us, helped keep the spirit of the Italian immigrants alive.

And thank you to our great-grandfather Savino and our grandparents Concetta and Luigi, for having the courage to come to America, giving us the opportunity to make a better life and to preserve our Italian heritage.

PHOTO CREDITS

Interior Photos:
All photos by Evan Sung except the following:
Page xii: Marie behind counter (Christopher Bierlein)
Page 15: Fruit cart on Mott St. across from Di Palo's [from PR020 (Geographic File),
Box NYC 21, Folder: Mott Street; neg #89262d. Photography © New-York Historical Society]
Page 16: Young Lou (Stanley Rosenblum)
Page 17: Viola, Sam, Lou, and Anna Nicosia (Stanley Rosenblum)
Page 18: Magazine cover of Lou, Sal, and Marie (MYKO Photography, INC. NYC)
Pages 2, 5, 8, 10, 11, 12, 16, and 19: Family photos (Courtesy of the Di Palo family)
Pages iv-v, xvi, 110, 128, 231: (Barbara M. Bachman)

••

*Photo Insert: All food photography is by Evan Sung with the exception of
the middle spread of regional photographs*

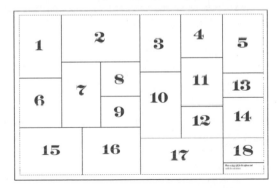

All photos in the middle spread by CAITLIN SANTOMAURO except where noted.

1. *Mario Vaccaro, a cheesemaker/farmer in Basilicata.*

2. *Fresh anchovies and sardines at Scalia in Sciacca.*

3. *In the mountain cheese-aging room of the bunker-turned-cheese cave run by Hancie Baumgardener of Degüst.*

4. *Scooping out the curds for Grana Padano at Latteria PLAC in Cremona.*

5. *Vincenzo Spinosi's signature pasta dish, made at his home in Campofilone.*

6. *Cesare Lopez giving me his fresh sheep's milk ricotta made near Rome.*

7. *Mario Vaccaro churning fresh butter for manteca.*

8. *A batteria of balsamic vinegar in the Giuseppe Giusti aceteria.*

9. *Sopravissana sheep in the fertile pasturelands of Lazio.*

10. *Prosciutto cured with the hoof at Negroni's prosciuttificio in San Daniele.*

11. *Vincenzo Spinosi and I pose with his freshly made Spinosini.*

12. *In the hills of Basilicata with the area's podolica cows.*

13. *Hand-harvested Sicilian fiore di sale in the salinas of Trapani.*

14. *Clockwise, my son, Sam; Franz Mitterutzner; Paul Yorg; and I pose on top of Suldenspitze in Alto Adige– Südtirol.* PHOTO BY TONI STOCKER.

15. *The hills of Basilicata.*

16. *Mario Vaccaro and his son making caciocavallo in their cheese-making cave.*

17. *The cantina of Rifugio Crucolo in Trentino.*

18. *Sicilian olive trees in Trapani.*

INDEX

Lou Di Palo grew up behind the counter at Di Palo's, the 104-year-old family-run specialty store in New York's Little Italy. Beloved by both his customers and those in the food community and media, Lou Di Palo is considered to be a preeminent Italian-food expert. In addition to running Di Palo's (for forty years and counting) with his brother, Sal, and sister Marie, he works as an Italian-food educator and consultant for supermarkets, trade associations, and various Italian commerce, tourism, and business groups, from whom he has received a number of awards for his efforts in educating Americans in the ways of Italian food. He lives with his wife, Connie, in New York City.

Rachel Wharton has nearly twenty years of experience as a writer, reporter, and editor, including four and a half years as a features food reporter and features food editor at the New York *Daily News*. She is a contributing editor of *Edible Manhattan* and *Edible Brooklyn* magazines, and a James Beard Foundation award-winning food writer with a master's degree in Food Studies from New York University.

ABOUT THE TYPE

This book was set in Bulmer, a typeface designed in the late eighteenth century by the London type cutter William Martin (1757–1830). The typeface was created especially for the Shakespeare Press, directed by William Bulmer (1757–1830)—hence the font's name. Bulmer is considered to be a transitional typeface, containing characteristics of old-style and modern designs. It is recognized for its elegantly proportioned letters, with their long ascenders and descenders.

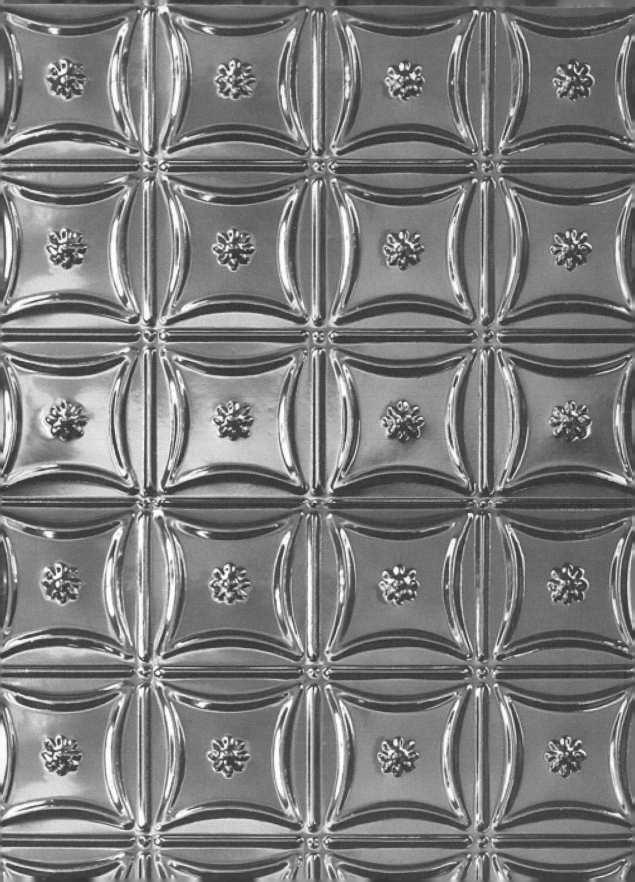